THE DAGUERREOTYPES OF
SOUTHWORTH
&
HAWES

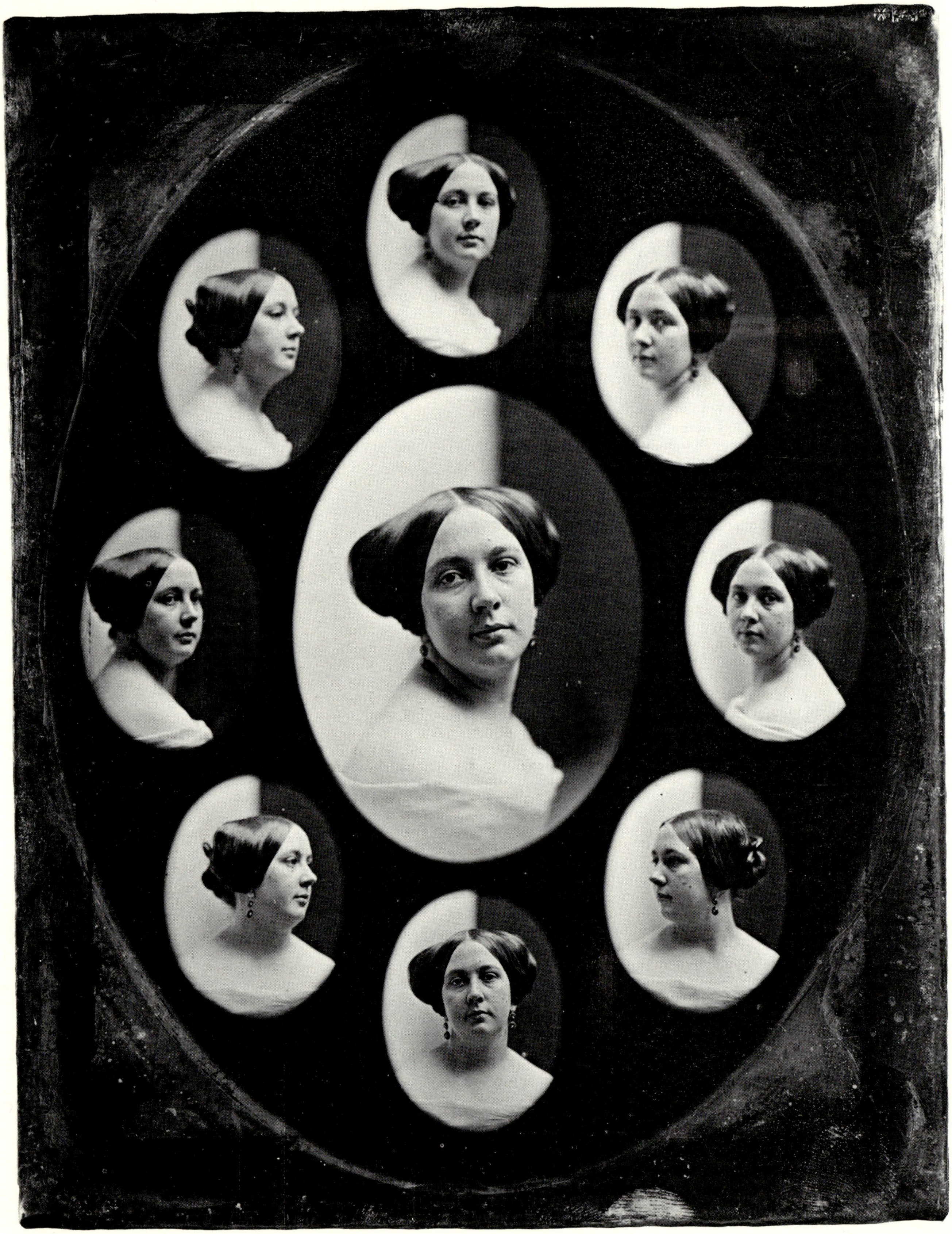

THE DAGUERREOTYPES OF SOUTHWORTH & HAWES

ROBERT A. SOBIESZEK
&
ODETTE M. APPEL

With the research assistance of Charles R. Moore

DOVER PUBLICATIONS, INC.
NEW YORK

Published in Canada by General Publishing Company, Ltd., 30 Lesmill Road, Don Mills, Toronto, Ontario.
Published in the United Kingdom by Constable and Company, Ltd., 10 Orange Street, London WC2H 7EG.

This Dover edition, first published in 1980, is an unabridged and revised republication of the work originally published jointly by David R. Godine and the International Museum of Photography at the George Eastman House (Rochester, N.Y.) in 1976 under the title *The Spirit of Fact: The Daguerreotypes of Southworth & Hawes, 1843–1862.* The Dover edition is published by special arrangement with David R. Godine, 306 Dartmouth Street, Boston, Massachusetts 02116.

Book design by Carol Belanger Grafton

International Standard Book Number: 0-486-23841-5
Library of Congress Catalog Card Number: 79-51887

Manufactured in the United States of America
Dover Publications, Inc.
180 Varick Street
New York, N.Y. 10014

PREFACE TO THE DOVER EDITION

The Daguerreotypes of Southworth & Hawes is an unabridged reprint of the book first published by David R. Godine, entitled *The Spirit of Fact.* The Dover edition, while containing all the images and text of the original, hardbound edition, has been redesigned and corrected. It is intended that as a modestly priced paperback this edition will reach a far wider audience than the original.

The Godine edition was published in 1976 as part of the Bicentennial observances. It was co-published by the International Museum of Photography at the George Eastman House in connection with the first major retrospective exhibition of the work of Southworth & Hawes. This exhibition was housed at the George Eastman House in Rochester (February–June, 1976), the National Portrait Gallery in Washington (July–December, 1976), and the Museum of Fine Arts in Boston (January–February, 1977). Prior to this retrospective, daguerreotypes by Southworth & Hawes had only been seen in substantial numbers twice in the previous two generations: at Holman's Print Shop in Boston and at the Metropolitan Museum of Art in New York, both exhibitions taking place in the 1930s.

After the dissolution of the firm of Southworth & Hawes in 1862, the thousands of remaining daguerreotypes were retained by Josiah Hawes, and later by his estate, until the majority found their way into the collections of three museums: the Museum of Fine Arts (Boston), the Metropolitan Museum of Art and the George Eastman House. The purpose of both the exhibition and this volume was to attempt to re-establish the reputation of Southworth & Hawes by presenting their work as a vital aspect of American art. The exhibition and this volume were the result of the interest in early 19th-century American photography on the part of Robert A. Sobieszek, Associate Curator of Photography at the George Eastman House, who, along with Odette M. Appel, Research Assistant for the project, jointly selected the images for the exhibition and authored the textual material of the catalogue. Special thanks are due Charles R. Moore, who kindly supplied the project with the fruits of his doctoral dissertation research on Southworth & Hawes.

Among the many individuals and institutions whose cooperation and encouragement in this project were invaluable, a number must be specifically thanked: the late John McKendry, Colta Fella Ives and Weston Naef of the Metropolitan Museum of Art; Eleanor A. Sayre and Clifford S. Ackley of Boston's Museum of Fine Arts; Mrs. Ropes Cabot and Thomas W. Parker of the Bostonian Society, Old State House; Abbott L. Cummings and Daniel H. Lohnes of the Society for the Preservation of New England Antiquities, Boston; the Massachusetts Historical Society, Boston; Jack Jackson of the Boston Athenaeum; Arnold H. Crane and Richard Parker who so willingly loaned material to the exhibition; and Norman J. Brouwer of New York's South Street Seaport Museum, E. H. Davis of the Scovill Manufacturing Co., Professor Rita K. Gollin of Rochester, Edward L. Hawes, Richard Holman of Holman's Print Shop and Duncan W. Munro of Mt. Auburn Cemetery. All gave freely and generously of their time and expertise.

We are grateful to the National Endowment for the Arts whose grant to the George Eastman House made this project possible. We are also most grateful to those institutions and private collectors who were willing to part with their fragile and rare daguerreotypes for over a year; both the trust and the spirit of cooperation that these loans represent are duly appreciated.

Last, but by no means least, sincere appreciation is extended to the members of the archive, clerical, conservation, exhibition design, photography, publicity and registration staffs of the International Museum of Photography. Although not named here, their enthusiastic labors and expertise were in many ways responsible for the exhibition's existence. George Pratt, editor of publications for the museum, is especially thanked for his efforts in the preparation of the manuscript.

ROBERT J. DOHERTY
Director
International Museum of Photography at George Eastman House

CONTENTS

INTRODUCTION

Every natural fact is a symbol of some spiritual fact. Every appearance in nature corresponds to some state of mind, and that state of mind can only be described by presenting that natural appearance as its picture.

—Ralph Waldo Emerson, *Nature,* 1836

Nineteenth-century American culture exhibited a faith in nature that superseded even its hope in progress and technology. In the midst of urban growth, new railways, factories, and inventions such as the telegraph, the typewriter and photography, the American vision of nature was at once materialistic and idealized. Nature was not only to be domesticated and settled, but its realities were viewed as keys to greater meanings. Landscape painters like Thomas Cole, Asher B. Durand and Fitz Hugh Lane; poets like Walt Whitman, William Cullen Bryant and John Greenleaf Whittier; and essayists like Ralph Waldo Emerson, Margaret Fuller and Henry David Thoreau—all these figures representing the poetic strain of American thought interpreted the phenomenal realities of nature as emblems of both material existence and spirituality. Emerson in particular, the outspoken leader of 19th-century American thinking, saw nature as a vast compendium of facts to be directly observed and appreciated[1] as a means to understanding the "ideal" reality. In his *Poetry* Emerson stated, "the higher use of the material world is to furnish us types or pictures to express the thoughts of the mind." As Whitman also pointed out in "Song of Myself," "All truths wait in all things/They neither hasten their own delivery nor resist it."

A culture so preoccupied with the factual aspects of the world could hardly fail to be enthralled by the unmitigated naturalism of photography. The 19th-century viewer accepted the photographic image as a completely true depiction of nature. Lecturing in 1840, Samuel F. B. Morse claimed that the first photographs were pictures "painted by Nature's self with a minuteness of detail [and which] *cannot be called copies of nature but portions of nature herself.*"

Photography provided the American public with a plethora of images. How were these images to transcend a mere replication of those "portions of nature herself" to attain the level of "pictures to express the thoughts of the mind"? According to Marcus Aurelius Root, a Philadelphia daguerreotypist and theorist, the photographer who was to be more than a mere copyist of nature had to possess, like his fellow artist, those intellectual and moral qualities that allowed him to find and delineate the proper expression of his subject:

To represent, in their just proportions, the beautiful and sublime in natural scenery; to reproduce in like manner the creations of inspired human genius; and especially to delineate the human face and figure pervaded by an *expression*, that bids the soul shine glowingly out through the same; are to transcribe the matchless pencillings of the Divine Proto-Artist. To do this, how imperfectly soever, demands qualities, alike of head and of heart, in rapt accordance with the Infinite Spirit.[2]

In short, American photography had to be like all American art:

To be alike true and great, American art must be America's spirit and life, with all their individualities, idealized and encircled with the magic halo of beauty![3]

Among those who succeeded in elevating photography to the level of art were Albert Sands Southworth and Josiah Johnson Hawes. Celebrated in its time as *the* portrait salon in America,[4] their studio produced an enormous body of pictorial images that included not only portraits but landscapes, marines and art reproductions. Remarkable as both technical achievements and aesthetic interpretations of nature, their work can be seen essentially as an American art expression. Progressive in the newness of the technology used to produce them, Southworth & Hawes's daguerreotypes are direct and clear depictions of the material world expressive of the subject's internal reality—the spirit of fact that transcends mere appearance.

Early Years of Daguerreotype Portraiture

Developed in France during the 1830s by Louis Jacques Mandé Daguerre and publicly announced in August of 1839, the daguerreotype was the first commercially feasible photographic process. Finely delineated on a highly polished sheet of silver-plated copper that was customarily modest in size, the image was difficult to view because of its reflective surface and was extremely sensitive to surface abrasions. Each image was a unique photographic specimen, for there was no negative for reproduction. The factual and precise details of the daguerreotype image rendered the process an immediate success as a mode of visual communication. The success, however, was essentially an American phenomenon. Although the process was invented in France and was popular in Great Britain, the daguerreotype was supplanted during the late 1840s by various negative/positive paper processes throughout the Continent. From 1840 to about 1850 the American photographer and public, on the other hand, responded to the daguerreotype with unrivaled enthusiasm. All varieties of subject matter were depicted on the silvered plate, but the portrait remained the culmination of the photographers' efforts.

The question of the author of the first daguerreotype portrait remains open. A Frenchman by the name of Susse is reputed to have captured a human likeness by daguerreotype in early September of 1839, only some fifteen days after the publication of Daguerre's process.[5] In America Professor John William Draper of New York claimed to have first made a daguerreotype portrait later that same month.[6] What is clear is that after the initial resolution of the process, its capacity for recording fact mandated the making of portraits.

The difficulties with making camera portraits at the time rested chiefly with lengthy exposure times. A sitting required as long as fifteen to twenty-five minutes, most often resulting in showing the sitter with eyes closed, or vacant if he had blinked repeatedly during the exposure. One of the first attempts to shorten the exposure time was painting the sitter's face white in order to increase the light's reflectivity,[7] which proved a makeshift and undesirable solution. The earliest lenses simply failed to allow enough light onto the photographic plate. Developments in lens design and refinements in the chemical process ultimately made daguerreotype portraits practical. A meniscus lens, faster than Daguerre's simple achromatic, enabled the French photographer Abel Rendu to sufficiently shorten the exposure time in 1839 to obtain portraits of men and women with the eyes open. According to François Gouraud, Rendu's and his own use of this lens allowed exposures of "ONE *minute to* TWO *minutes twenty-seven seconds*"—a phenomenal claim when nearly every other daguerreotypist was working under the limitations of half an hour or so. From 1840 to 1841 various other lenses and chemical accelerators such as bromine and chlorine helped further decrease exposure time. In September of 1840, Draper reported that in full daylight he could make a portrait in about twenty to ninety seconds with a double convex non-achromatic lens.[8] Less than a year later, on March 30, 1841, G. W. Prosch wrote to Albert Sands Southworth that with a plate sensitized with a bromine and iodine mixture he "was able to take pictures in an ordinary room with diffused light in 25 seconds, without the Bromine it required 4 minutes." As soon as exposure time was measured in seconds rather than minutes, portraiture became feasible and developed into the most widespread of all 19th-century photographic activities.

Despite the difficulties of portraiture in comparison to the relatively easy control of still lifes, landscapes and architectural views, approximately ninety-five percent of all daguerreotypes were portraits. By 1849, T. S. Arthur remarked:

> If our children and children's children to the third and fourth generation are not in possession of portraits of their ancestors, it will be no fault of the Daguerreotypists of the present day; for verily, they are limning faces at a rate that promises soon to make every man's house a Daguerreian Gallery. . . . In our great cities, a Daguerreotypist is to be found in almost every square; and there is scarcely a county in any state that has not one or more of these industrious individuals busy at work in catching 'the shadow' ere the 'substance fade' . . . it is hard to find the man who has not the shadowy faces of his wife and children done up in purple morocco and velvet, together or singly, among his household treasures.[9]

The 1840s and 1850s represent the first period in social history when portraiture was not restricted to the aristocratic or upper classes. Even those with moderate income could now afford portraits of themselves, their friends and families. The inexpensiveness and easy availability of photographic images led to a mania for forming portrait collections, ranging from modest family likenesses to large-scaled compendia of human images.

When Southworth and Hawes formed their partnership in Boston in 1843, the basic technical problems of making daguerreotype portraits had been resolved. Stressing quality rather than speed, the two partners concentrated on producing portraits that were immediately recognized as both technical feats and aesthetic achievements which clearly demonstrated the distinction between a poor and a first-rate daguerreotype:

> In the former everything is hard, dry, rigid, and disagreeable, the flesh, mere blotches of light and shade, the eyes glaring or completely dead, the action of the figures stiff and constrained, the folds of the draperies, hard as though carved in wood. In the latter, the flesh is preserved in all the beautiful gradations of form and texture, the most delicate lights playing over its surface in a thousand different degrees of intensity, the fabrics are soft, easy, and graceful, the action and expression natural and refined.[10]

The partners did not hesitate to let their customers know their work was first-rate. As the following advertisement from about 1850 indicates, they addressed themselves to those who could afford their prices and their personal attention:

> As no cheap work is done, we shall spend no time in bantering about prices; and wish to have all understand that ours is a one-price concern.[11]

The personalities who sat for their cameras represented a full spectrum of 19th-century American culture: writers, statesmen, scientists, musicians, actors and actresses. Southworth & Hawes's popularity among this class and the superiority of their work resulted from the collaboration of two individualistic and forceful personalities—Hawes, solid, conservative, serious and reticent; Southworth, opportunistic, adventuresome and gregarious.

EARLY LIFE OF ALBERT SOUTHWORTH

Little is known about the personal life of Albert Sands Southworth. He was born in West Fairlee, Vermont, on March 12, 1811, and had two brothers, Asa and Samuel Niles, and a sister named Nancy Niles. The 1829 catalogue of the Bradford Academy lists Albert Southworth among its student body. He attended Phillips Academy, Andover, Massachusetts, from 1833 to 1835, where he was a member of the Social Fraternity. After having tried teaching, Southworth established a drugstore in Cabotville (now Chicopee), Massachusetts, in 1839.[12] A letter to Nancy dating from this period reveals Southworth's dissatisfaction with the easy niche of his "snug little office" in Cabotville and indicates his interest in daguerreotypy, newly discovered through a series of lectures given by François Gouraud in 1840:

> Professor Goraud [Gouraud] soon lectured in Boston. His illustra-

tive experiment resulted in his producing a dimmed and foggy plate instead of the architectural details of buildings, and the definite lines and forms of street objects. It happened to be a misty day attended with both snow and rain.

The Professor appeared highly elated, and exhibited his picture with great apparent satisfaction, that he had it in his power to copy the very mist and smoke of the atmosphere in a stormy day. Many a photographer has often wished for some natural phenomenon that might serve as a pretext for attributing to some apparent cause the faults of imperfectly understood chemical combinations, or partially polished plates.[13]

Jean Baptiste François Fauvel-Gouraud, a pupil of Daguerre, arrived in New York as the representative of Alphonse Giroux & Cie., the sole company licensed by Daguerre to sell his manual and camera. In New York, and then later in Boston and Providence, Gouraud gave lecture demonstrations of the process and exhibited daguerreotypes previously prepared in both America and France.

The presentation apparently stimulated Southworth to further investigate the new phenomenon. He soon traveled to New York at the written invitation of Joseph Pennell, his former roommate at Phillips Academy, who was then assisting Samuel F. B. Morse in the experiments with daguerreotypy and the telegraph. A meeting with Daguerre had sparked Morse's interest in the daguerreotype, and he became one of the first in America to establish a studio offering instruction in the process. Although he knew of Gouraud's presentations, Morse thought the Frenchman's data primitive and less than practical, remarking, "All the instruction professed to be imparted by M. Gouraud, I have felt it necessary to forget."[14]

Morse had begun experimenting with the daguerreotype in his New York studio, and it was here with Morse that Southworth first learned the rudiments of the daguerreian process. Both Southworth and Pennell soon returned to Cabotville and commenced a series of costly experiments with the hope of improving the new photographic technique.[15] In a letter dated May 21, 1840, Southworth shared with his sister Nancy his intense excitement in this new endeavor:

You have read of the daguerreotype, an apparatus for taking views of buildings, streets, yards, and so forth. I had an invitation to join Mr. Pennell, one of my roommates in old Phillips, in getting one, and partly to gratify my curiosity, and partly with the hope of making it profitable, I met Mr. Pennell in New York and purchased one. I cannot in a letter describe all the wonders of this apparatus. Suffice it to say, that I *can* now make a perfect picture in one hour's time, that would take a painter weeks to draw. The picture is represented in *light and shade*, nicer by far than any steel engraving you ever saw. The colors of objects are *not* given; but the picture is shown in light and shade.

It is a letter rife with confidence of a young man about to venture into a new business, for Pennell had already suggested that he and Southworth enter into partnership to establish a daguerreotype studio. Southworth's continuing correspondence with his sister provides the only record of his progress in the new profession. More importantly, the letters reveal something of Southworth's personality and motivations. Ambitious for financial gain and personal recognition, he appears to have been imbued with a sense of idealism which, combined with his perfectionism, created a tension which always left him dissatisfied.

Albert Southworth and Joseph Pennell

By September of 1840, Southworth and Pennell had formed a partnership and had established a daguerreotype studio. The studio's experiments were again shared with Nancy:

I have just succeeded in managing the Daguerreotype so as to make perfect likenesses, and if I should leave it now, those who have assisted me would not be pleased. Besides, I have not now funds to bear expenses. . . . You would like to know my prospects for making money, and so forth. It must be to somebody a profitable business. Mr. Pennell is with me and we have very far surpassed anybody in this country, and probably in the world, in making miniatures [daguerreotypes]. We have exchanged with some of the New Yorkers, and have sent some to Boston. They are as far beyond the one I sent home as that is beyond one you could make with a *pen*. I shall send you one by mail before long in a newspaper to Uncle A. B. and you must settle the postage with him. I have not time to tell you how it is done now. We make them not larger than a five cent piece [i.e., a half-dime, which measures ten-sixteenths of an inch in diameter] or as large as the one you have. Since we commenced, the opinions of people with regard to our success have changed about as many times as the weather, but all give it up now. In a fair day it requires three minutes sitting and we know positively that we can have an apparatus that will not require more than thirty seconds.[16]

The type of camera Southworth and Pennell were using had been patented by Alexander Wolcott. Of wooden construction with a circular opening at one end, the camera received the light reflected from the sitter on a concave mirror (speculum) at the back. The speculum then focused the rays upon the sensitized plate facing the mirror near the front of the camera body. Three decades later, Southworth reminisced:

We made progress in 1840 in adapting apparatus to views and to miniatures from life. For the purpose of more rapid action by increased light, we planned and made a speculum thirteen inches in diameter, thirty inch focus, and weighing fifty-five pounds.[17]

Whether Southworth and Pennell were responsible for the reflector mirror is questionable. Southworth never publicly acknowledged that he had paid Amasa Holcomb, a manufacturer of reflecting telescopes at Southwick, Massachusetts, to develop a reflector for him. In a letter dated 1841, Holcomb reminded Southworth of this commission and its success, claiming, "It seems to us that the present state of perfection of your Daguerreotype so far as the optical part is concerned is endebted to our experiments *principally.*"[18]

In time, gradual improvements in lens designs and the use of chemical accelerators for shorter exposures rendered Wolcott's camera obsolete. Southworth described the results of some of these innovations:

Improvements in apparatus and the use of bromine had helped us to use a light comfortable to the eyes, and permit us to work in about one minute in the best light in the day. We now began to electrotype our plates, improving their polish, and thus greatly improving our pictures. [Electroplating was used to add more silver to the daguerreotype plate.] We invented and perfected and patented our swing polishing plate-holder. For us this was a great acquisition, for it enabled us to finish our plates with great perfection.[19]

According to Holcomb's letter, the time and materials required for the research and construction of these mechanical innovations totaled one thousand dollars. Such expenditures drove Southworth into debt by the spring of 1841. Fortunately, a number of businessmen and manufacturers came to his aid, contributed to the studio's financial solvency and insured its survival.[20]

Southworth had meanwhile decided to establish a daguerreotype studio in Boston. On November 29, 1840, he wrote to his sister Nancy:

I am about going into company with the two first rate mechanics. Mr. Pennell and myself think there is no other way for us to get along. We shall probably leave Cabotville soon and go to Boston and Lowell. Perhaps we shall need the assistance of two or three Females in our business and if we should and I should go to Boston, I want you to come there for a while.

Besides expressing his desire to move to Boston and requesting his sister to join the studio staff, he also stated his intention to admit two unidentified "first rate mechanics" as partners in his business. Although his earlier partnership with Pennell was begun with capital of less than fifty dollars and he now needed substantially more to survive, Southworth hardly lacked self-confidence. A letter to Nancy dated April 22, 1841 reveals his barely concealed optimism:

We are about removing our miniature apparatus to Boston. Our prospects are at present flattering. Our miniatures are by far the best in America, probably in the world. We sent specimens to England last October [1840] and have just heard from them. None near as good there. . . . We hope to get our room ready in less than a month. . . . My partners are in Cabotville and will remain there until I get fitted up here. . . .

Despite the optimism, the going was not easy:

The spring of 1841 found us in Boston deeply in debt contracted in our experiments during the previous year. We were among strangers, without funds, and often unable to take our letters from the post office. Postage was not in those days required to be prepaid, and business letters were usually 12½ or 18¾ cents each. Our whole expense of living was sometimes as low as seventy-five cents per week. In almost any established business, with the same industry and economy, we should have accumulated money.[21]

In light of Boston's role as the hub of the commercial, financial, cultural and social activity of New England, the move was a wise calculated risk. Southworth was fully aware that Boston's educated class of wealthy businessmen, socially prominent families, and leading intellectuals offered ideal patrons for the quality of portraiture he was determined to maintain.

THE FORMATION OF THE SOUTHWORTH & HAWES PARTNERSHIP

The early years of Southworth's Boston studio brought major changes as the business prospered. In 1842, Southworth moved the studio from its initial location atop Scollay's building to a new and more permanent one in Tremont Row. In 1843, Pennell left the firm and moved South.[22] That same year Southworth replaced Pennell with a new full partner of the studio, Josiah Johnson Hawes.

The early life of Josiah Johnson Hawes parallels that of Southworth. The first of the eight children of Edward and Martha Johnson Hawes, Josiah was born on February 20, 1808, in East Sudbury (now Wayland), Massachusetts.[23] Three out of his four brothers, interestingly enough, practiced daguerreotypy during at least one stage in their careers. Like Southworth, Hawes had a varied career before becoming a daguerreotypist. Initially apprenticed as a carpenter, he taught himself how to paint. From 1829 until about 1841 he earned his living as an itinerant portrait artist and frequently lectured about electricity in various New England towns. He described his conversion from journeyman carpenter to itinerant artist in the following words:

Happening one day to come across an ordinary oil painting which I was admiring, a friend of mine asked me to close one eye and look at the picture through my hand with the other eye. The surprising change which took place, from its being an ordinary flat canvas to a realistic copy of nature with all its aerial perspective and beauty so affected me, that from that time I was ambitious to become an artist. I purchased books, colors, and brushes and commenced the study of art.

I practiced miniature painting on ivory, likewise portraits in oil, landscapes, etc., with no teacher but my books.[24]

His training in art was later to become an important influence on his work with Southworth.

In March of 1840, Hawes attended François Gouraud's lectures on the daguerreotype process—ironically the same series of talks in Boston at which Southworth was presumably present. Hawes later described his introduction to the new picture-making technique:

About this time—1840—the excitement of the discovery of the daguerreotype took place: and some specimens of it which I saw in Boston changed my course entirely. I gave up painting and commenced daguerreotyping in 1841.[25]

Like Southworth, Hawes felt the necessity to improve upon the daguerreotype process as described by Gouraud in 1840. Reluctant to abandon a proven source of income, however, Hawes continued to paint until 1841.

During an interview in 1896, Hawes described in detail how he first began in his new profession:

I immediately commenced the business of making the daguerreotype, and went out to Arlington and got the biggest window I could find, and commenced taking pictures. I moved around from place to place. It used to take an hour to take a picture in those days; but people were willing to sit an hour for their likeness. Now they can't keep still a moment.[26]

As a fledgling itinerant daguerreotypist, Hawes must have traveled through the same territory where he had previously plied his trade as a portrait artist. He daguerreotyped in Arlington and Lowell, Massachusetts, and tested the market in Providence, Rhode Island.[27] An undated trade card reads: "Superior Colored Daguerreotypes by Hawes & Somerby. Electro-Type Gilding and Silvering."[28] This would imply that Hawes had combined resources with a partner sometime prior to joining Southworth in 1843. Years later, the Hawes children could recall having heard the name

Somerby mentioned at home, but could not supply further facts.[29]

If Southworth and Hawes were acquainted prior to forming the partnership, no record can be found to substantiate it. However, statements by both Southworth and Hawes and existing correspondence date the partnership from November of 1843.

Despite the two partners' tremendous volume of business, Southworth & Hawes were plagued for several years with continual debts and meager earnings. A note from the Scovills, dated October of 1843, hints that part of the problem was the expense of Southworth & Hawes's continuing experiments to improve the quality of their daguerreotypes. The Scovills approved of the "decision to try less experiments" and went on to say "[we] trust you will make more Money for the year to come than the last."[30] The continuing fluctuation of the business activity level in the studio and a general decline in the firm's solvency soon discouraged Southworth.

Hawes was determined to see things through, but Southworth saw new opportunities spring up in the West. Impressed by the talk of gold just waiting to be picked up off the ground in California, Southworth set out for the West in 1849 in search of gold.[31] His letters after his arrival in California reveal not only a zest for adventure but also a fascination with the topography.

Prudently, Southworth did not abandon all ties with his studio. Prior to his departure, he drew up a partnership agreement with Hawes whereby the two men could follow separate professions but share profits and losses equally.[32] Following the example of many who remained in the East, Hawes expressed interest in Southworth's Californian venture by investing in half of his partner's share in the joint-stock company he had joined, the Bunker Hill Trading and Mining Association. While in California, Southworth remained faithful to his contract with Hawes. In a letter dated 1850, he apologized for not having time to detail an account of his "pecuniary affairs" for Hawes's benefit. Nevertheless, he sent his letter with a sum of about $120.00 in gold to be divided equally between his wife and his sister.

In the meantime, back in Boston, Hawes confessed to Nancy in 1850 that "Business is very dull. I have not much more than paid expenses for last fortnight. . . ." The business downturn was probably attributable to cloudy skies, of which Mrs. Hawes complained that year. There must have been some good days as well, for she wrote to her brother on February 11, 1850: "Our business is going on smoothly, and we have plenty to do in good weather."

GRAND PARLOR STEREOSCOPE

Southworth returned to Boston in January of 1851. The profits of the Californian venture had been minimal.[33] Resuming his partnership with Hawes, Southworth focused his activities on the invention and patenting of technical equipment relating to the interest of the firm. Among the most widely acclaimed of these inventions was the Grand Parlor Stereoscope which won the firm a gold medal at the Fair of the Massachusetts Charitable Mechanics Association in 1853. Listed among the "Machinery and New Inventions," this Stereoscope, proclaimed the judges' report, surpassed "all its predecessors in the beauty and perfection of the results which it attains."

Theirs was not the first such machine by any means. As early as 1832, the British physicist Sir Charles Wheatstone had described stereoscopic principles and had constructed a practical viewing apparatus by 1838.[34] Wheatstone's instrument presented the reflections of two slightly dissimilar images to the viewer's eyes by a pair of mirrors. The differences between the two images were identical to the variations of the two images perceived by each of the two eyes. Combined optically behind the viewer's eyes, these two images created an illusion of virtual depth. In 1844 Sir David Brewster perfected a different type of viewer which used photographs instead of drawings. Brewster's lenticular stereoscope, which allowed the two pictures to be directly seen and coalesced by means of two lenses, superseded Wheatstone's reflective type and became the basic design for nearly all 19th-century stereoscope viewers. Unable to do much more than exhibit his apparatus during the late 1840s, Brewster finally convinced the Paris opticians Duboscq and Soleil in 1851 to manufacture stereoscopes. Once the viewers were mass produced and photographers began to make binocularly paired images, the stereoscope gained a tremendous success and popularity.

Southworth's stereoscope was significant for two reasons. First, it was not fashioned after the Brewster model but was constructed with a set of mirrors which were placed at forty-five degree angles to the viewer's sight, which in turn reflected two dissimilar binocular daguerreotype images. Southworth had reverted to the older Wheatstone design because it would allow the daguerreotypes to be placed in darkened boxes with perfectly controlled light. This control would then minimize the distracting and unwanted reflections from the plates. Secondly, the sheer size of the instrument was impressive and unique. Whereas most stereoscopes, whether using daguerreotypes or paper photographs, were scaled for relatively small sixth-plate images, Southworth's was built to use his customary full-plate daguerreotypes. A large cabinet resting on a decorative cast-iron stand designed to sit fairly permanently in front of a parlor window, this apparatus achieved considerable publicity for the firm. On January 8, 1853, *Gleason's Pictorial* reported that the Grand Parlor Stereoscope "so vastly improved upon Professor Wheaton's [sic] stereoscopic principle and discovery, as to have perfected an invention which may be said to have made the whole discovery their own."

Southworth & Hawes were so confident of the impressive qualities of their new invention that their advertising copy made the following claims:

> The Parlor and Gallery Stereoscope (the only one yet made) is now on exhibition at the "ARTISTS' DAGUERREOTYPE ROOMS," 5½ Tremont Row, opposite Brattle Street. A spacious Room has been purposely fitted up, making in addition to the usual exhibition, the largest and finest display of Daguerreotypes ever shown. Visitors, either day or evening, will be sure of a rich treat. . . . A large list of names, interesting to the public, might be mentioned, whose likenesses are on exhibition; . . .

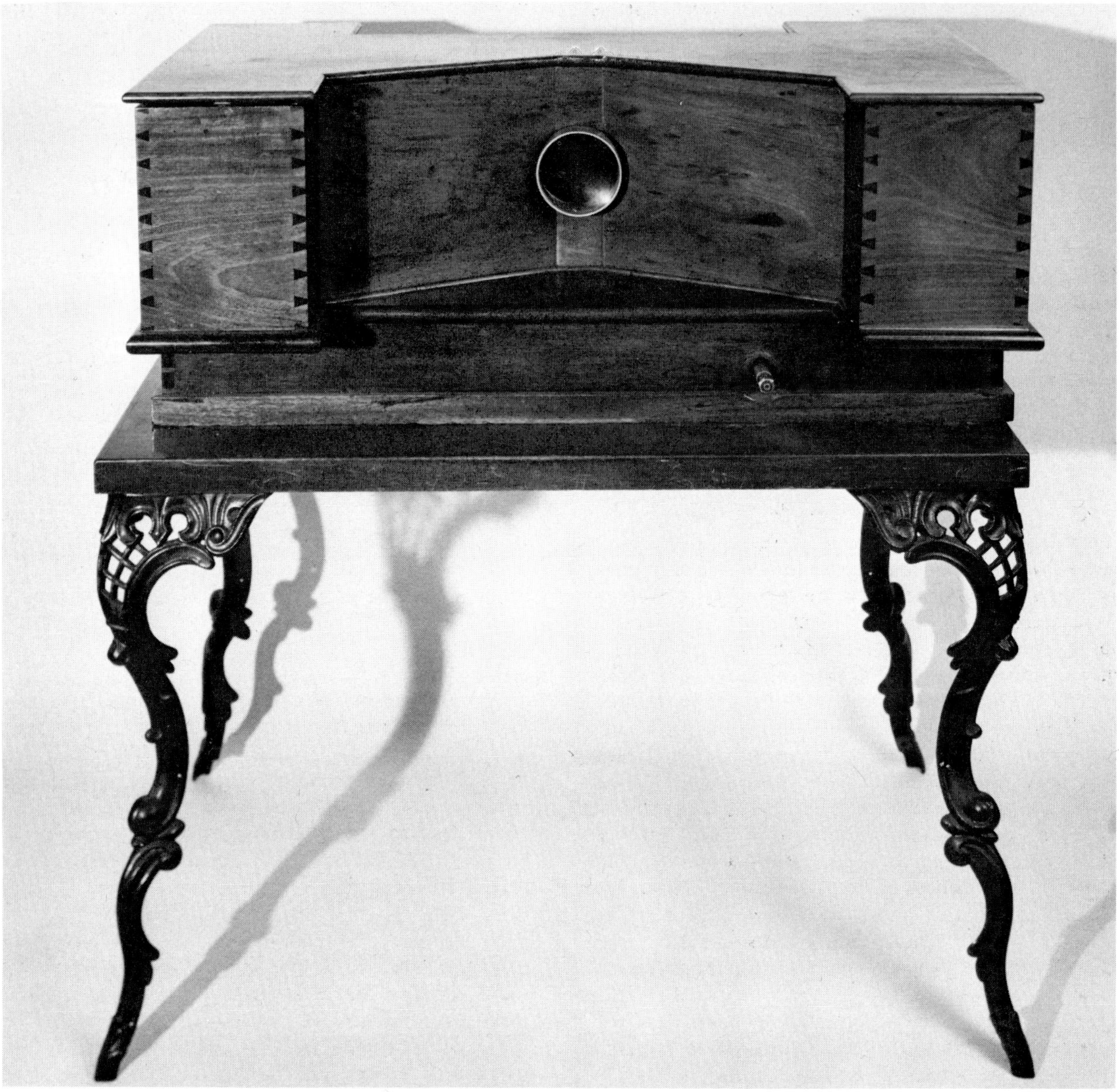

Southworth & Hawes's Grand Parlor and Gallery Stereoscope. Collection of the IMP/GEH.

Messrs. Southworth & Hawes would gratefully acknowledge the many favors of their friends, and of the artists and lovers of art in Boston and vicinity. It is with great satisfaction and perfect confidence, that we are again able to invite them to an examination of the last most wonderful and most beautiful improvement in Daguerreotypes; the transformation of shadows into substance—the change of pictures upon a plain surface into statuary and solidity.[35]

A few scenes selected for stereoscopic presentation were literally statues: the *Laocoön Group,* the *Apollo Belvedere, General Joseph Warren* (Plate 104), a statue of *Clytie* (Plate 105), and a funerary monument from Mount Auburn Cemetery (Plate 103).[36] Finding the spatial illusion absolute, a writer for the magazine *To-day* commented in June of 1852: "the effect of the *Laocoön* in this stereoscope is really finer than one often gains in looking at the statue." Other views, such as those of Brattle Street (Plate 100), the Roebling Suspension Bridge at Niagara (Plate 96), and the interior of the Boston Athenaeum (Plates 102a, 102b) make use of viewpoint and natural forms to exaggerate or emphasize the stereoscopic effect of deep, perspectival space.

Southworth & Hawes were granted their patent on July 11, 1854, for a camera which varied the exposures for stereoscopic effect both horizontally and vertically, "in which the two positions of the camera are upon a line making an angle of forty-five degrees with the horizon." Another method of producing an appearance of deep focus was described in the patent specifications:

We sometimes, however, take the first picture with the focus adjusted to nearer objects, and the second to distant ones, with a fine effect, the two coalescing in the stereoscope and forming a perfect picture, presenting at the same time the perfect foreground and the perfect background, the imperfections of the individual pictures not being apparent.[37]

According to Hawes, an additional patent for the camera was secured in Europe. A second patent was issued to Southworth & Hawes on June 19, 1855, for the stereoscope viewer or "Grand Parlor and Gallery Stereoscope."[38]

Such major photographers as Platt D. Babbitt and Marcus Aurelius Root[39] attested to the ultimate realism of Southworth & Hawes's stereoscopic views, and many prominent Bostonians bought season tickets to see these simulated three-dimensional images at the Tremont Row studio. The firm's confidence in the apparatus, however, was scarcely enough to guarantee its financial success. Priced at $1,160.00, the Grand Parlor Stereoscope was out of reach of all but the wealthy.[40]

Daguerreotype Supplies from the Southworth & Hawes Studio

Southworth also improved photographic techniques and manufactured cameras and coating boxes. The letterhead on the firm's invoices reminded the customers that among supplies furnished were "Cameras which will not reverse pictures, and every variety of Apparatus, Chemicals, and Materials, furnished and warranted." In addition, there were manufacturers, technicians and distributors involved with the firm's sales business. The Scovill Manufacturing Company of Waterbury, Connecticut, began retailing Southworth's camera within a month of its display at the 1842 fair of the American Institute of the City of New York.[41] The Scovills continued to place orders for cameras with Southworth & Hawes at least through 1845. It is difficult to say precisely who constructed these cameras, but some were probably built at the studio. Existing evidence indicates that a certain E. N. Coburn was responsible for several—the same E. N. Coburn who built daguerreian equipment for another leading Boston daguerreotypist, John Adams Whipple.[42] For lenses, Southworth & Hawes dealt with George Prosch, a reputable lens-maker who had produced Samuel F. B. Morse's camera equipment.

Second in importance on the list of Southworth & Hawes's daguerreotype supplies were the type and quality of the plates. The Scovill Manufacturing Company supplied most of the plates used in the studio and sold through the business. Hallmarks on some of the plates, however, reveal that the supply came from several other manufacturers as well, including Edward White, Christofle and Gaudin (Appendix B). The Scovill Manufacturing Company was contracted as the sole producer of Southworth & Hawes's swing polishing plate-holder,[43] patented in 1846 and designed to facilitate the buffing and polishing of the silvered copper plate to a mirror finish.

If Southworth's chief interest was the invention and development of new articles for distribution and retail, Hawes concentrated on mechanical aids that improved the appearance of his portraits. Hawes took great pride in his finest daguerreotypes. His famous portrait of Chief Justice Lemuel Shaw (Plate 10) as well as another of Miss Hodges of Salem (probably Plate 26) were each insured for $1,000.00 when they were shown at the fair of the Massachusetts Charitable Mechanics Association.[44] Hawes even went so far as to copyright some of his portraits.[45]

The prominence of Southworth's name in the studio during his lifetime creates the danger of underestimating Hawes. When Hawes spoke of the inventions produced in the studio, he revealed his active involvement in perfecting several of them. Among the inventions Hawes probably helped develop were the vignette used to make "bust" type portraits, a modified head screw to hold the sitter's head steady during the exposure, the curtain slide for plate-holders, and the swing-back camera,[46] an innovation allowing the plate frame to tilt and thereby compensate for the distortion of parallel lines. He perfected what appears to be a prototype of the later Dallmeyer lens, a triple lens designed to reduce aberration to a minimum which was especially useful in copying flat work (Plates 106, 107).[47]

Although a far less visible member of the firm, Hawes was an equal partner until the firm's dissolution in 1862, after which he advertised solely under his own name, referring in passing to "the old firm of Southworth & Hawes."[48] He maintained the studio until his final trip to Crawford Notch, New Hampshire, where he died on August 7, 1901.[49] Southworth worked as an independent for the remainder of his career, lecturing and studying the photographic applications to graphology. He finally retired to Charlestown, Massachusetts, where he died on March 3, 1894.[50] Both artists had devoted most of their lives to photography and had made significant contributions to the aesthetics of portraiture.

Aesthetics of Portraiture

The economic and social need for photographic portraiture stemmed basically from the traditional desire for the portrayed human face. Photography did not create the public desire for portrait collections, as evidenced in the immense popularity of Lavater's *Essays on Physiognomy,* a late 18th-century "picture gallery executed by some of the leading painters and engravers of the century and containing admirable likenesses of many of the famous figures of the day."[51] The photographic portrait simply reinforced the existing need and perhaps made Lavater's Gallery more objective. In 1844, the New York daguerreotypist Mathew B. Brady began to collect and publish what he called *Gallery of Illustrious Americans.*[52] Similarly, John Plumbe, Jr., a Philadelphia daguerreotypist, issued his *National Plumbeotype Gallery* in 1847.[53] Both of these collections consisted of lithographs copied from daguerreotype portraits.

The entire aesthetic premise of portrait images was founded upon two related yet different ideas: likeness and expression. By far the majority of daguerreotype portraits are simple, unassuming presentations of the sitters' appearance. Usually lacking in emotional intensity, the faces blankly stare out of the portrait frame with mindless endurance. The sitter was either suspicious of the machinery and alchemy or simply discomfited by having to hold a rigid posture for upwards of thirty seconds without moving, blinking or breathing. The resulting record of the physical appearance, with little interpretation of an inner character of the human subject, was primarily a document that could be used for memory's ruminations when the mind forgot the details. On this documentary level, most daguerreotype portraits were undistinguished. Melville's Pierre in the novel *Pierre; or The Ambiguities* (1850/51) knew this well:

For he considered with what infinite readiness now, the most faithful portrait of anyone could be taken by the Daguerreotype, whereas in former times a faithful portrait was only within the power of the moneyed, or mental aristocrats of the earth. How natural then the inference, that instead of, as in old times, immortalizing a genius, a portrait now only *dayalized* a dunce. Besides, when everybody has his portrait published, true distinction lies in not having yours published at all. For if you are published along with Tom, Dick, and Harry, and wear a coat of their cut, how then are you distinct from Tom, Dick, and Harry?

Pierre was not alone in seeing little value in the likenesses produced by the daguerreotype camera. Phoebe Pyncheon, in Hawthorne's *The House of the Seven Gables* (1850/51), shared his view completely: "I don't much like pictures of that sort—they are so hard and stern; besides dodging away from the eye and trying to escape altogether. They are conscious of looking very unamiable, I suppose, and therefore hate to be seen."

For portraiture in general, likeness was the major aim of the photographer. According to Marcus Aurelius Root, who was thinking no doubt of the majority of his sitters, "faithful likeness is the chief desideratum in portraiture, the mere head and bust are preferable to a larger proportion of the figure."[54] He added further that if an ordinary portrait was simply a faithful likeness, an artistic portrait was an expression of "livingness" and "individuality." "For a portrait . . . however splendidly colored, and however skillfully finished its manifold accessories, is worse than worthless if the pictured face does not show the *soul* of the original,—that *individuality* or *self*-hood, which differentiates *him* from all beings, past, present, or future."[55] "Expression," Root added, "is a *sine qua non* towards what a man really is, whether in an original or a portrait."[56] The manuals and literature on portrait photography, the critics as well as the photographers, all called for the camera artist to pay careful attention to the forms of expression, the posing of the sitter and the use of evocative lighting. By observing the transitory nuances of the physiognomy—smiles, tilts of the head, and fugitive movements of the lips and eyes—the artist photographer had to discover the just expression, the eloquent expression that proffers the character of the sitter.

A mere likeness was easily accomplished by anyone who could handle the equipment and chemicals, but combining the appearance with expression took a certain amount of genius on the part of the artist photographer, as Root pointed out: "To do all this is the prerogative of *genius* exclusively; mere *talent* cannot effect it, neither can industry, nor the highest mechanical aptitude."[57]

The work of Southworth & Hawes perfectly exemplifies the product of such a "genius." Their studio was best known for its portraits of Boston's intelligentsia and cultured upper stratum. Many who considered a visit to Boston a necessity thought their trip incomplete without a sitting at the Southworth & Hawes studio. The two partners welcomed as patrons such notables as Ralph Waldo Emerson (Plate 3), Nathaniel Hawthorne, Henry Wadsworth Longfellow (Plate 6), Oliver Wendell Holmes, Daniel Webster (Plates 19, 20), Louis Kossuth (Plate 65) and Jenny Lind (Plate 66). On several occasions, Charles Dickens visited the studio in the company of the Boston publisher James T. Fields but unfortunately failed to sit for his portrait.[58] He had probably come to share in the congeniality of the studio, which had become a gathering place for Boston's elite—much as Nadar's was the center of the Parisian intellectuals.

THE MAKING OF THE PORTRAIT

What was it like to have one's portrait taken in the Southworth & Hawes studio? When the customer arrived at the studio, he was received in the exhibition room on the third floor where, amidst props creating a mock-parlor setting, examples of the studio's finest work were displayed. As each customer's turn came, Asa Southworth, Albert's brother, would announce the appropriate name. The actual camera exposure was carried out in the operating room, located at least one story higher than the exhibition room, among the several rooms connecting fourth floor suites, the last of which was illuminated by a large skylight. Since the only source of light was the sun, business depended heavily upon the atmospheric conditions and the amount of available natural light. Here, in the operating room, at least one of the partners personally posed the sitters and manipulated the plates and camera.[59]

Not all aspects of the portrait making were accomplished by the partners. Southworth's sister Nancy was responsible for the hand coloring of the daguerreotypes.[60] Nancy Niles Southworth had come from Vermont around the winter of 1841 to help her brother with his new business and had stayed with the studio to marry his partner Josiah in 1849. As early as 1843 the firm furnished colored images, and by 1845 Southworth was giving instructions in the art.[61] The studio did not exaggerate when it boasted of the superiority of its colored daguerreotypes:

We blend artistically, our lights and shadows; and, when we color, avoid the harsh, but, patternlike outline, or semblance of a paper profile, or theorem.[62]

Another advertisement for the studio's colored daguerreotypes reads:

All persons, without exception, pronounce our Coloring unequalled. Artists themselves say it is as true to nature as it can possibly be.[63]

Applied dry with extreme care, their colors are subtle and beautiful.[64] The tints are usually flesh colored, often enhanced by pastel blouse fronts and monochrome backgrounds. Every so often some spectacular background effects lend a romantic aura to the portrait that is the partners' unique trademark (Plate 32). Only occasionally did the prevailing Victorian exuberance induce them to garishly color the entire plate, as in the half plate of a dishevelled unidentified young woman seated within a simulated landscape of ice floes (Plate 43).

Although Nancy assisted in the coloring of the finished plates, there were no assistant cameramen or operators in the studio—a fact in which Southworth & Hawes took great pride. Hawes was most likely the more practical artist in the firm. While his partner had been a proprietor of a drugstore, Hawes had been a practicing painter. Southworth was the theorist of the two and at times publicly aired his thoughts on the aesthetics of photography. In his speech delivered in June of 1870 to the National Photographic Association of the United States in Cleveland, Ohio, Southworth discussed the photographer as a potential artist and stressed his mental qualifications as more important than any facility with the tools at hand:

> The artist, even in photography, must go beyond discovery and the knowledge of facts; he must create and invent truths and produce new developments of facts. . . . He should not only be familiar with nature and her philosophy, but he should be informed as to the principles which govern or influence human character. History and poetry should be to him mere *pastime*; observation of nature, cause and effect, should be his employment. . . . The mere manipulations, the handling of brush or chisel, is as mechanical and in no respect beyond adjusting the camera or retouching correctly. The mind must express the value and mark and impress resemblances and differences. It must be instructed and directed by impressions, at the time, emanating from the subject itself.

Southworth proceeds to discuss the elements of good portraiture:

> What is to be done is obliged to be done quickly. The whole character of the sitter is to be read at first sight; the whole likeness, as it shall appear when finished, is to be seen at first, in each and all its details, and in their unity and combination. Natural and accidental defects are to be separated from natural and possible perfections; these latter to obliterate or hide the former. Nature is not all to be represented as it is, but as it ought to be, and might possibly have been; and it is required of and should be the aim of the artist-photographer to produce in the likeness the best possible character and finest expression of which that particular face or figure could ever have been capable. But in the result there is to be no departure from truth in the delineation and representation of beauty, and expression, and character.[65]

Southworth & Hawes faithfully applied these precepts to their portraiture. Nowhere in all of their approximately 1,500 extant daguerreotypes is a formula pose or a facial gesture repeated. The only possible exception to this rule is the vignetted oval portraits of females that were one of their leitmotifs; but even in those of the same sitter (Plates 35a-d), subtle angles of the head and direction of the eyes modulate the particular character of the woman. The full range of individual treatments of the sitters can be studied in comparing various poses: the portraits of Daniel Webster (Plate 20) and an unidentified gentleman (Plate 23); the sensuously colored "Boston Beauty" (Plate 32) and the vignetted version of the same woman in profile (Plate 33); or the informal and eccentric arrangements of the figure in the portraits of Lola Montez (Plates 27, 28) and the quiet, formal pose of Harriet Beecher Stowe (Plate 29).[66]

Portraits of both the famous and lesser-known subjects reveal the same respect and sensitivity in treatment. Although differing in results, dramatic spotlighting and Rembrandtesque light effects are similarly utilized in the portrait of the unidentified female with white bonnet (Plate 36) and in the well-known portrait of Justice Lemuel Shaw (Plate 10). It was undoubtedly Southworth & Hawes's intention to fashion each portrait in accordance with the personality of the individual sitter that accounts not only for the relatively high cost of their portraits but also for the studio's fame and reputation.

ACHIEVEMENTS OF SOUTHWORTH & HAWES

Compliments, accolades and official awards were constantly accorded them despite their lack of participation in the established photographic community. When Southworth & Hawes did exhibit, it was not at photographic salons, nor were they often mentioned in the popular photographic press. In short, they were not commercially aggressive the way Brady or Plumbe was. Rather, their reputation was the product of informal, personal recommendations and the publicity resulting from the portraits engraved from their daguerreotypes which appeared repeatedly in *Gleason's Pictorial Drawing Room Companion* (later *Ballou's Pictorial Drawing Room Companion*). Secondly, their reputation was the result of the exposure of their work to the general public at such trade shows as the Massachusetts Charitable Mechanics Association fairs and at the displays they mounted in the reception rooms of their studio.

Evidence, however, indicates that Southworth & Hawes did not always exhibit their "best" work. As Southworth stated emphatically: "The best specimens are always taken by the customers; three-fourths of those exhibited are second-best, or rejected ones."[67] If the subject was of public interest, the firm could sometimes make copies for sale. In these instances, for example, as with the portrait of Daniel Webster in profile, the firm even assumed some of the manufacturing expense.[68] The majority of the portraits displayed either at a fair or at the studio were not always the best version of a given likeness. Likewise, nearly all of the daguerreotype portraits by Southworth & Hawes presently in public collections are of this "reject" category. A few examples of choice quality exist in private collections, but access is often difficult and most have not yet been catalogued. What is therefore most surprising is that their reputation is so easily assured by what was considered not their finest work at the time. What has come down to us—mainly from the studio's collection through the Hawes family—remains so powerful, so compelling that it is difficult to imagine that better examples could exist.

Although portraits were by far their most important concern, Southworth & Hawes's fame did not rest completely on their work in portraiture. Their landscapes and views equal the portrayals of the human subject in their expressive interpretations and clarity of depiction.[69] The views of Niagara Falls in the winter (Plates 94, 95), the Roebling Suspension Bridge (Plate 96) and Mount Auburn Cemetery (Plates 89-93) are at once documents of appearance and distillations of the essential meanings of the scenes. Very few daguerreotypists could have selected a detail of the suspension bridge which so powerfully communicates the interrelated meanings of the man-made product and its natural surroundings. The monuments at Mount Auburn, on the other hand, are surrounded with a kind of arcane ambiguity resulting from the theatrical chiaroscuro effects.

Southworth & Hawes strove to record and interpret everything they daguerreotyped. They achieved Emerson's ideal of "the higher use of the material world . . . to furnish us types or pictures to express the thoughts of the mind." How closely the two partners shared in the spirit of this view is evident in the following statement by Southworth:

> The artist is conscious of something besides the mere physical, in every object in nature. He feels its expression, he sympathizes with its character, he is impressed with its language; his heart, mind, and soul are stirred in its contemplation. It is the life, the feeling, the mind, the soul of the subject itself.[70]

As records of 19th-century America, the daguerreotypes from the Southworth & Hawes studio are unquestionably the quintessential product of the period. More importantly, they are testaments to the partners' attempt to define those truths that Whitman felt waited in all things. Their work presents to the modern viewer the meaning and the expressive spirit of the facts they documented.

NOTES

Much of the primary research on the lives of Southworth & Hawes was conducted by Charles L. Moore for "Two Partners in Boston: The Daguerreian Artistry of Albert Southworth and Josiah Hawes," a dissertation submitted in partial fulfillment of the requirements for the degree of Doctor of Philosophy in the Department of American Culture at the University of Michigan, 1974.

1. The relationship between Emerson's emphasis on direct observation of nature and early photography was first pointed out by Richard Rudisill, *Mirror Image: The Influence of the Daguerreotype on American Society,* Albuquerque: University of New Mexico Press, 1971, pp. 16-17.
2. Marcus Aurelius Root, *The Camera and the Pencil; or The Heliographic Art . . .,* Philadelphia: M. A. Root, 1864, p. xvi.
3. *Ibid.,* p. 24.
4. The list of Southworth & Hawes's correspondents comprises a who's who of famous American daguerreotypists: Platt D. Babbitt, Mathew Brady, Alexander Hesler, John Mayall, John Plumbe, Marcus Aurelius Root, William Shew, Robert H. Vance, Edward White. The partners' correspondence and business records consist of dialogues with other photographers and students having difficulties with processing and equipment, as well as orders for cameras and accessories and complaints regarding unsatisfactory merchandise.
5. Mentioned in François Gouraud, "Manner of Taking Portraits," *Boston Daily Advertiser and Patriot,* 26 March 1840. Reprinted in Gouraud's *Description of the Daguerreotype Process or A Summary of M. Gouraud's Public Lectures, According to the Principles of M. Daguerre, with a Description of a Provisionary Method for Taking Human Portraits,* Boston: Dutton & Wentworth's Print, 1840, p. 14. (See Appendix A.) Susse was also responsible for writing the first directions for making portraits, which was published as an appended chapter to the November 1839 edition of Daguerre's manual.
6. See the undated letter from Draper to Marcus Aurelius Root in the latter's *The Camera and the Pencil; or The Heliographic Art . . .,* Philadelphia: M. A. Root, 1864, pp. 341–342. Root's book is the first full-length artistic treatise on photographic portraiture to be published in this country. Also cf. *ibid.,* pp. 346–348 for Samuel F. B. Morse's account of the beginning of photographic portraiture in America.
7. Cf. Helmut and Alison Gernsheim, *L. J. M. Daguerre: The History of the Diorama and the Daguerreotype,* 2nd revised ed., New York: Dover, 1968, p. 117.
8. Cited in Robert Hunt, *A Popular Treatise on the Art of Photography, Including Daguerreotype . . .,* Glasgow: Richard Griffin, 1841, p. 64. Hunt cites an article published by Draper in the *London and Edinburgh Philosophical Magazine,* September 1840.
9. T. S. Arthur's article appeared in *Godey's Magazine Lady's Book,* 1849. Cited in Beaumont Newhall's Introduction to the reprint of Root's *The Camera and the Pencil . . .,* Pawlet, Vt.: Helios, 1971, p. 5
10. Judges' Report, Massachusetts Charitable Mechanics Association, 1847, Southworth & Hawes Collection, International Museum of Photography at George Eastman House (hereafter: S&H, IMP/GEH).
11. Undated advertisement, S&H, IMP/GEH. Southworth & Hawes's minimum price for a medium-sized daguerreotype portrait was $5.00, according to *Humphrey's Journal,* V (November 1853), p. 223. In contrast, Brady's price for the same-sized portrait was only $2.00; cf. Beaumont Newhall, *The Daguerreotype in America,* 3rd. revised ed., New York: Dover, 1976, p. 63.
12. Cf. Newhall, *op. cit.,* pp. 28–30. Information pertaining to Southworth's early life is in the documents and miscellaneous clippings in the Hawes's family papers, collection of Edward L. Hawes, Springfield, Illinois. Also cf. letter, Albert Southworth, Beals Bar, Calif., to Nancy Hawes, Boston, 15 March 1850, S&H, IMP/GEH.
13. Albert Southworth, "An Address to the National Photographic Association of the United States," *The Philadelphia Photographer,* VIII (October 1871), p. 316. (Hereafter referred to as "An Address.")
14. Samuel F. B. Morse, *Evening Star* (New York), 24 February 1840, cited in Newhall, *The Daguerreotype,* p. 30.
15. Southworth, "An Address," p. 317.
16. Letter, Albert Southworth, Cabotville, Mass., to Nancy Southworth, Boston, 30 September 1840, S&H, IMP/GEH.
17. Southworth, "An Address," p. 317.
18. Letter, Amasa Holcomb, Southwick, Mass., to Albert Southworth, Boston, 25 May 1841, S&H, IMP/GEH.
19. Southworth, "An Address," p. 318.
20. *Ibid.,* p. 317.
21. *Ibid.,* pp. 317–318.
22. Cf. *ibid.,* p. 318; and letter, Thomas Norris, Boston, to Messrs. Southworth and Hawes, Boston, 26 November 1843, S&H, IMP/GEH. Norris's order is addressed to "Messrs. Southworth and Hawes" rather than to "Mr. A. S. Southworth and Co.," the earlier designation. Also, with regard to Pennell, cf. letter, S. Eaton, Milledgeville, Georgia, to Albert Southworth, Boston, 11 March 1844, S&H, IMP/GEH.
23. Reminiscences, Hawes children, Boston, 1930s, S&H, IMP/GEH.
24. [Josiah Johnson Hawes], "Stray Leaves from the Diary of the Oldest Professional Photographer in the World," *Photo Era,* February 1906, p. 105.
25. *Ibid.,* p. 106.
26. "Among Ye Ancients," *Sunday Journal* (Boston), 15 March 1896, S&H, IMP/GEH.
27. "One of the Oldest," *Snap Shot,* III (June 1896), p. 317, annotated copy, property of Edward L. Hawes, Springfield, Illinois.

28. I. N. Phelps Stokes, *The Hawes Stokes Collection of American Daguerreotypes by Albert Sands Southworth and Josiah Johnson Hawes,* New York: The Metropolitan Museum of Art, 1939, p. 8.

29. Cf. newspaper clipping, unidentified Boston newspaper, 20 February 1898; and letter, Edward S. Hawes, Boston, to I. N. Phelps Stokes, New York, 15 January 1935, both in S&H, IMP/GEH.

30. Letter, J. M. L. & W. H. Scovill, Waterbury, Conn., to Albert Southworth, Boston, 30 October 1843, S&H, IMP/GEH.

31. Southworth read extensively about the West before his departure; he owned at least one publication on Western America. See receipt, five dollars paid by Albert Southworth, Boston, to Thomas O. Walker, Boston, for purchase of ". . . a new work entitled *The Exploring Expedition,*" 3 May 1845, S&H, IMP/GEH.

32. Articles of Agreement, signed by Albert Southworth and Josiah Johnson Hawes, Boston, 2 March 1849, S&H, IMP/GEH.

33. The decision summary of a lawsuit in the Circuit Court of the United States, Western District of Michigan, heard on 25 January 1876 and decided upon on 5 April 1876 by Judge Withey, stated: "In 1849 he [Southworth] went to California and remained nearly two years, till January, 1851, during which time he worked in the mines, and gave no attention to the art of photography." The decision was published in *Western Photographic News,* April 1876, pp. 233–236. This indicates that the view of San Francisco, customarily attributed to Southworth (Metropolitan Museum of Art, accession #37.14.42), is probably by another photographer, as yet unidentified. The probability is further strengthened by the fact that the view is clearly a part of the five-piece panorama of San Francisco dating from the winter of 1851/52, approximately a year after Southworth had departed from California. See Anita Ventura [Mozley], "Gold Rush Panoramas: San Francisco—1850 to 1853," *Sea Letter,* vol. II, 2 & 3 (October 1964), unpaginated. An expression of gratitude is due to Beaumont Newhall for calling our attention to the lawsuit.

34. Cf. Robert Taft, *Photography and the American Scene, A Social History, 1839–1889,* reprint of the 1938 edition, New York: Dover, 1964, p. 170; also cf. Helmut and Alison Gernsheim, *The History of Photography from the Camera Obscura to the Beginning of the Modern Era,* New York: McGraw-Hill, 1969, pp. 253–254, 256.

35. Advertisement for the Southworth & Hawes studio, n.d. [ca. 1853], S&H, IMP/GEH.

36. Cf. studio account book of Southworth & Hawes, listing views shown in the stereoscope as well as the purchasers of the seasons tickets to the Grand Parlor Stereoscope, 14 October 1852, S&H, IMP/GEH.

37. Patent Specifications for U.S. Patent No. 11,304, dated 11 July 1854, U.S. Patent Office, Washington, D.C.

38. Patent Specifications for U.S. Patent No. 13,106, dated 19 June 1855, U.S. Patent Office, Washington, D.C.

39. See letters: Platt Babbitt, Niagara Falls, to Albert Southworth, Boston, 23 October 1856; and Marcus Root, Philadelphia, to Albert Southworth, Boston, 26 May 1855, both in S&H, IMP/GEH.

40. Stokes, *op. cit.,* p. 11: "Filled with daguerreotypes and supplied with a dozen extra plates, it was advertised at $1,160.00."

41. Cf. letter, David J. Harris, New York, to Albert Southworth, Boston, 28 October 1842, S&H, IMP/GEH. Scovill and Co. purchased the patent rights "presumably to one or more of Southworth's camera developments" in 1842. Cf. unpublished manuscript on "The History of the Scovill Manufacturing Company." Courtesy of E. H. Davis, Plant Historian, Scovill Manufacturing Co., Waterbury, Conn., p. 92, n. 46.

42. E. N. Coburn's role in constructing cameras for Southworth & Hawes is difficult to determine. Few of his letters are clear. It is, however, fairly safe to assume that Coburn did perform work for Southworth from 1845 to 1847. Cf. "Good News for Backsliders," *Western Photographic News,* II (April 1876), p. 234; and letter, E. N. Coburn, Post Mills, Vt., to Albert Southworth, Boston, 14 January 1847, S&H, IMP/GEH.

43. Agreement between Southworth & Hawes, Boston, and J. M. L. & W. H. Scovill, Waterbury, Conn., 6 March 1846, S&H, IMP/GEH.

44. See "Among Ye Ancients," *Sunday Journal* (Boston), 15 March 1896; and "Oldest in the World," *Boston Herald,* 10 August 1901, S&H, IMP/GEH.

45. See unidentified newspaper clippings, 20 February 1898, S&H, IMP/GEH.

46. *Ibid.*

47. [Hawes], *op. cit.,* pp. 106–107.

48. Stokes, *op. cit.,* pp. 9–10. He cites an advertisement from *Russell's Horse Railroad Guide for Boston and Vicinity,* July 1862.

49. Newspaper clippings, thirty-six obituary notices on the death of Josiah Johnson Hawes, collection of Edward L. Hawes, Springfield, Illinois.

50. For Southworth's later career, cf. "An Address," pp. 318–319; for death date, cf. Newhall, *op. cit.,* p. 154.

51. Cited in John Liggett, *The Human Face,* New York: Stein & Day, 1974, p. 190. J. C. Lavater's *Physiognomische Fragmente zur Beförderung der Menschenkenntnis und Menschenliebe* appeared between 1775 and 1778 in Germany; by 1789 a number of English editions were published and the first French edition was underway. Lavater's work underwent many English and American editions during the 19th century. American portrait photographers could thus freely draw upon Lavater's theories. Cf. Root, *op. cit.,* p. 85.

52. Cf. Beaumont Newhall, *The History of Photography from 1839 to the Present Day,* rev. ed., New York: Museum of Modern Art, 1964, p. 26.

53. Cf. Taft, *op. cit.,* p. 50.

54. Root, *op. cit.,* p. 110.

55. *Ibid.,* p. 143.

56. *Ibid.,* p. 161.

57. *Ibid.,* p. 144.

58. Related in "Oldest American Photographer," *Transcript* (Boston), 9 August 1901. S&H, IMP/GEH.

59. For information on the practices of Southworth & Hawes, cf., among others, the letters: Albert Southworth, Boston, to George Dexter, Boston, 12 June 1844; Nancy Southworth Hawes, Boston, to Albert Southworth, city unknown, Calif., 11 February 1850; and Josiah Hawes, Boston, to Nancy Southworth Hawes, West Fairlee, Vt., 24 January 1853, all in S&H, IMP/GEH.

60. A label on the reverse of a framed daguerreotype portrait of Cassius Marcellus Clay by Southworth & Hawes (Museum of Fine Arts, Boston, no accession number) bears the following: "Hand-tinted by Mrs. Hawes."

61. Letter, L. C. Champney, Pittsfield, Mass., to Albert Southworth, Boston, 22 February 1843; also cf. letter, John Mayall, Philadelphia, to Albert Southworth, Boston, 14 December 1845, both in S&H, IMP/GEH.

62. Broadside advertising the Southworth & Hawes studio, n. d. [1850s], S&H, IMP/GEH.

63. Advertisement for the studio of Southworth & Hawes, n. d. [1850s], S&H, IMP/GEH.

64. The general method of coloring daguerreotypes consisted of mixing finely ground pigments with dissolved gum arabic and straining the mixture which was then allowed to dry and applied with a soft camel's hair brush. Atmospheric humidity appears to have been sufficient to activate the adhesive quality of the gum arabic. The majority of the daguerreotype manuals, while discouraging hand-coloring on the grounds that the straight daguerreotype was preferable, conceded that the public demanded hand-coloring. Cf. S. D. Humphrey, *American Hand Book of the Daguerreotype* . . ., New York: S. D. Humphrey, 1858, pp. 48–49: "Of all the so-called improvements in the Daguerreotype, the coloring is the least worthy of notice. Yet the operator is often, in fact most generally, called upon to hide an excellent specimen under *paint.* I can conceive of nothing more perfect in a Daguerreotype than a finely-developed image, with clearness of lights and shadows, possessing the lively tone resulting from good gilding."

65. Southworth, "An Address," pp. 320–321.

66. Rudisill, *op. cit.,* p. 178.

67. Broadside advertising the studio of Southworth & Hawes, n. d. [1850s], S&H, IMP/GEH.

68. Advertisement for the studio of Southworth & Hawes, n. d. [early 1850s], S&H, IMP/GEH.

69. Any consideration of Southworth & Hawes's daguerreotype views must include mention of their daguerreotypes of an eclipse taken in April or very early May of 1846. While not the first to photograph an eclipse, they produced images that were well-received. Cf. letters, Joseph Pennell, Waterbury, Conn., to Albert Southworth, Boston, 21 May 1846; and Joseph Tracy, Boston, to Albert Southworth, Boston, 6 May 1846, both in S&H, IMP/GEH. Unfortunately, none of these plates appear to be extant.

70. Southworth, "An Address," p. 322.

THE PLATES

The reproductions are faithful to the original appearance of the daguerreotype plates. The surface abrasions and scratches which have accumulated over the years and are now considered part of the photographic artifact have been reproduced along with the image proper. Because Southworth & Hawes chose not to use the corrective prisms or mirrors which were then available, most of their daguerreotypes are laterally reversed, from right to left, as in a mirror image. This reversal, too, has been faithfully reproduced. In some cases, the reproductions have been enlarged from the original daguerreotypes to show detail. The plate-size designation in the caption can be consulted to determine the original size.

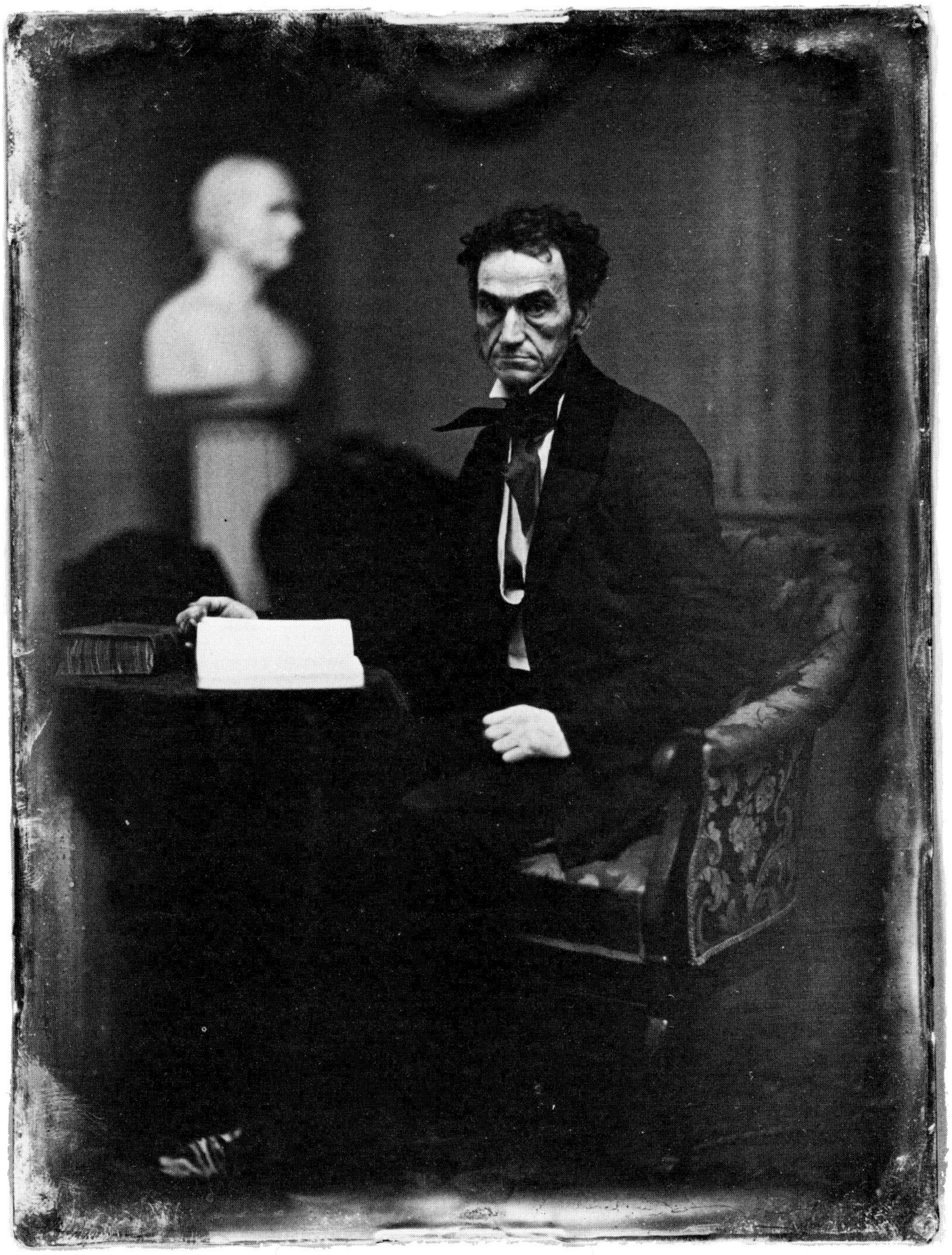

1. RUFUS CHOATE

Date: c. 1851. Whole plate. Hallmark: l.r.: S & F in lozenge. Metropolitan Museum of Art. Gift of I. N. Phelps Stokes and the Hawes Family. 37.14.48.*

One of America's most capable lawyers, Rufus Choate (1799–1859) was among the most scholarly of 19th-century public figures. His career included several appointments in state government as well as in the United States Congress and Senate where he became famous for his classical orations. Except for a short term during 1853–54 as attorney general of Massachusetts, from 1845 on he maintained a law practice directly adjoining the studio of Southworth & Hawes. After the two partners repeatedly requested a sitting, Choate agreed to pose for a portrait, provided he should not be kept waiting and the sitting take no more than fifteen minutes. On the appointed day he rushed in, posed four or five times in the allotted quarter hour and rushed back to his client-filled office. The resulting likeness appropriately expresses his character by using law books and a classical bust of an orator as symbols of his intellectual power.

[''Among Ye Ancients,'' *Boston Sunday Journal,* 15 March 1896.]

* The abbreviations for the hallmark locations are traditional to most art catalogues: ''l'' refers to ''lower'' when used first, ''u'' is ''upper''; when second in abbreviation, ''l'' refers to ''left'' while ''r'' is ''right.'' Where the plate has been hand-colored, mention has been made. In addition, each entry cites the collection from which the daguerreotype was borrowed and the accession number, when available.

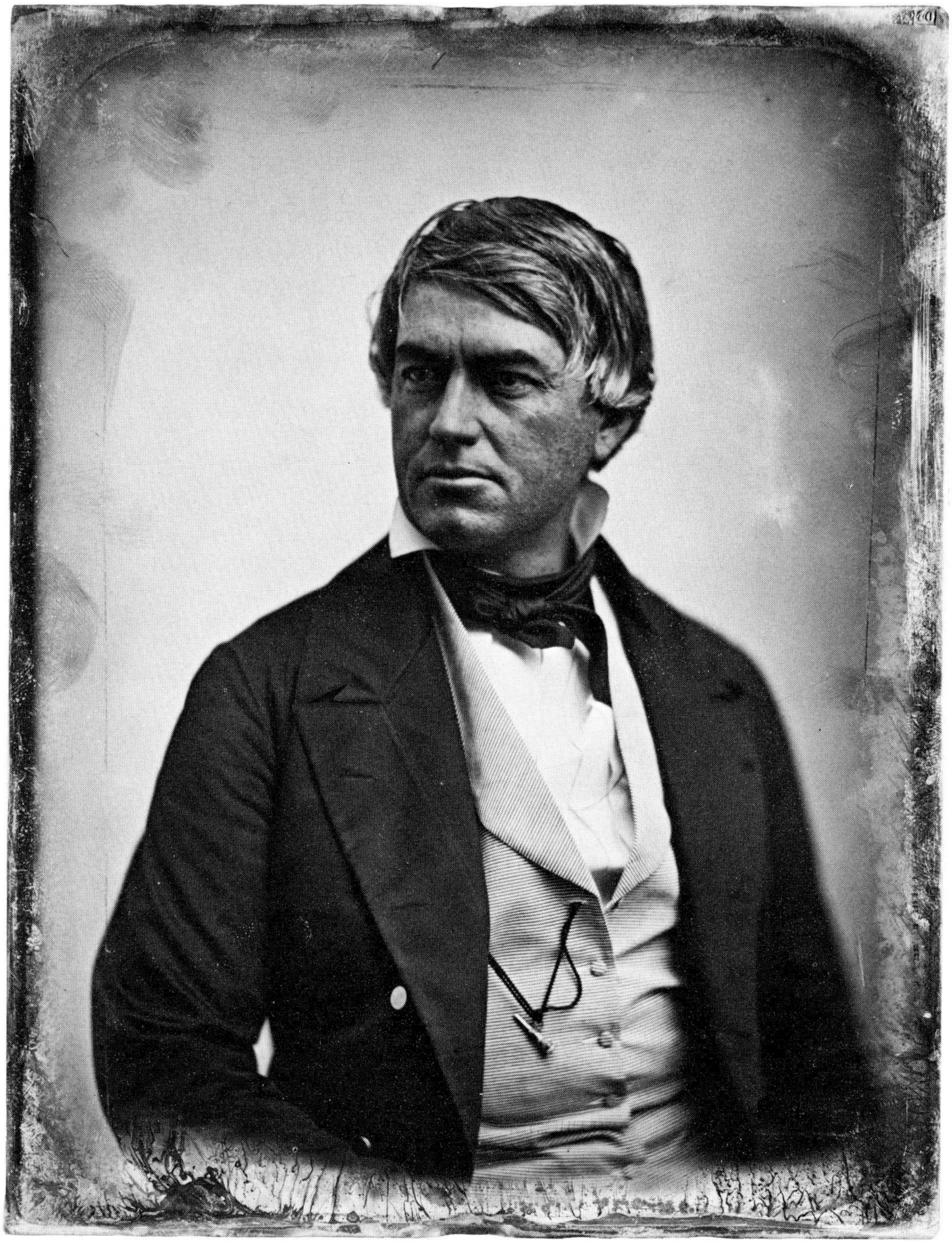

2. Cassius Marcellus Clay

Whole plate. Hallmark: u.r.: Doublé J. P. Society for the Preservation of New England Antiquities, Boston. Gift of Herbert F. Otis. 1964.257h.

Cassius Marcellus Clay (1810–1903) is said to have presented a strange mixture of "manly vigor, unfaltering honesty and indiscreet pugnacity." When his advocacy of the abolition of slavery cut short a political career in his native Kentucky, he volunteered for the Mexican War of 1848. Under the Lincoln administration, he accepted a diplomatic post to Russia in 1861. Clay spent the last twenty years of his life in relative seclusion writing his memoirs. His eccentric behavior and wild temper resulted in a Kentucky court declaring him legally insane shortly before his death in 1903.

Although documents date Clay's only visit to the North in 1844 when he delivered campaign speeches for Henry Clay, Boston's Museum of Fine Arts retains a hand-colored version of this portrait, questionably dated 1840 and inscribed: "Hand-colored by Mrs. Hawes." Nancy Southworth married Hawes only in 1849 and the inscription most likely even post-dates the marriage. The hallmark identifies the origin of the plate as French, and French plates were imported into the States only in the late 1840s. Thus both of the above dates appear inaccurate. Possibly, a few of the French plates entered the Southworth & Hawes studio in the mid-40s, but the lack of more precise evidence leaves the dating of the portrait uncertain.

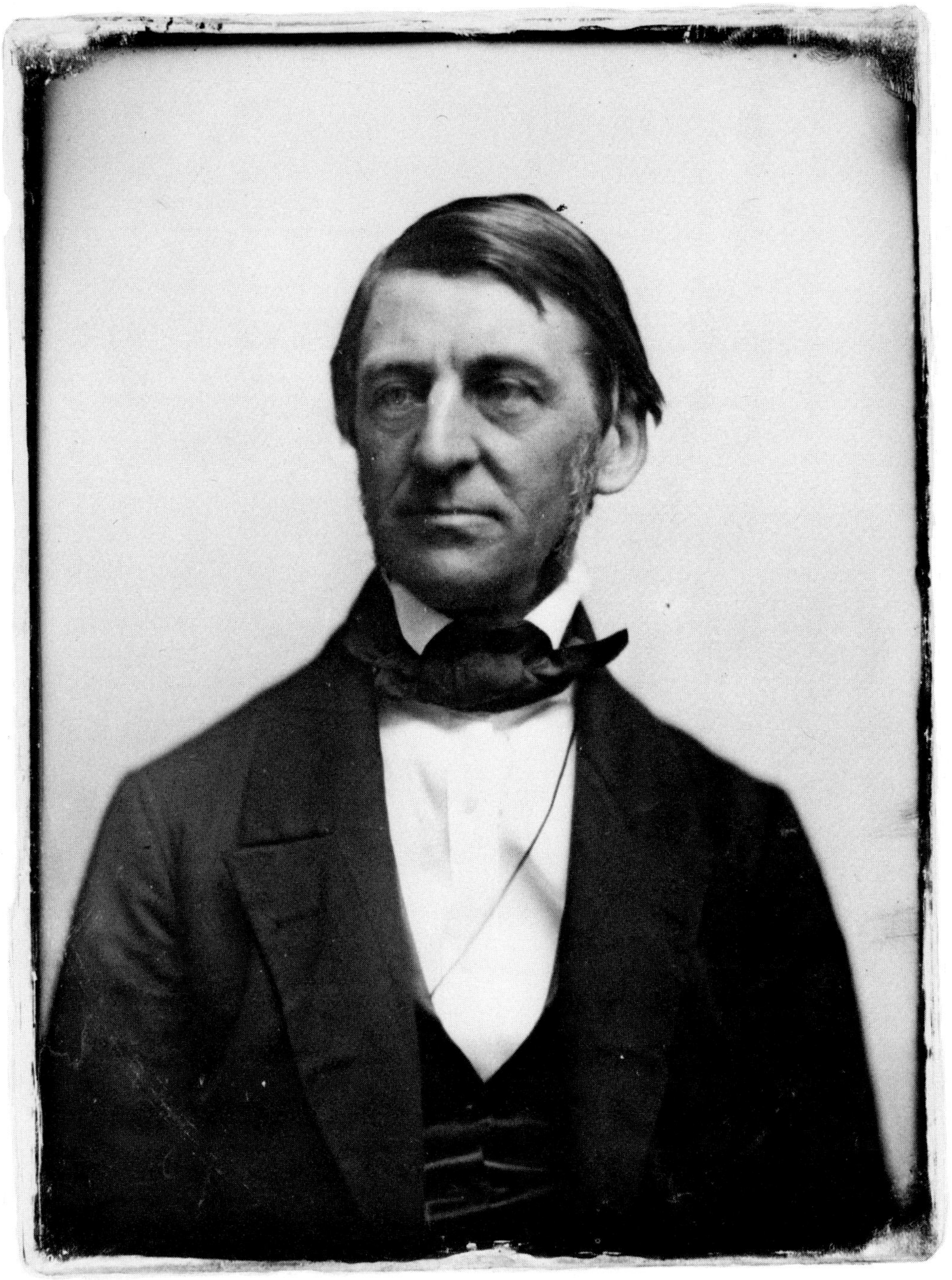

3. Ralph Waldo Emerson

Date: 1857. Whole plate. Hallmark: u.l.: Christofle. Society for the Preservation of New England Antiquities, Boston. Gift of Miss Mary Woodman, Boston. 1920.321.

A rare portrait of America's greatest philosopher, essayist and poet, this daguerreotype of a middle-aged Emerson is an uncompromising depiction of the "sage of Concord" at the height of his public career and personal development. In active pursuit of his beliefs in the divinity of man and self-reliance, he had left the Second Unitarian Church of Boston in 1832 and had broken ties with the ministry, his chosen calling since he had entered Harvard Divinity School in 1825. Primarily known for *Nature* (1836) and *Essays* (1841 and 1844), Emerson (1803-1882) authored twelve volumes of collected writings.

The simplicity of the portrait is a visual analogue to the spirit of Transcendentalism, the New England brand of Idealism Emerson helped define. The Transcendental Club, whose members included Thoreau, Margaret Fuller and Bronson Alcott, met at Old Manse, Emerson's house in Concord, beginning in 1836. From 1842 to 1844, Emerson served as the editor of the Club's magazine, *The Dial*. Around 1850, Emerson began to turn his attention to politics and social problems, notably the question of slavery. He spent the remaining twenty years revising his earlier work until his death in 1882.

[Rusk, Ralph L. *The Life of Ralph Waldo Emerson.* New York: Charles Scribner's Sons, 1949, passim.]

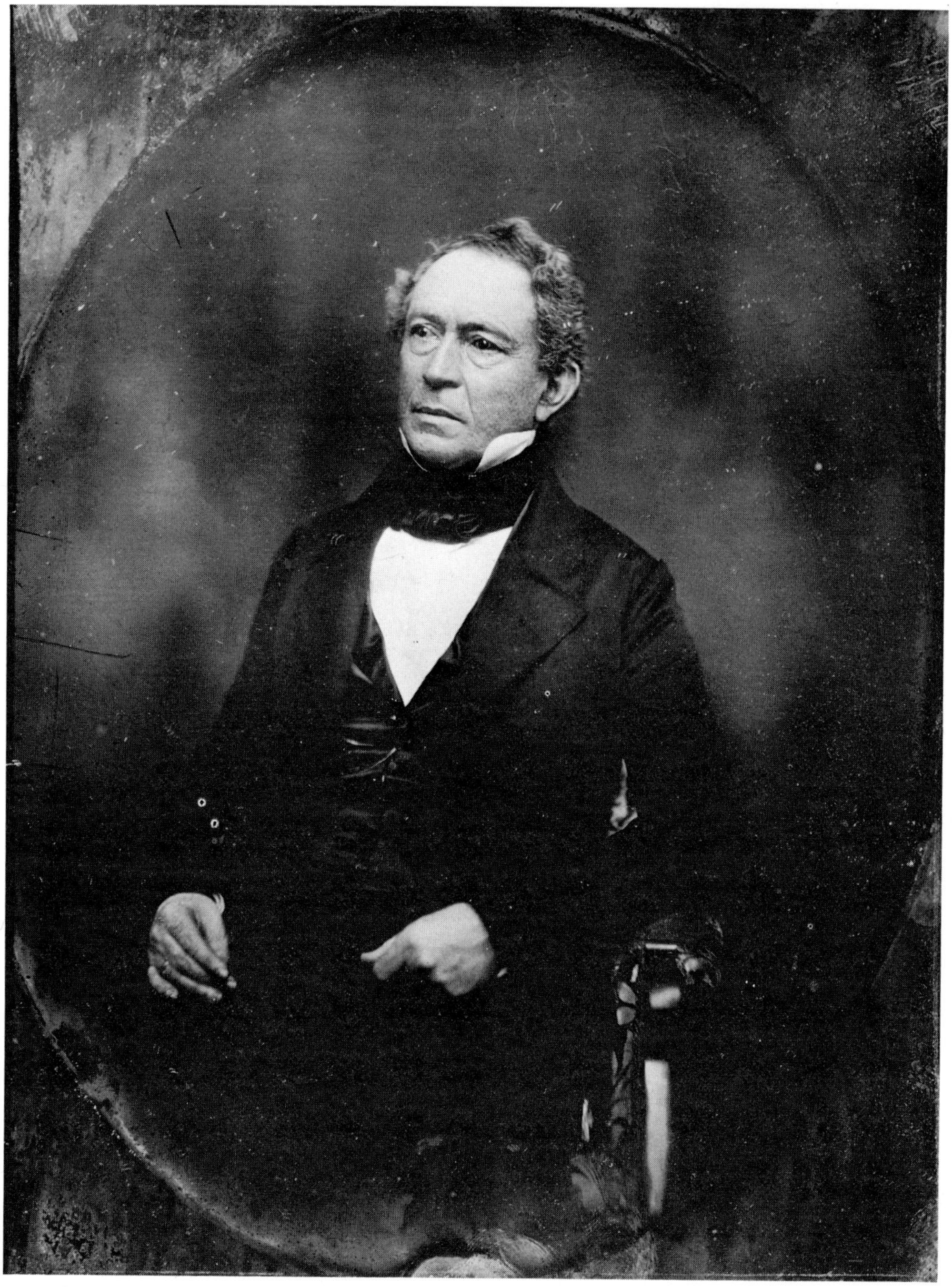

4. Edward Everett

Whole plate. Hallmark: u.l.: 40 in square; u.r.: H. S. in rectangle. Metropolitan Museum of Art. Gift of I. N. Phelps Stokes and the Hawes family. 37.14.21.

Although neglected in modern histories of 19th-century America, Edward Everett (1794–1865) had a distinguished career in ministry, politics and literature. Graduating from Harvard with highest honors as the youngest member of his class, he was appointed pastor of Boston's largest and most fashionable church, the Brattle Street Church, at the age of nineteen. A year later, he was offered a professorship in Greek literature for which he prepared himself with four years in Germany where he earned the first doctoral degree awarded an American. He was elected governor of Massachusetts in 1835, named United States minister to Great Britain in 1841, and from 1846 to 1849 served as president of Harvard College. His appointment to the Senate under the Fillmore administration was interrupted by an illness in 1853 which forced him to retire into private life. The remaining ten years of his life, however, proved instrumental in establishing his influence and reputation throughout the United States as a scholarly and powerful orator.

[Russell, Foster W. *Mount Auburn Biographies.* Wakefield, Massachusetts: Murray Printing Co., 1953, pp. 57–58.]

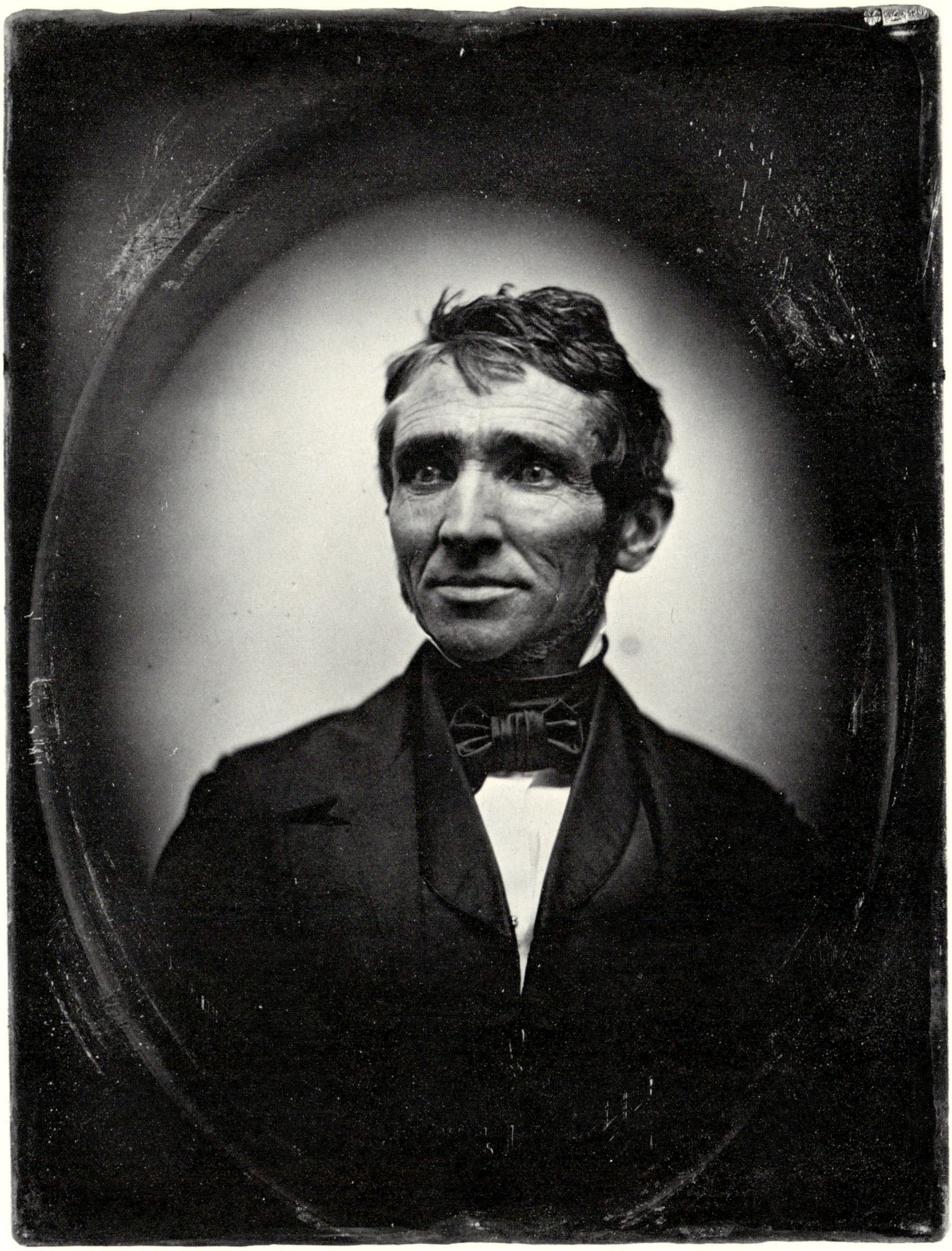

5. Charles Goodyear

Whole plate. Hallmark: u.r.: Doublé J. P. Society for the Preservation of New England Antiquities, Boston. Gift of the New England Historic Genealogical Society, Boston. 1964.269.

The inventor of vulcanized rubber, Charles Goodyear (1800–1860) began experimenting as early as 1830 with methods of making india rubber impervious to extremes in temperature. He dedicated the next ten years of his life to the solution of this problem despite repeated failures and poverty which led him to debtor's prison several times. He was finally granted a patent in 1844, but numerous infringements on his patent rights and ensuing court cases left him little profit. This dramatic daguerreotype portrait of Goodyear might well be viewed as a celebration of his most decisive court victory of 1852 in which Daniel Webster (cf. Plates 19, 20) defended his case and Rufus Choate (cf. Plate 1) prosecuted. The use of backlighting to emphasize Goodyear's rusticated features is comparable to the lighting effects in the portrait of Lemuel Shaw (cf. Plate 10) which were quite accidentally achieved when Shaw arrived at the studio.

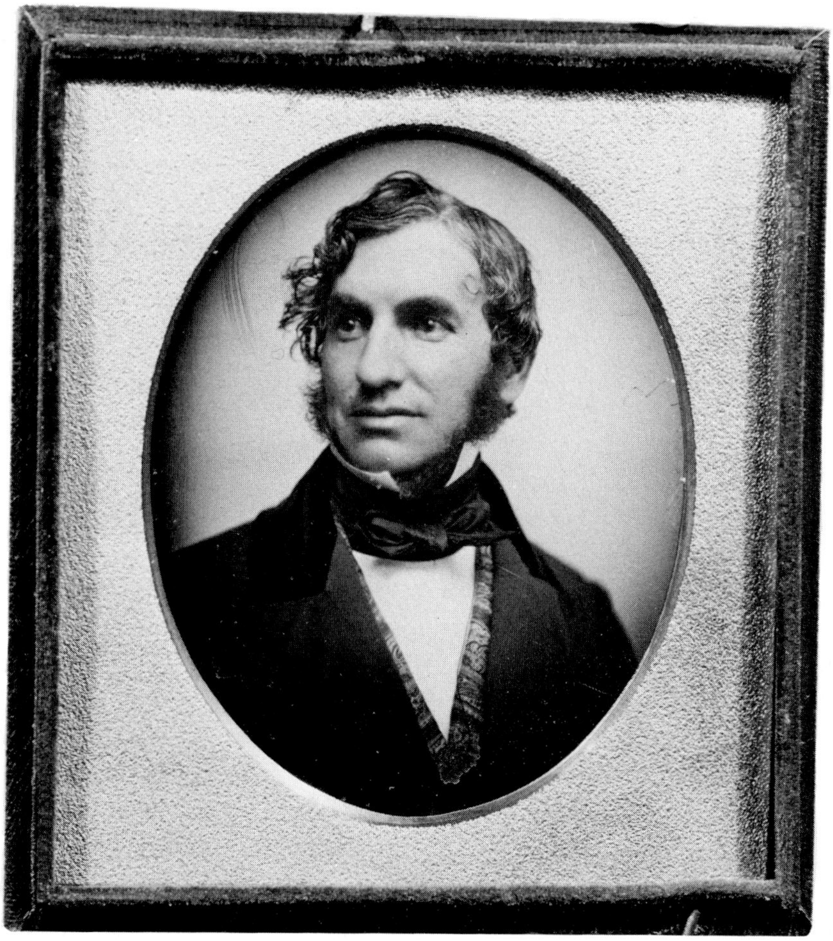

6. Henry Wadsworth Longfellow

Quarter plate. Hallmark: u.r.: Scovill Extra. Metropolitan Museum of Art. Gift of I. N. Phelps Stokes and the Hawes family. 37.14.31.

A celebrated author and an impressive dandy, Henry Wadsworth Longfellow (1807–1882) was perhaps the most frequently limned and photographed man of his time. Often annoyed by the numerous requests for sittings from painters and photographers, he remarked once to a friend that if he had to choose between good looks and a good likeness, he was all for good looks.

About 1847 when this portrait was taken, Longfellow was teaching at Harvard and had just published *Evangeline*, his first epic and most popular poem. This likeness seems to have well captured a contemporary description of the poet: "his complexion light and delicate as a maiden's . . . his nose rather prominent, his eyes clear and blue and his well-formed head covered with a profusion of brown hair waving loosely."

[Wagenknecht, Edward. *Henry Wadsworth Longfellow.* New York: Oxford University Press, 1966, passim. Newhall, Beaumont. "First American Masters of the Camera," *Art News Annual,* XLVI, no. 9 (November 1947), p. 98.]

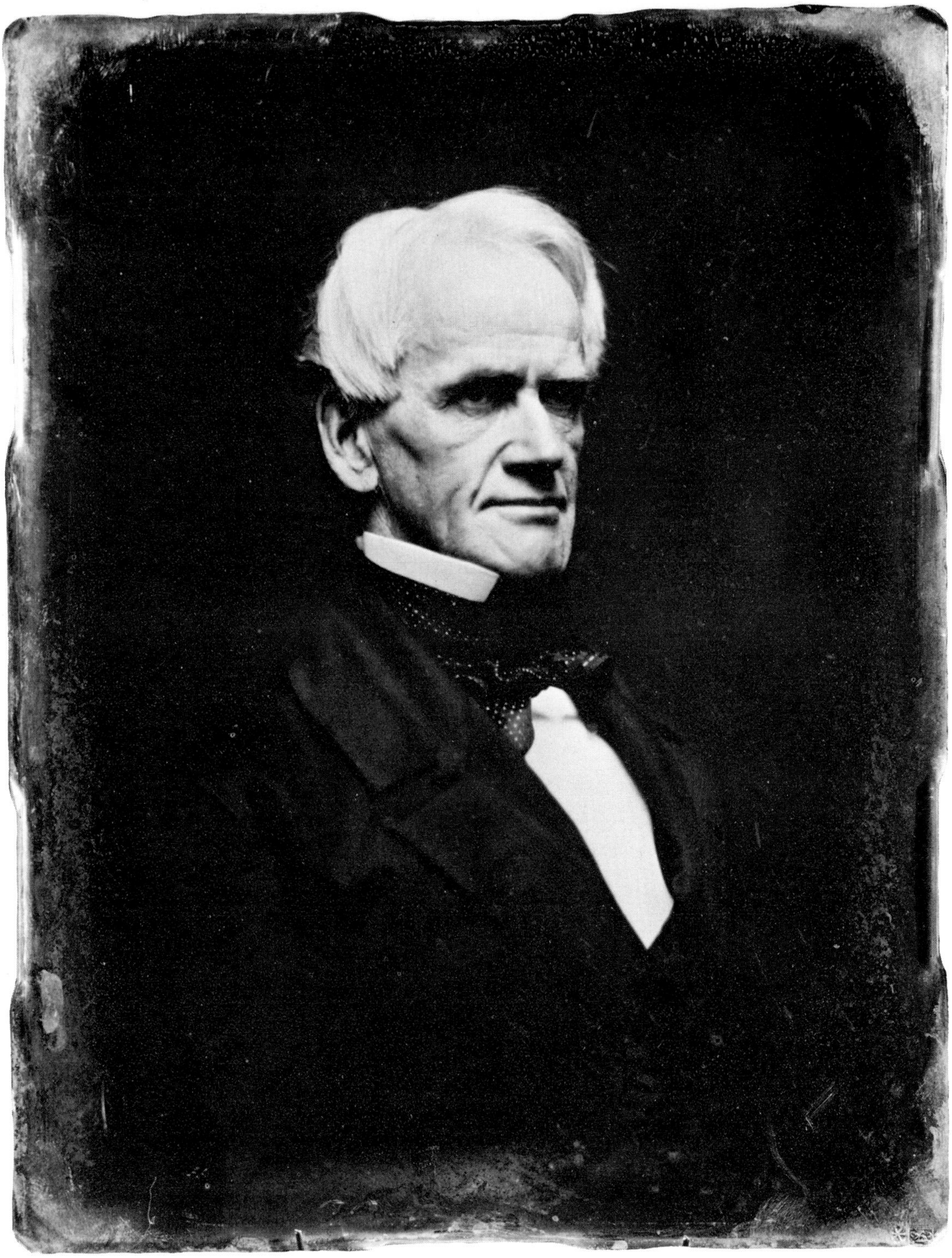

7. Horace Mann

Date: c. 1851. Whole plate. Hallmark: l.r.: Doublé J.P. Metropolitan Museum of Art. Gift of I. N. Phelps Stokes and the Hawes family. 37.14.25.

Taken on the eve of his assuming presidency of Antioch College, this portrait of Horace Mann (1796–1859) conveys a sense of the stern discipline and rigid dignity which he sought to instill in his fellow man. Self-educated, Mann matriculated at Brown University and upon graduation in 1819 entered a career in law. His legal acumen and oratorical skill soon won him a seat in the state legislature, and from 1835 to 1837 he served in the Massachusetts State Senate. His real dedication, however, lay in public education. In 1837 he forsook his promising legal career to accept the secretaryship of the newly formed state board of education. Except for his five-year service as U.S. senator (1848-1853), Mann pursued these aims relentlessly. In 1853 he left Boston for Yellow Springs, Ohio, and spent the remaining six years of his life there as president of Antioch College. He had at last found an institution which shared his beliefs in coeducation, nonsectarianism and equal opportunities for Blacks.

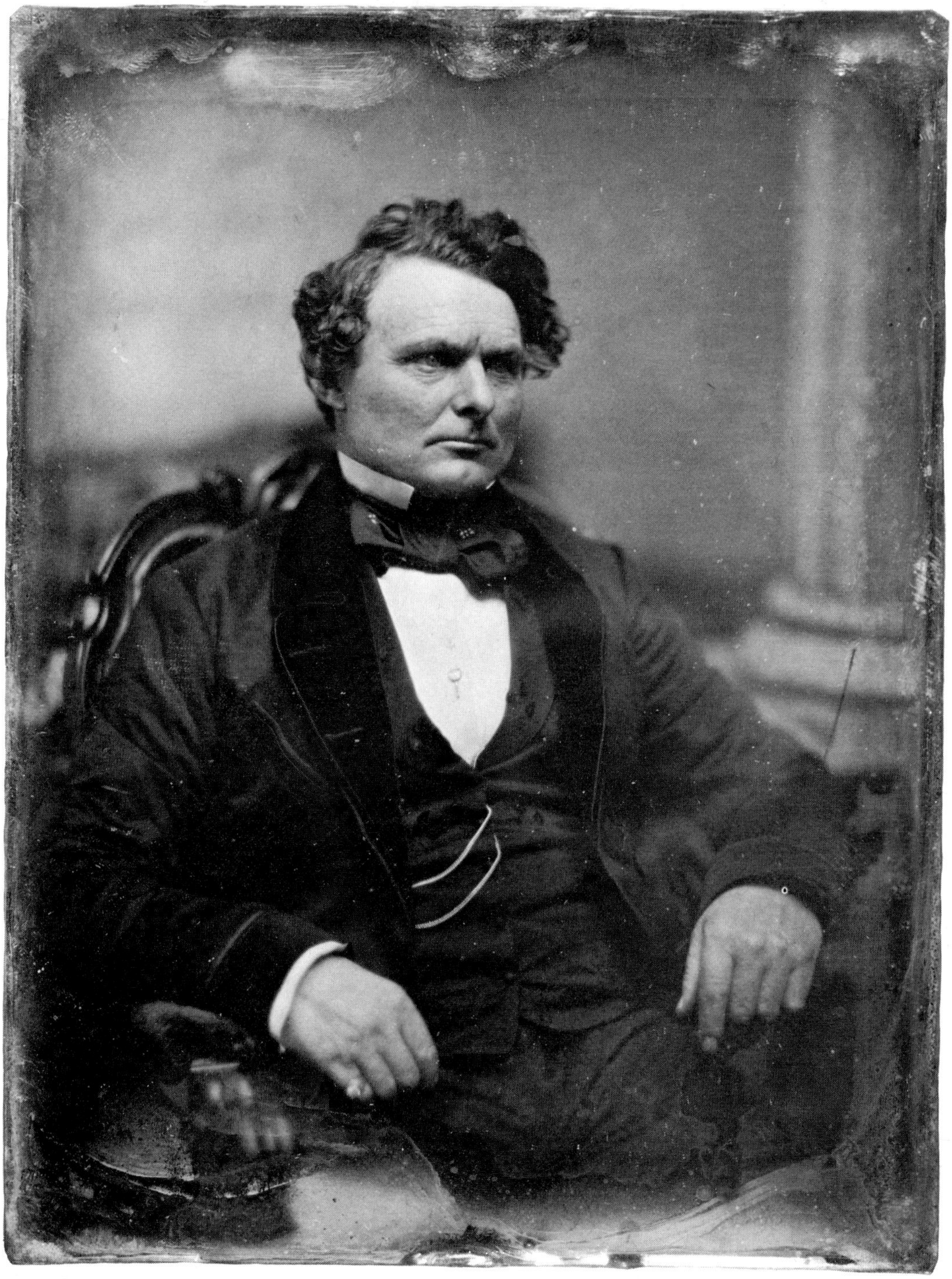

8. DONALD MCKAY

Date: 1854. Whole plate. Hallmark: u.l.: Doublé J.P. Metropolitan Museum of Art. Gift of I. N. Phelps Stokes and the Hawes family. 37.14.1.

A native of Nova Scotia, Donald McKay (1810–1880) learned the shipbuilding trade in New York. He began business in Newburyport, Massachusetts, before establishing a shipyard in East Boston. Famed for its prolific output, the yard produced as many as seven vessels a year and provided clippers for trade in California, England and Australia until McKay's retirement to farming in 1874. Several of his vessels can be seen in the views taken by Southworth & Hawes of the Boston harbor area (cf. Plates 86–88). This portrait is said to have originally hung over the transom sofa of McKay's ship, *Champion of the Seas,* launched in 1854.

[Wilson, James Grant, ed. *Appleton's Cyclopedia of National Biography.* New York: Appleton & Co., 1888, IV, p. 126. Untitled article, *Daily Atlas* (Boston), 20 May 1854.]

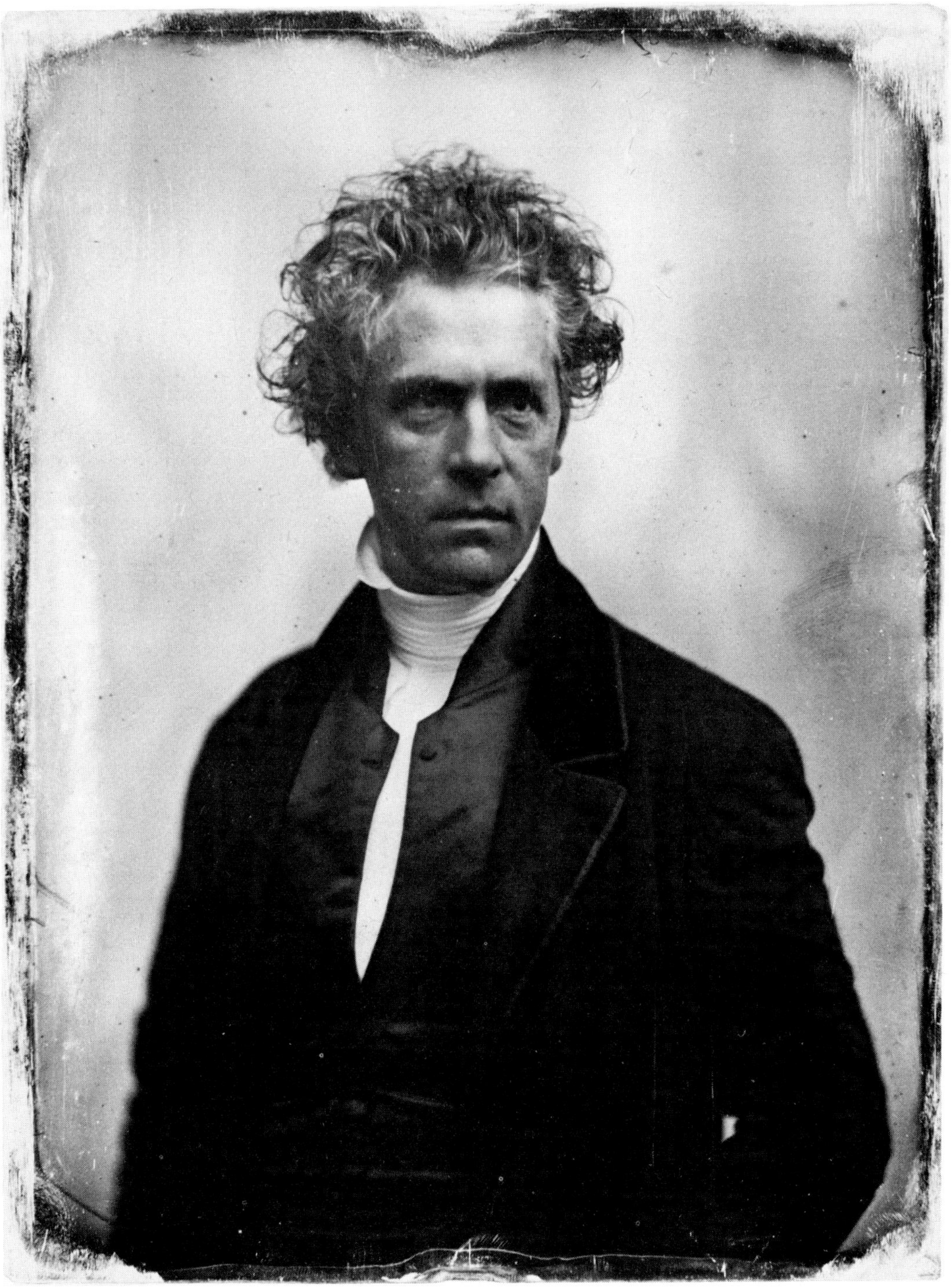

9. Rollin Heber Neal

Date: c. 1853. Whole plate. Hallmark: l.r.: S & F in lozenge. International Museum of Photography at George Eastman House. Southworth & Hawes Collection. 74:193:141.

For nearly forty years, Rollin Heber Neal (1808–1879) was the pastor of the First Baptist Church located on the corner of Hanover and Union Streets in Boston. One of the most eloquent and successful preachers of his day, Neal received two degrees of Doctor of Divinity, one from Brown University in 1850 and another from Harvard in 1857. His long relationship with the First Baptist Church began in 1837, while he also served as an overseer of Harvard College and published many of his sermons and addresses. Neal's portrait is reproduced as an engraving in *Gleason's Pictorial Drawing Room Companion.* Southworth & Hawes's daguerreotype portraits were often used to illustrate articles on various Boston congregations of the time.

This portrait shows an extreme in the male hair fashion which seems to have been popular during the early 1850s. A similar hairstyle, unruly, tossed and waving loosely, is seen in a number of Southworth & Hawes's portraits of men (cf. Plates 5, 6, 10). Just what species of transcendental, anti-materialistic romanticism this style signaled is not clear.

[*Gleason's Pictorial Drawing Room Companion*, V (November 1853), p. 348.]

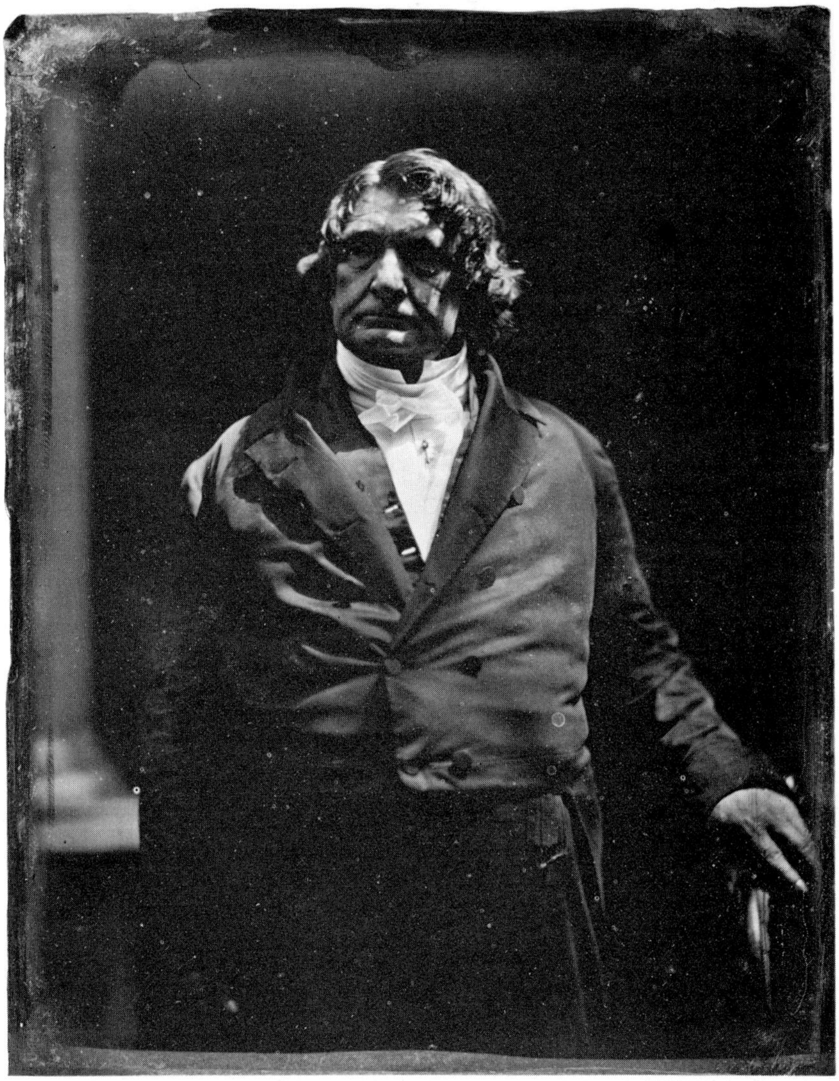

10. LEMUEL SHAW

Half plate. Hallmark: inaccessible. Metropolitan Museum of Art. Gift of Edward S. Hawes, Alice Mary Hawes and Marion A. Hawes. 38.38.34.

A testament to the two partners' artistic genius for previsualizing effects, this masterpiece portrait was achieved entirely by chance. When Chief Justice Lemuel Shaw (1781–1861) arrived at the studio for a sitting, he happened to stand under the studio skylight while waiting for the preparation of the daguerreotype plate. Realizing the powerful effect of the overhead light on his rugged features, the photographers—and one would like to think it Hawes—begged him to remain where he was. In a matter of seconds, they secured this portrait of the Massachusetts Chief Justice whom a contemporary described as "the absolute power of a crag vitalized by a human spirit."

According to a Worcester newspaper journalist writing in 1886: "More magnificent than any other is a large standing photograph of Chief Justice Shaw. . . . It is wonderfully artistic, with brilliant lights and deep shadows, as if it were taken from a marble statue. It is a majestic picture, with 'the front of Jove himself,' and the masses of wavy hair are very effective. . . . It is one of the most remarkable photographs in existence . . . [making] beauty in a man seem paltry and almost contemptible. . . . [It is] the expression of great power, splendid intellect and mighty will."

[Untitled article, *Boston Transcript*, 27 November 1888. "Portraits of Noted Men," *Worcester Spy,* 6 January 1886.]

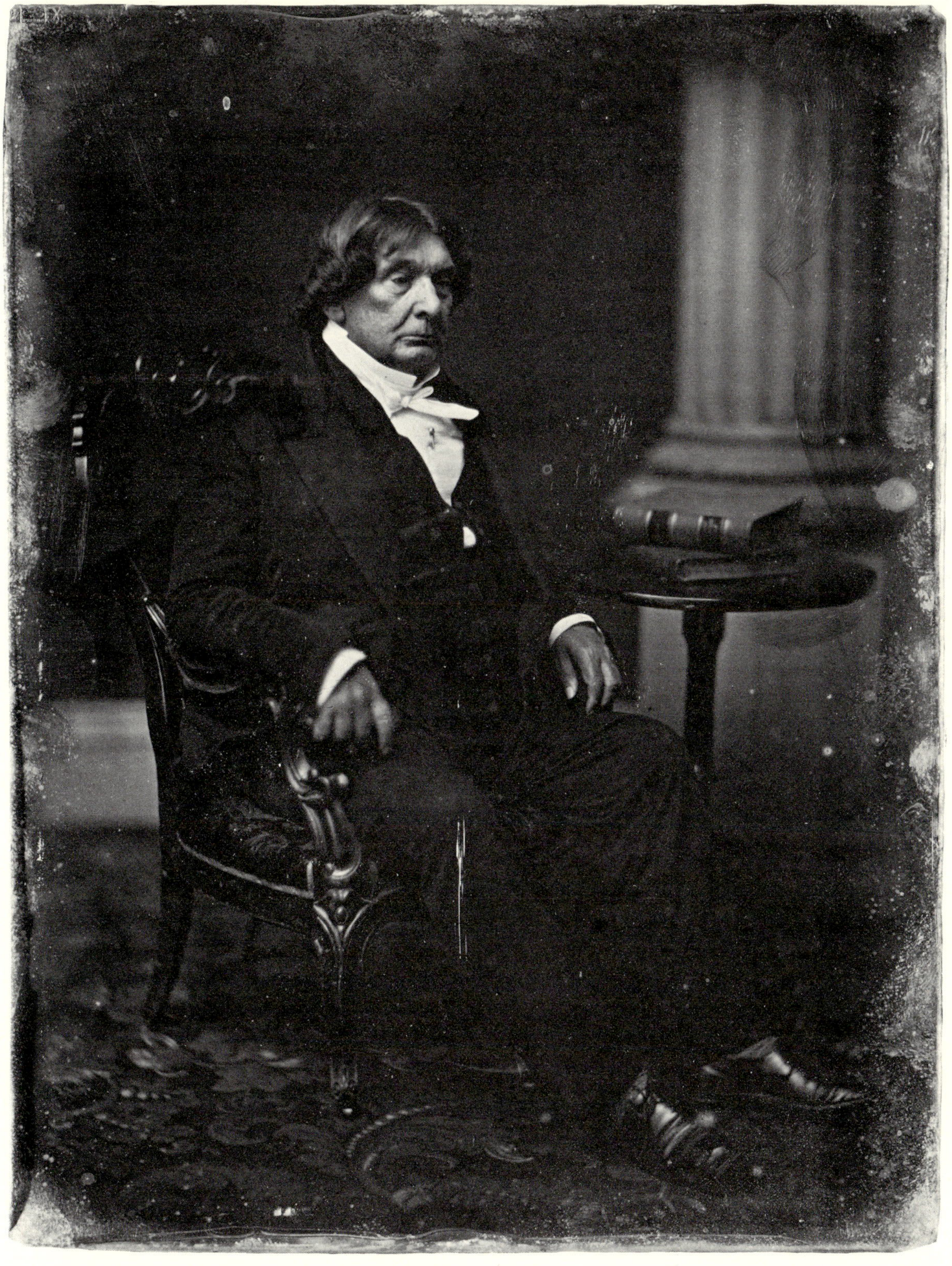

11. Lemuel Shaw

Whole plate. Hallmark: u.l.: Doublé J. P. Society for the Preservation of New England Antiquities, Boston. Gift of Herbert Foster Otis. 1964.257a.

Although less spontaneous, this portrait of Shaw fully captured the powerful presence of the sitter. The partners probably posed Shaw carefully for this exposure but skillfully avoided a static effect by catching the sitter in a moment of seeming contemplation. No attempt was made to correct his unruly hair or to smooth his wrinkled coat. The portrait is a sympathetic likeness of Shaw as both a private individual and an eminent American jurist.

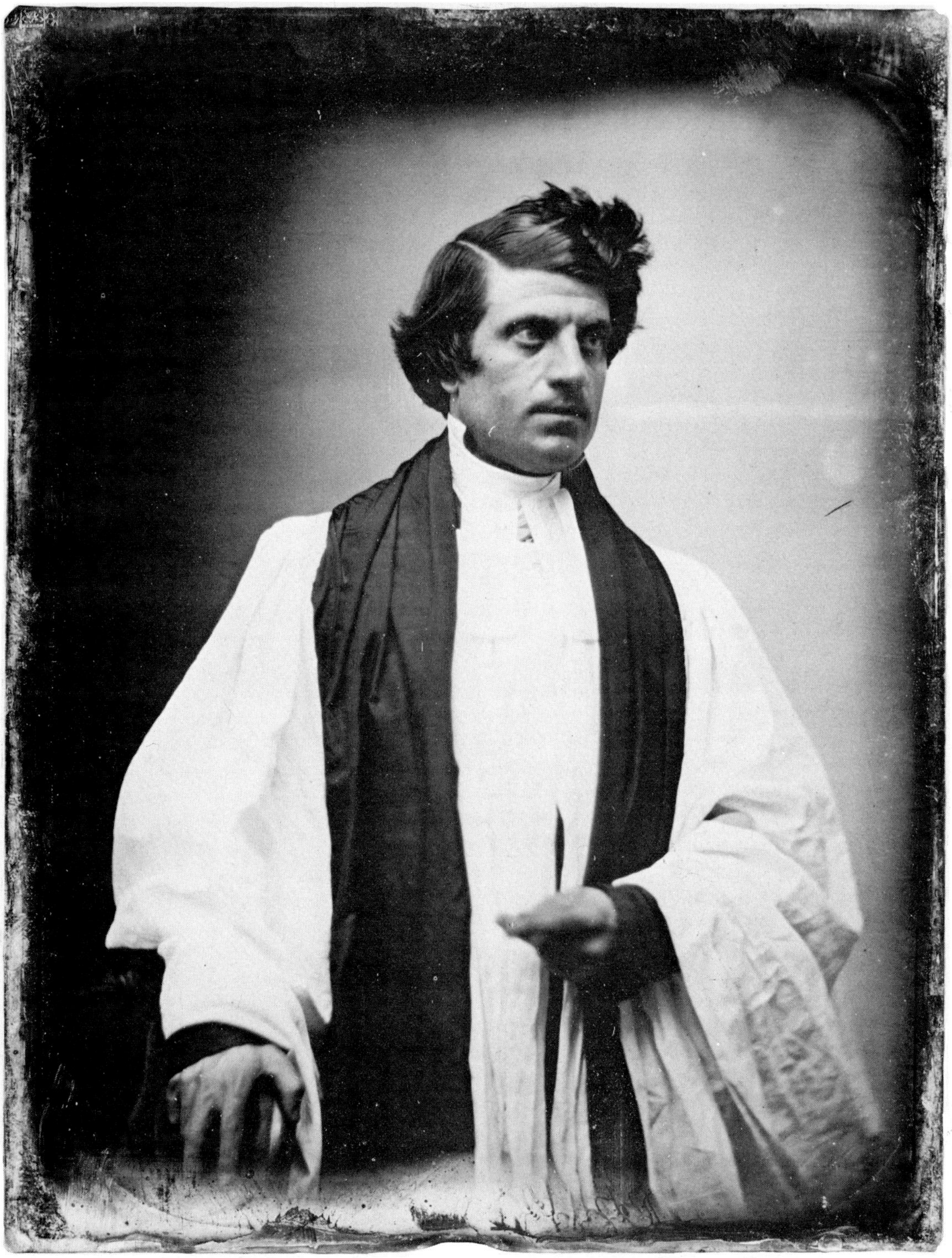

12. REVEREND WILLIAM T. SMITHETT

Date: 1853. Whole plate. Hallmark: u.l.: Doublé J. P. Museum of Fine Arts, Boston. Gift of Edward Southworth Hawes in memory of his father, Josiah Johnson Hawes. 43.1391.

This imposing figure was long thought to represent Bishop Clarke of Rhode Island. An engraving of a daguerreotype by Southworth & Hawes in *Gleason's Pictorial Drawing Room Companion* finally identified the sitter as Reverend William T. Smithett (1822–?), rector of the Christ Church in Boston. The *Gleason's* article provides a brief biographical sketch of Reverend Smithett. He was born in Dover, England, and raised in France. When the revolution broke out in 1830, he returned to England until his departure for a diocese in the Barbados in the winter of 1840/41. Arriving in the United States at an unknown date, he spent time in parishes in Pennsylvania and New York before coming to Boston in 1851.

[*Gleason's Pictorial Drawing Room Companion*, date unknown, p. 172.]

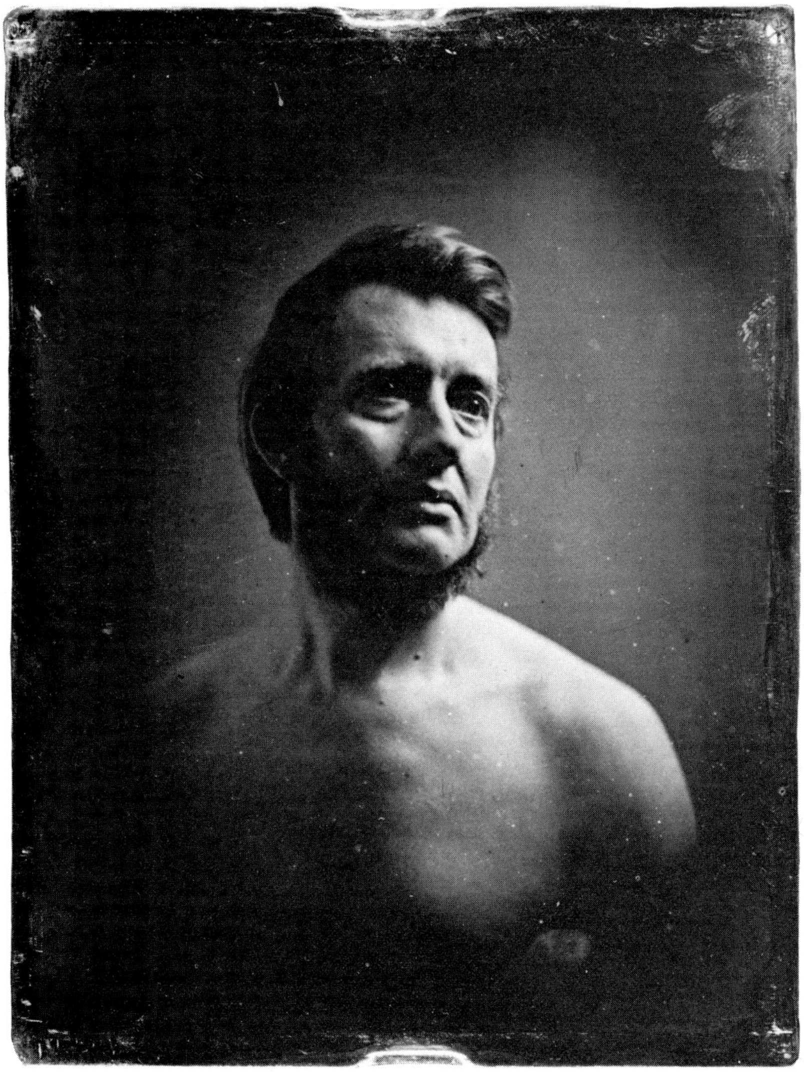

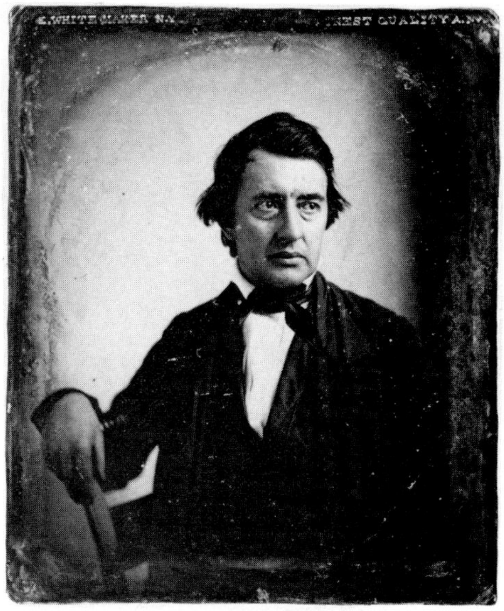

13. ALBERT SANDS SOUTHWORTH

Half plate. Hallmark: u.r.: star; u.l.: 40. International Museum of Photography at George Eastman House. Southworth & Hawes Collection. 74:193:1127.

14. ALBERT SANDS SOUTHWORTH

Sixth plate. Hallmark: upper edge: E. White. Metropolitan Museum of Art. Gift of I. N. Phelps Stokes and the Hawes family. 37.14.16.

This surprising and bizarre portrait of the daguerreian artist as an ideal bust (cf. Plate 105) is the only extant vignetted male portrait from the Southworth & Hawes studio. Whether this is a self-portrait or an idealized likeness by Hawes is unknown, as is the specific iconographic reference, if any. Perhaps a flight of vanity on the part of a romanticizing artist, the portrait is an attempt to create an ideal type through such classicizing motifs as the lilt of the head, the distantly gazing eyes, and the bust terminating at midchest and upper arms. All that is needed is a circular plinth. The forced dramatic lighting, however, and the daguerreotype's penchant for naturalistic details accentuate the deep shadows beneath Southworth's eyes, thereby detracting from the smooth perfection of a neoclassical ideal.

Southworth (1811–1894) appears somewhat younger in the second small-plate daguerreotype which may have been a souvenir for either his sister Nancy or his wife Louise. Oddly enough, this portrait lacks the usual touch of the partners' genius, while the former clearly exemplifies their capacity to create

> the most beautiful and worthy [portraits] of any on exhibition. Indeed, the best of them are at least equal to any ever produced. In composition, arrangement of their various parts and expressions, many of them, by each of several Exhibitors, are equal to some of the best portraits produced by our Painters, and in some respects, of course, they are beyond all rivalry by painting . . .the flesh is preserved in all the beautiful gradations of form and texture, the most delicate lights playing over its surface in a thousand different degrees of intensity, the fabrics are soft, easy, and graceful, the action and expression natural and refined . . .the works of Messrs. Southworth and Hawes and Mr. Whipple are by far the finest in the Exhibition . . . [and] the last subtle gradations of tint and expression are better given the best specimens of Messrs. Southworth and Hawes.

[Judges Report, Fine Arts, *Fifth Fair and Exhibition for Premiums of the Massachusetts Charitable Mechanics Association,* Boston, 1847, typescript, S&H, IMP/GEH.]

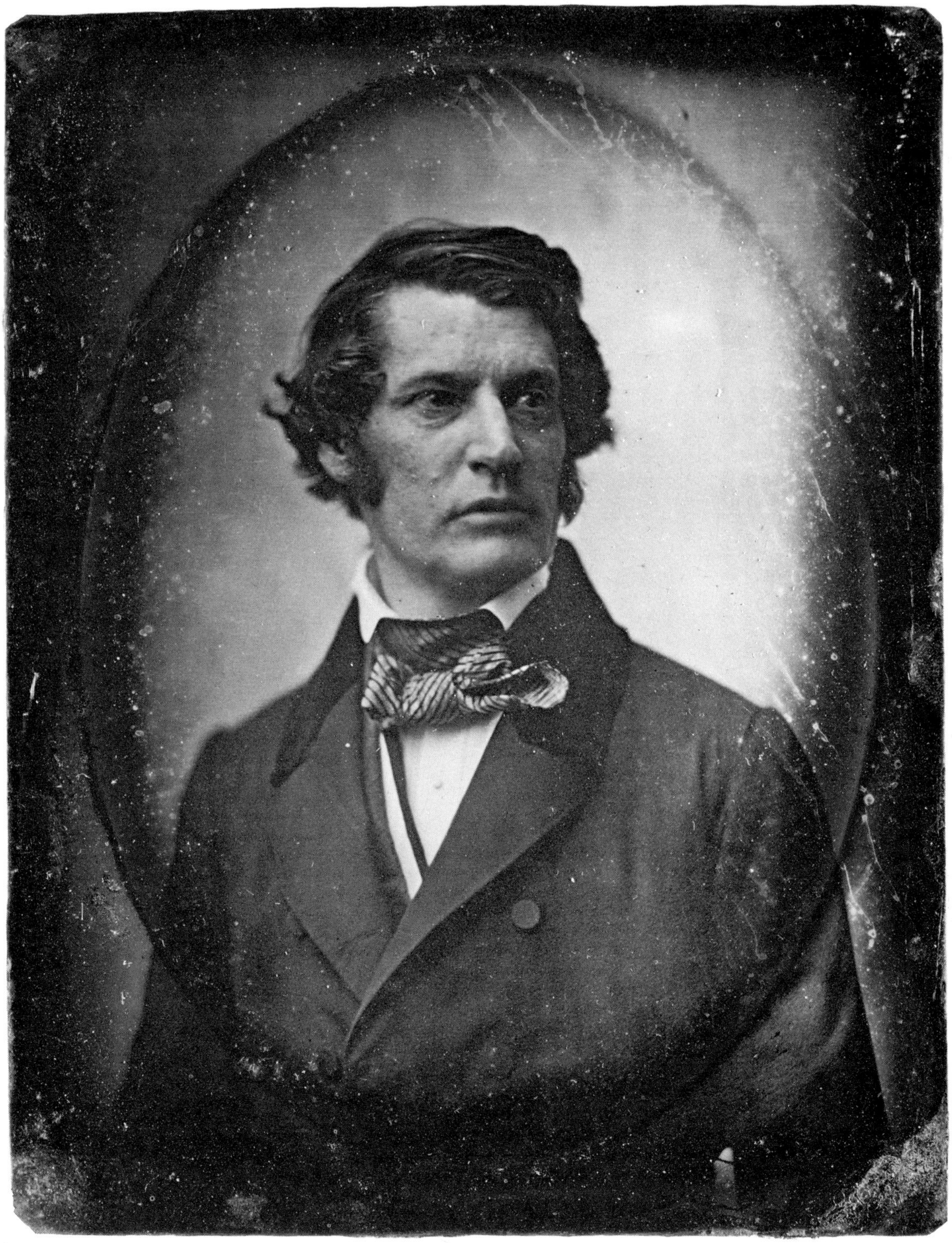

15. Charles Sumner

Date: 1856. Whole plate. Hallmark: none. The Bostonian Society, Old State House, Boston. Gift of Edward L. Pierce, 1894.94.58.

Six feet, four inches tall and endowed with a powerful voice, Charles Sumner (1811–1874) was noted for his speech and bearing. Having studied law at Harvard and fluent in German, French and Italian, Sumner was among the most cultured and cosmopolitan of 19th-century American statesmen. In international affairs he did much to influence the maintenance of peace between the United States, Great Britain and France at a time when war with either nation would have greatly imperiled the Union. At home he was an outspoken abolitionist and did more than any other northern statesman to promote absolute human equality. Two other portraits of Sumner exist in Boston's Museum of Fine Arts: one showing the politician's earnest features playfully offset by a wildly striped neckerchief (54.716), the other by a gay polka-dotted one (43.1398).

[Russell, Foster W. *Mount Auburn Biographies,* p. 160.]

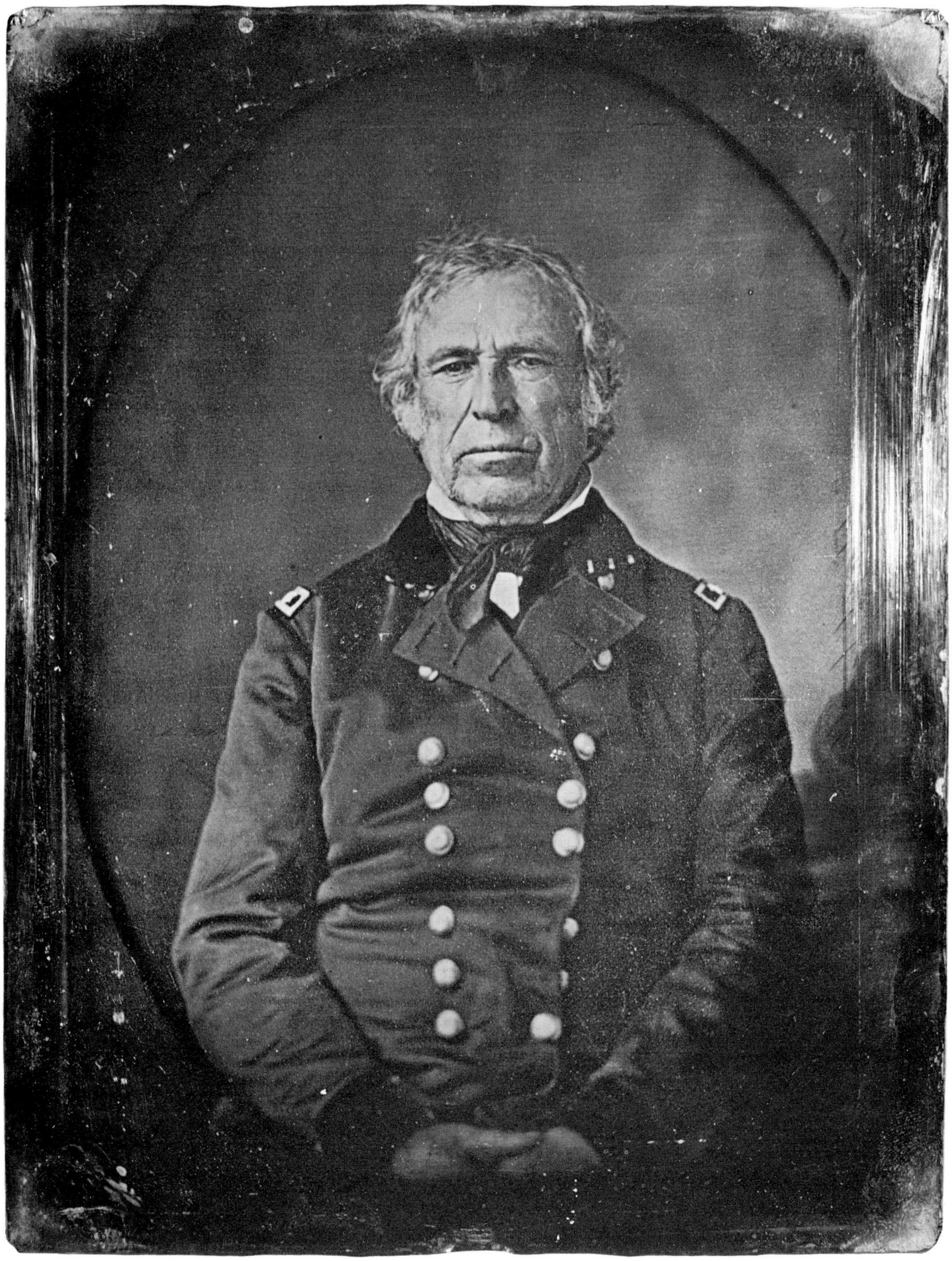

16. General Zachary Taylor

Whole plate, enlarged copy from a sixth plate (see Met. 37.14.22). Hallmark: u.l.: star; u.r.: 40. Society for the Preservation of New England Antiquities, Boston. Gift of Herbert Foster Otis. 1964.257b.

The Whig candidate for Presidency in 1848, General Zachary Taylor (1784–1850) was reputed to have been as plain and forthright as this portrait suggests. An authentic hero, General Taylor achieved his greatest victories as an Indian fighter and frontier soldier in Mexico. His achievements as President, however, were less remarkable. His honest and good intentions could not mask his lack of training, experience and aptitude for the position. Even so, his inglorious death from too much sun, ice water and raw fruit after only sixteen months in office was genuinely mourned by Americans as the loss of ''Old Rough and Ready.''

This portrait of General Taylor is an enlarged and laterally reversed copy of a sixth plate now in the Metropolitan Museum of Art collection (37.14.22). The clarity of the image, compared to the smaller original plate, has visibly suffered (cf. Plate 71).

[Ketchum, Richard M. ''Faces from the Past—XII,'' *American Heritage,* XIV, 6 (October 1963), p. 53.]

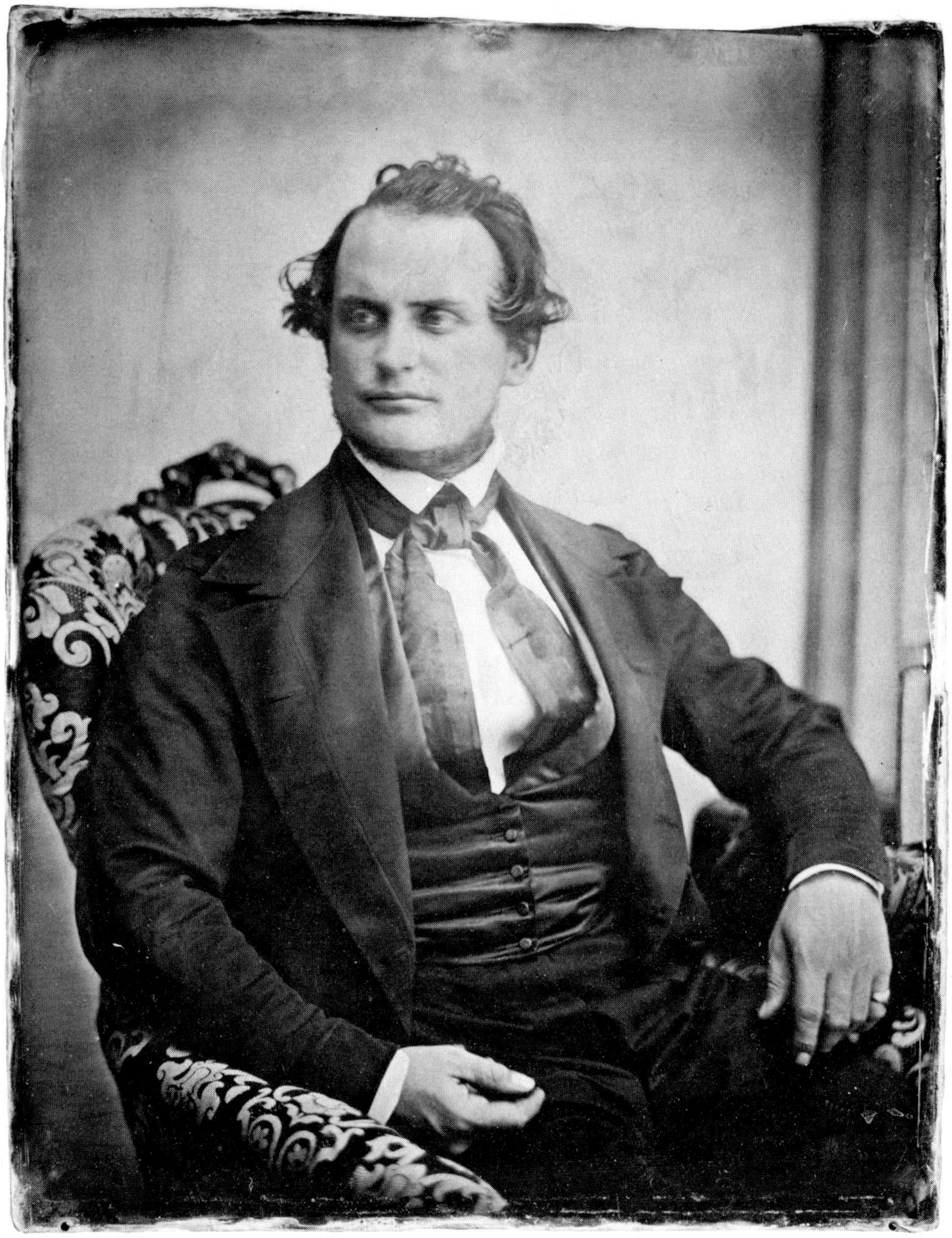

17. JOHN L. TUCKER

Date: c. 1851. Mammoth plate (12⅞″ x 16⅜″). Hallmark: u.l.: 20 Garanti in rectangle. Metropolitan Museum of Art. Gift of I. N. Phelps Stokes and the Hawes family. 37.14.57.

As the host of the prestigious Tremont House Hotel, John L. Tucker became a popular figure in Boston during the 1830s and 1840s. The news of his retirement in 1851 after twenty years at the hotel caused widespread lament throughout the city and was duly reported in Boston's journal, *Gleason's Pictorial Drawing Room Companion*. The report was accompanied by a portrait of Tucker engraved after a daguerreotype by Southworth & Hawes. A comparison between these two portraits reveals striking similarities in the sitter's expression and the casual style of his hair and tie. There is little doubt that the sitter in both pictures is John L. Tucker (see illustration at right) and that the published portrait is a direct, albeit reverse, version of the daguerreotype shown here.

[*Gleason's Pictorial Drawing Room Companion,* I, 4 (1851), p. 56.]

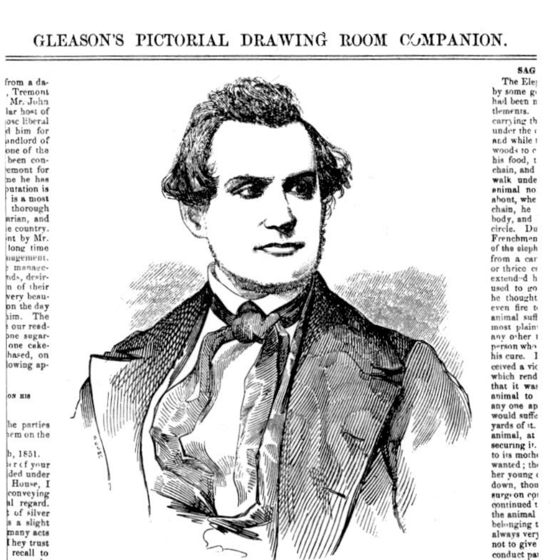
GLEASON'S PICTORIAL DRAWING ROOM COMPANION.

THE PORTRAIT OF JOHN L. TUCKER, ESQ.

OUR COUNTRY.

The United States have a sea-coast along the Atlantic and Gulf of Mexico of 3500 miles. On the Pacific the extent of coast is 1620 miles. According to an estimate by the superintendent of the coast survey, the length of the "shore line" of the United States, which includes bays, sounds, and small irregularities of the main shore and sea islands, is 33,063 miles. We have also a

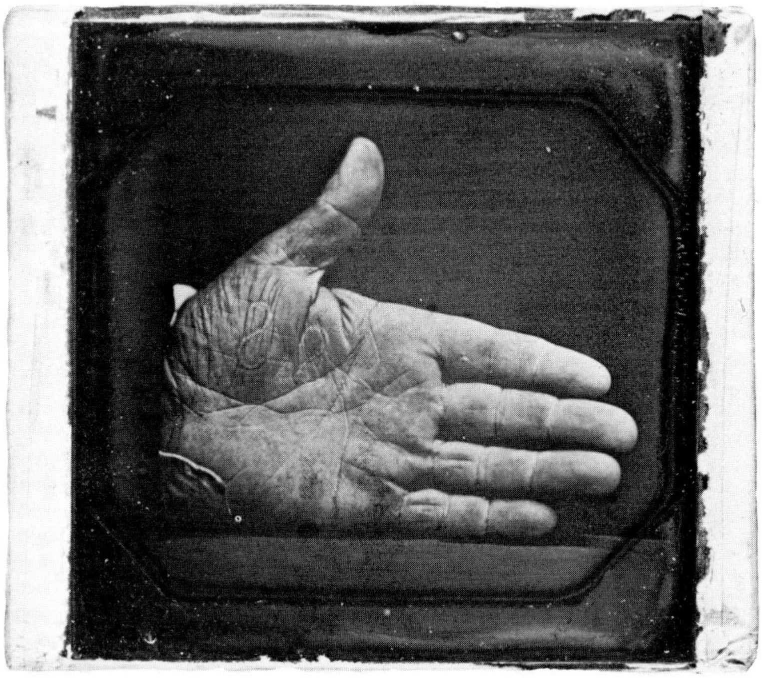

18. CAPTAIN JONATHAN W. WALKER'S BRANDED HAND

Date: 1845. Sixth plate. Hallmark: none. Massachusetts Historical Society, Boston. Bowditch Collection. MHS77.

Welcome home again, brave seaman! with
 thy thoughtful brow and gray,
And the old heroic spirit of our earlier, better
 day,—
With that front of calm endurance, on
 whose steady nerve in vain
Pressed the iron of the prison, smote the fiery
 shafts of pain!

Is the tyrant's brand upon thee? Did the
 brutal cravens aim
To make God's truth thy falsehood, his
 holiest work thy shame?
When, all blood-quenched, from the torture
 the iron was withdrawn,
How laughed their evil angel the baffled
 fools to scorn!

They change to wrong the duty which God
 hath written out
On the great heart of humanity, too legible
 for doubt!
They, the loathsome moral lepers, blotched
 from footsole up to crown,
Give to shame what God hath given unto
 honor and renown!

Why, that brand is highest honor!—than
 its traces never yet
Upon old armorial hatchments was a prouder
 blazon set;
And thy unborn generations, as they tread
 our rocky strand,
Shall tell with pride the story of their father's
 BRANDED HAND!

These stanzas from "The Branded Hand" (1846) by John Greenleaf Whittier and the small daguerreotype reproduced here both commemorate, if somewhat cryptically, Captain Jonathan Walker (1799–1878). A Florida seaman originally from Cape Cod, he was sympathetic to the plight of the slaves. In 1844 he made an unsuccessful attempt to aid a group of seven to freedom by sailing them to the West Indies. Walker paid for his part in the venture with a year in solitary confinement, a $600.00 fine, and the branded letters "s.s." for "slave stealer" on his right palm. The incident would probably have passed unnoticed had not Walker loyally pursued his beliefs as an effective anti-slavery lecturer after his release. Southworth & Hawes's closeup recording of the Captain's palm leaves us wondering what Walker himself might have looked like.

Taken about 1845 when Southworth met Walker, this image is one of the earliest conceptual portraits in that a body part can stand for the total personality. The picture predates by some eight years Charles Hugo's study of Victor's hand; it predates by over a decade Adolphe Braun's portrait of la Comtesse de Castiglione's feet; it also anticipates Hawes's medical photographs of 1868 by its clinical certainty and dryness.

[Wilson, James Grant, ed. *Appleton's Cyclopedia of National Biography.* New York: D. Appleton, 1889, p. 328. Unidentified Boston newspaper clipping, May 1878, Massachusetts Historical Society.]

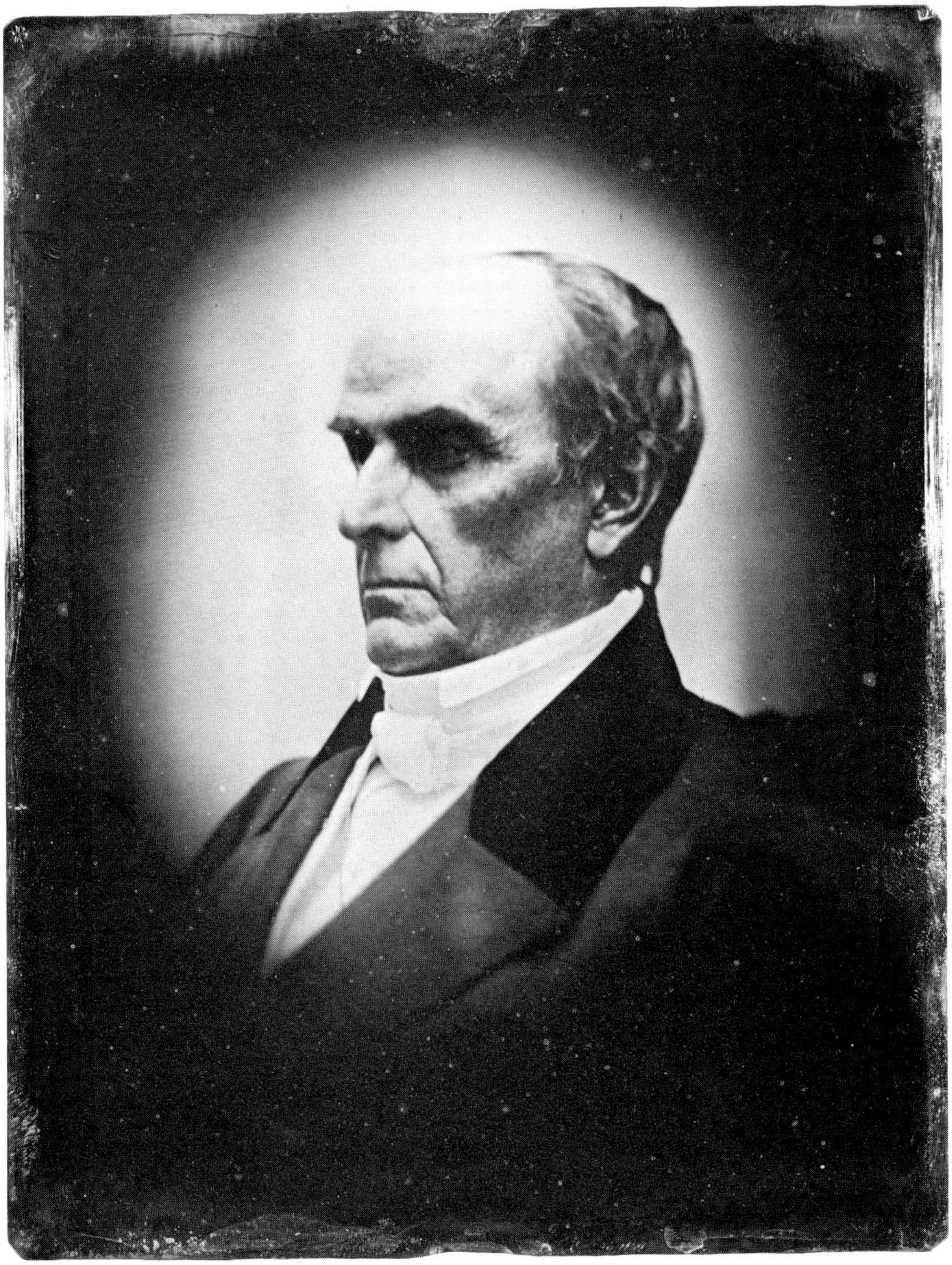

19. DANIEL WEBSTER

Date: April 22, 1851. Whole plate. Hallmark: u.l.: star; u.r.: 40. Museum of Fine Arts, Boston. Gift of Edward Southworth Hawes in memory of his father, Josiah Johnson Hawes. 43.1401.

Daniel Webster (1782–1852) had posed for Southworth & Hawes at least twice (cf. Plate 20). Among the requests for the studio's portraits of notables, those for copy daguerreotypes and, later, paper prints of Webster's portraits were by far the most frequent. In 1886 Josiah Hawes, who had continued to maintain a photographic studio after Southworth's retirement in 1861, ran the advertisement at the right in the *Boston Transcript.*

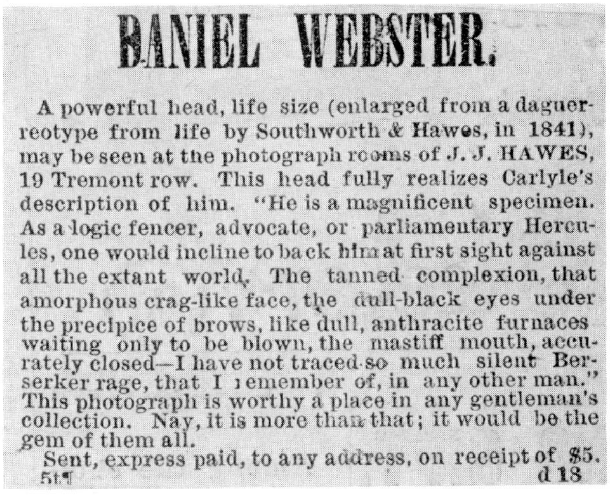

DANIEL WEBSTER.

A powerful head, life size (enlarged from a daguerreotype from life by Southworth & Hawes, in 1841), may be seen at the photograph rooms of J. J. HAWES, 19 Tremont row. This head fully realizes Carlyle's description of him. "He is a magnificent specimen. As a logic fencer, advocate, or parliamentary Hercules, one would incline to back him at first sight against all the extant world. The tanned complexion, that amorphous crag-like face, the dull-black eyes under the precipice of brows, like dull, anthracite furnaces waiting only to be blown, the mastiff mouth, accurately closed—I have not traced so much silent Berserker rage, that I remember of, in any other man." This photograph is worthy a place in any gentleman's collection. Nay, it is more than that; it would be the gem of them all.

Sent, express paid, to any address, on receipt of $5.

d 18

RIGHT: Advertisement, *Boston Transcript*, December 1886. Southworth & Hawes Collection, IMP/GEH.

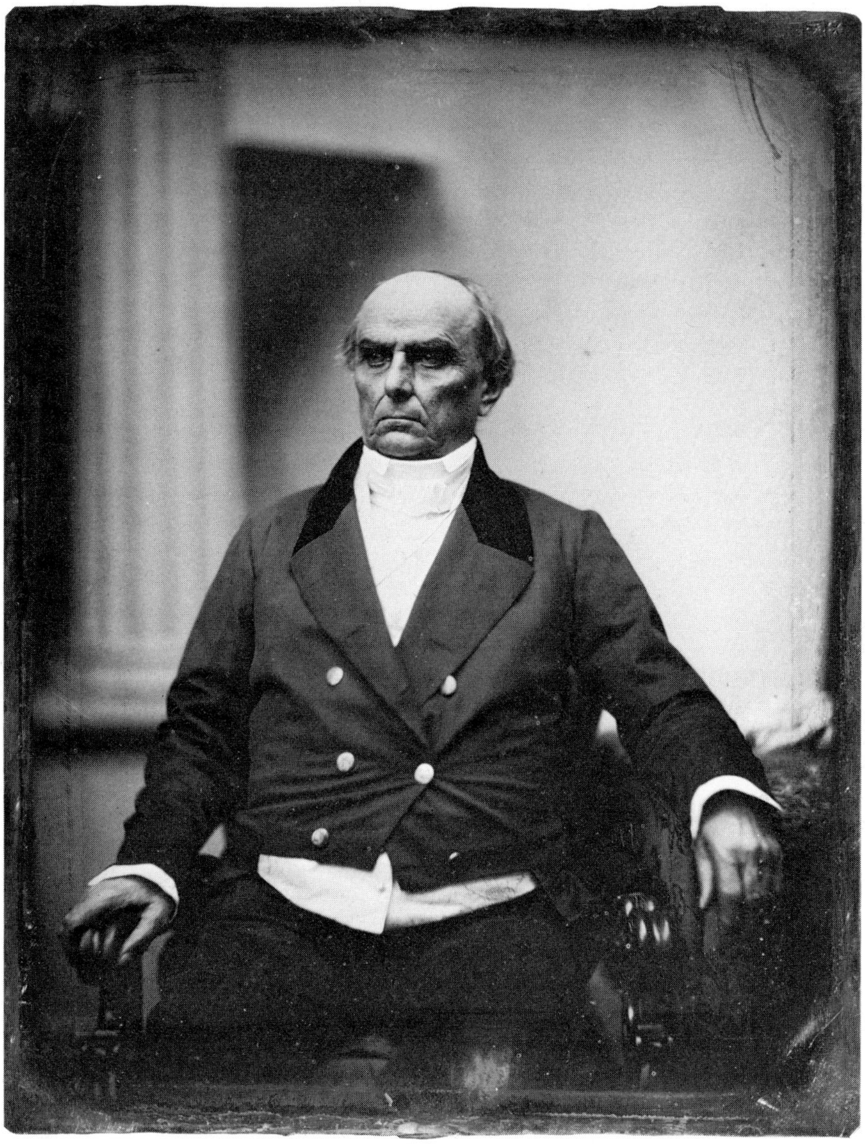

20. DANIEL WEBSTER

Date: April 22, 1851. Whole plate. Hallmark: u.r.: Doublé J. P. Museum of Fine Arts, Boston. Gift of Edward Southworth Hawes in memory of his father, Josiah Johnson Hawes. 43.1402.

The American painter William Willard arranged with Southworth & Hawes for Daniel Webster to sit for this portrait which he could then use as a model for his oil portrait painting. The painting now hangs in relative obscurity, but the daguerreotype has transcended its intended purpose to become one of the great renditions of the aging statesman. Webster projects his indomitable will and firm convictions in this portrait just as he had a month earlier when he shocked Boston with a speech upholding the law for the return of fugitive slaves. The figure presents itself to the viewer with all the judgmental gravity and hierarchic aloofness of a medieval deity enthroned. The low placement of the figure in the pictorial plane and the backlighting add to the weight and solemnity of Webster's appearance.

This is one of the few images from the Southworth & Hawes studio that can be definitely attributed to one of the partners. Since it bears the date of 1850, when Southworth was in California, only Hawes could have secured this likeness.

[Rudisill, Richard. *Mirror Image: The Influence of Daguerreotype on American Society.* Albuquerque: University of New Mexico Press, 1971, p. 178.]

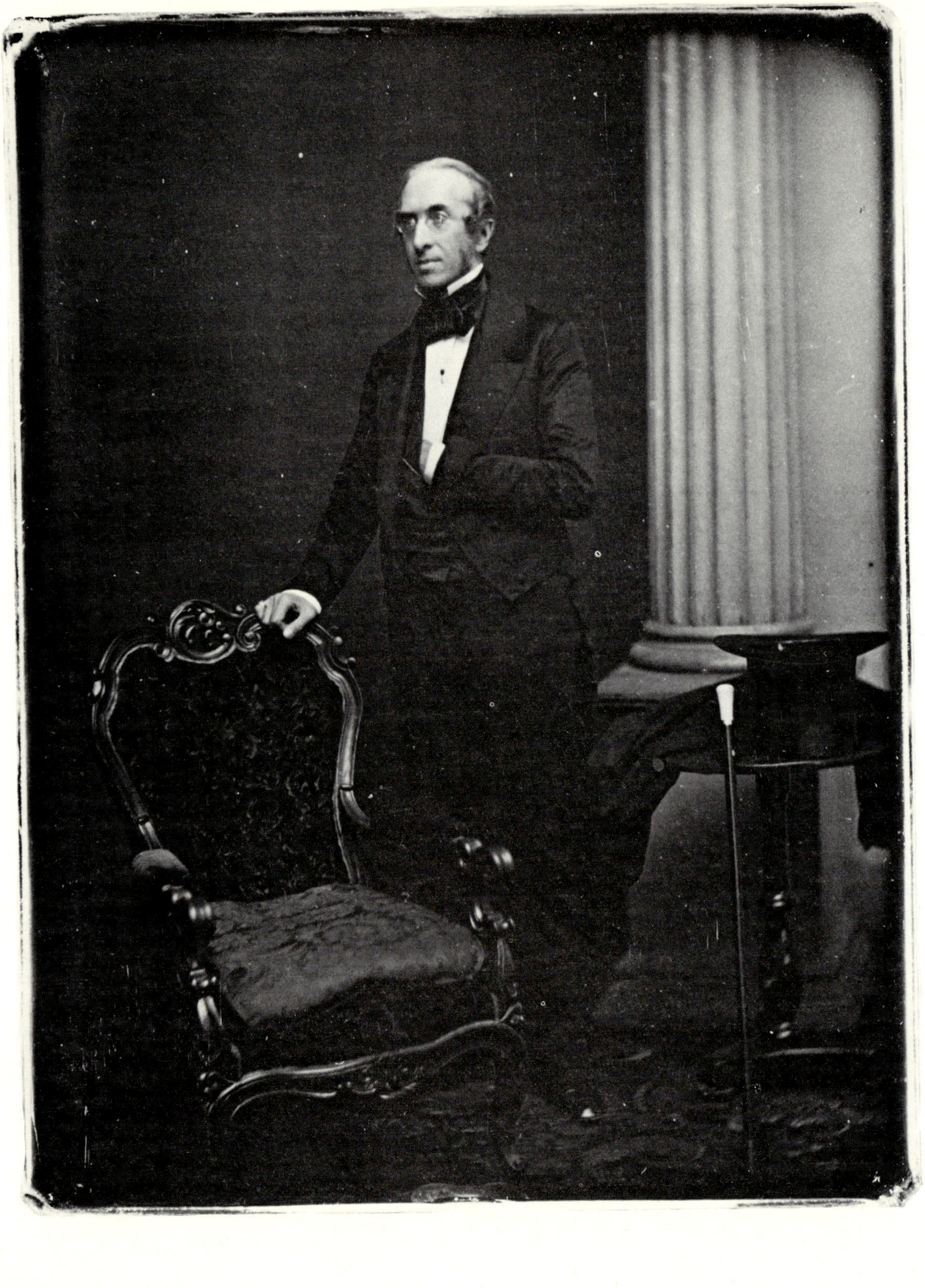

21. Unidentified Male

Whole plate. Hallmark: u.l.: Doublé J. P. International Museum of Photography at George Eastman House. Southworth & Hawes Collection. 74:193:256a.

Previously identified as a likeness of William Lloyd Garrison, this portrait of an unidentified gentleman is almost a parody of the Philadelphia photographer Marcus Root's wry comment:

Hands, hats, and numerous other accompaniments, e.g. landscape or fancy backgrounds, curtains, &c., should (in my opinion) be rigorously banished from the picture, as tending to impair the likeness. So a high chair-back behind the head both interferes (I think) with the effect of the face, and offends correct taste.

Yet in its rigidity and strict control of both posture and accessories, this portrait does evince a possible characterization of the sitter.

It has been suggested that the sitter might have been Robert Charles Winthrop (1809–1894), Massachusetts Senator and U.S. Representative.

[Root, Marcus Aurelius. *The Camera and the Pencil; or The Heliographic Art. . . .* Philadelphia: M. A. Root, 1864, p. 108.]

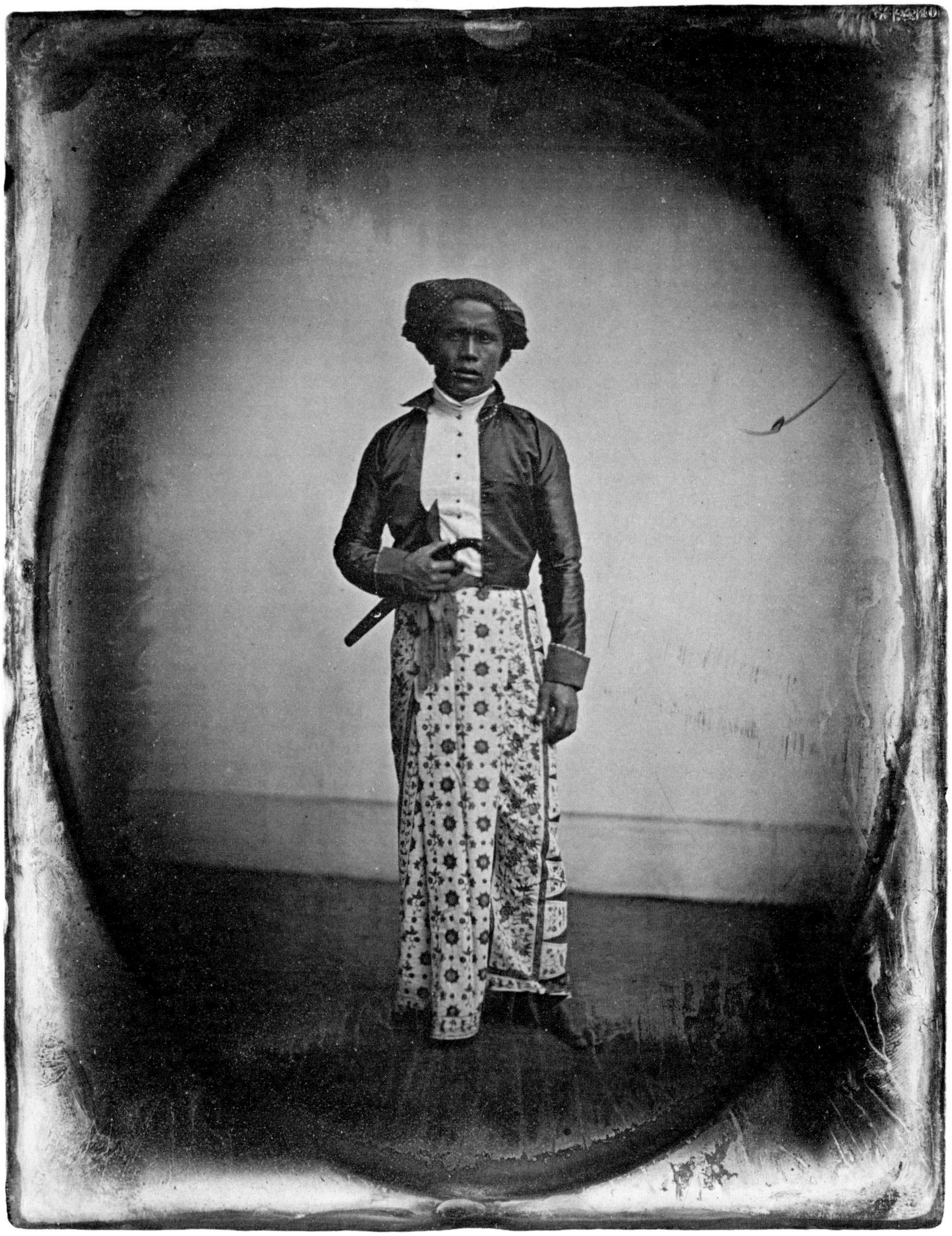

22. Unidentified Asian Male

Whole plate. Hallmark: u.r.: Doublé J. P. Museum of Fine Arts, Boston. Gift of Edward Southworth Hawes in memory of his father, Josiah Johnson Hawes. 43.1483.

Nothing is known about the circumstances surrounding the taking of this portrait. The subject appears to be a lascar, an East Indian sailor dressed in a typical 19th-century Indonesian sailor's uniform and holding a creese, a Malay dagger. The static, frontal pose, the distance between the figure and the camera, and the obviousness of the studio environment are uncharacteristic of Southworth & Hawes's style. The recording of the costume and the total appearance of the sailor was as much the objective of this photograph as the portrayal of the individual personality. A peculiar strength of expression, however, results from the purely photographic and analytic approach to the subject, somewhat akin to a dry ethnographic style.

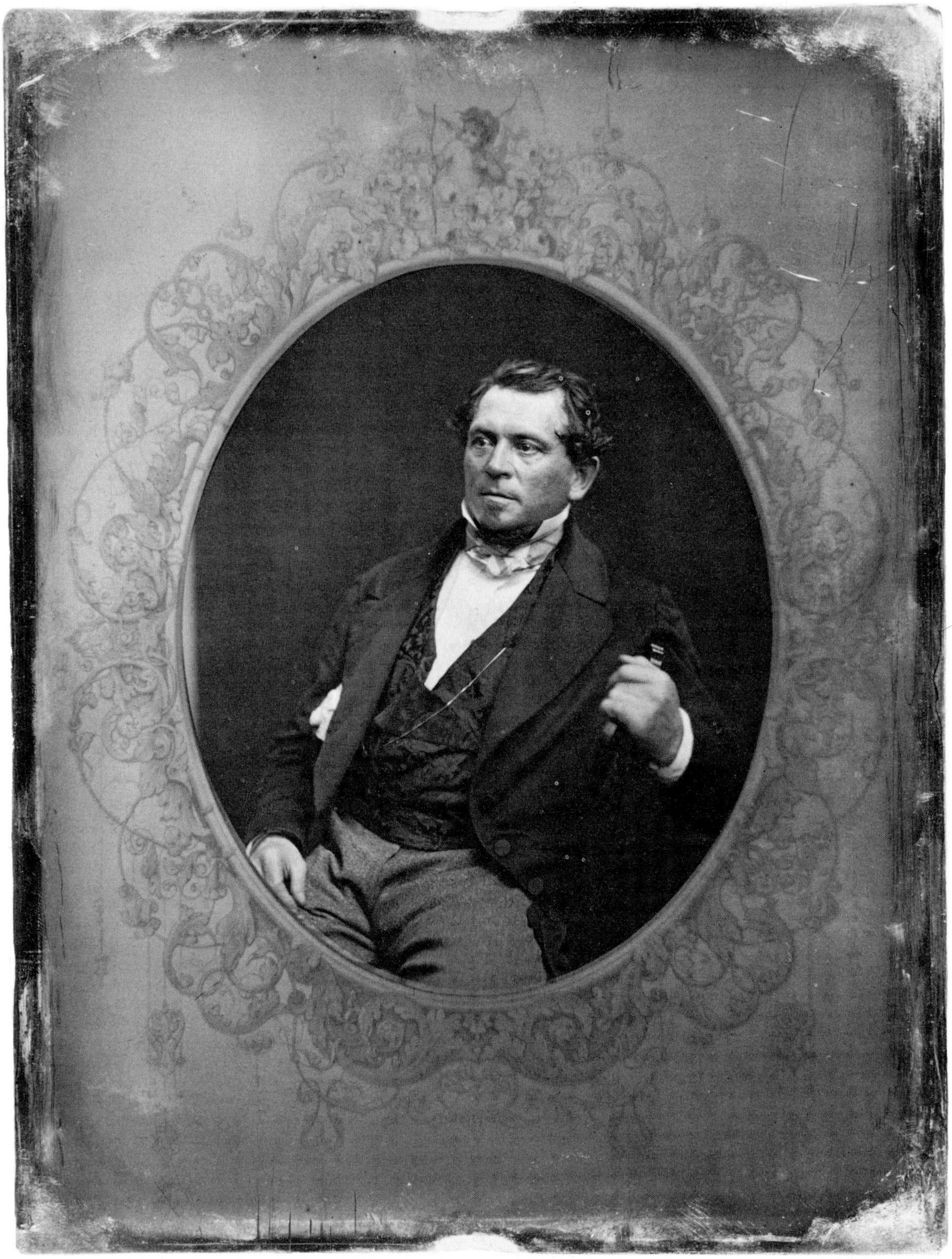

23. Unidentified Male with Engraved Border

Whole plate. Hallmark: none. International Museum of Photography at George Eastman House. Southworth & Hawes Collection. 74:193:120.

24. Unidentified Female with Engraved Border

Whole plate. Hand-colored. Hallmark: l.l.: star; l.r.: 40. International Museum of Photography at George Eastman House. Southworth & Hawes Collection. 74:193:50.

Writing to her brother then in California, Nancy Niles Southworth Hawes thus described the firm's use of decorative frames as exemplified by this pair of matrimonial portraits:

We have been getting up a new style for pictures, which I think will be rather pleasing. We have only made two, and they are liked well. They are made by covering the middle of a French plate, and copying on the outside border one of the borders from a picture in Moore's Book of Beauty then cover the border, and in the center take a likeness. It gives a very pretty finish to the picture and, by experimenting, I think we shall be able to make some very pretty things in this way.

Undoubtedly, her reference is to either the 1846 or 1847 edition of *The Beauties of Moore: A Series of Portraits of*

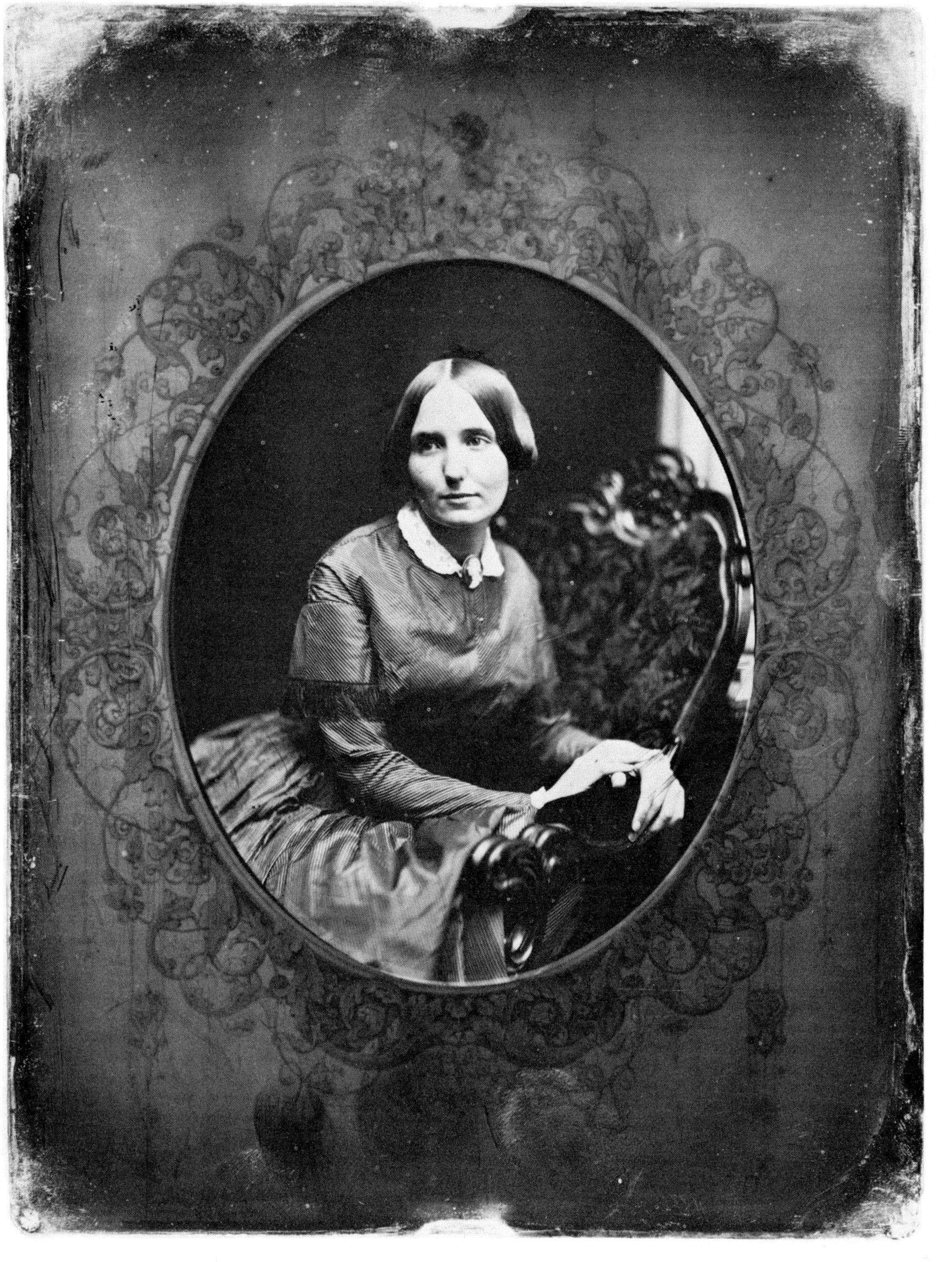

His Principal Female Characters. . . . The book is a compendium of the Victorian ideal of feminine beauty and of exemplary portrait poses and compositions. It reproduces a number of steel engraved plates with the verses by Thomas Moore (1779–1852), a fashionable poet and ballad composer during the Regency. The various female types to whom these amatory verses were often directed were idealistically rendered by such Victorian artists as Augustus Egg, William P. Frith and W. Maddox. These paintings were then translated into engravings, each with a different decorative border by J. Marchant. The border which Nancy Hawes used for these two portraits corresponds to an unnumbered plate entitled ''Black and Blue Eyes'' in Moore's book. The actual pose of the female sitter is close to *Fanny* by William P. Frith illustrating Moore's ''Pensive Thought.''

[Letter, Nancy Southworth Hawes, Boston, to Albert Southworth, n.p. [Beals Bar] 24 August 1849, S&H, IMP/GEH. *The Beauties of Moore: A Series of Portraits of His Principal Female Characters From Paintings by Eminent Artists, Made Expressly for the Work. Engraved by, or Under the Immediate Superintendence of, Mr. Edward Finden. With Descriptive Letterpress.* London: Chapman & Hall, 1846; *ibid*.: Chapman, 1847.]

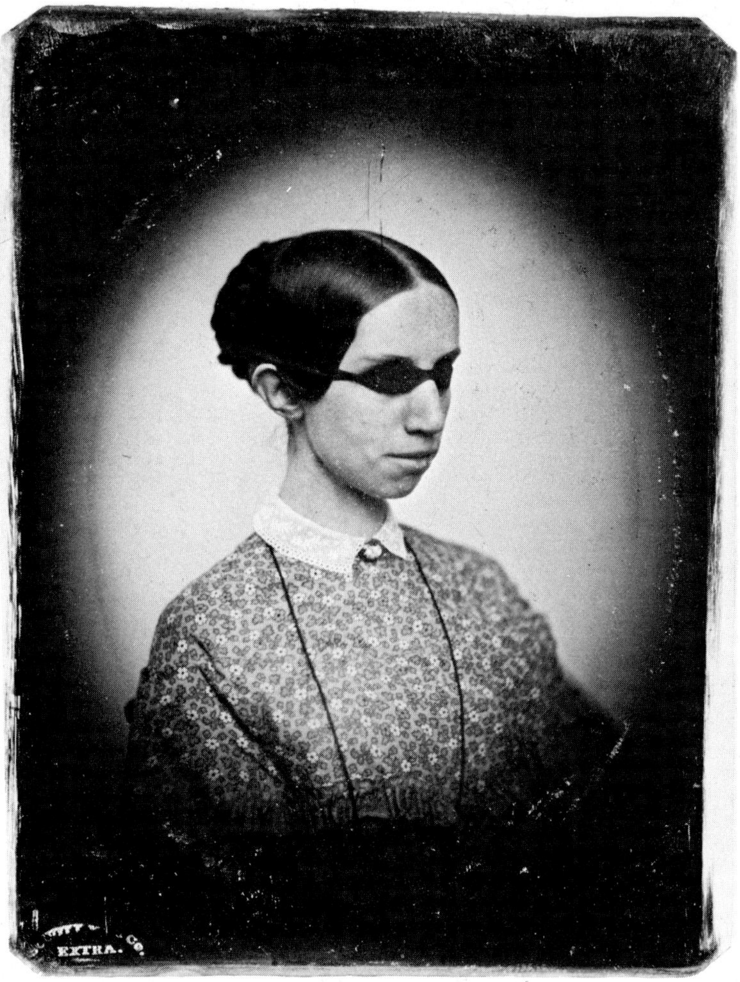

25. LAURA DEWEY BRIDGMAN

Quarter plate. Hallmark: l.l.: Scovill Extra. Museum of Fine Arts, Boston. Gift of Edward Southworth Hawes in memory of his father, Josiah Johnson Hawes. 43.1431.

Laura Dewey Bridgman (1829–1889) was brought to Boston in 1837 after friends of her family presented her case to Dr. Samuel G. Howe of the Perkins Institute for the Blind. At the age of two Laura had suffered a severe illness which left her deprived of both sight and hearing and thus her speech. Under Dr. Howe's care, however, she made remarkable progress in learning the manual alphabet and became the first blind-deaf-mute to be successfully educated in this country. Bridgman was to exert a profound influence on another blind-mute, Helen Keller, who, like Bridgman, also attended the Perkins Institute. After a visit to the Perkins Institute in 1842, Charles Dickens wrote about her extensively in his *American Notes.*

While many Southworth & Hawes portraits lack a definitive background and present the sitter against an empty foil, none implies the sense of complete alienation as this strange and compelling portrait of Bridgman. The effect is partially due to the eyeless countenance with the dark patches required of all patients at the Perkins Institute. However, the vignetting, backlighting and posing of the sitter are also crucial to the expression of utter isolation.

[Dickens, Charles. *American Notes and Pictures from Italy*. London and New York: Macmillan & Co., 1893, pp. 21–38.]

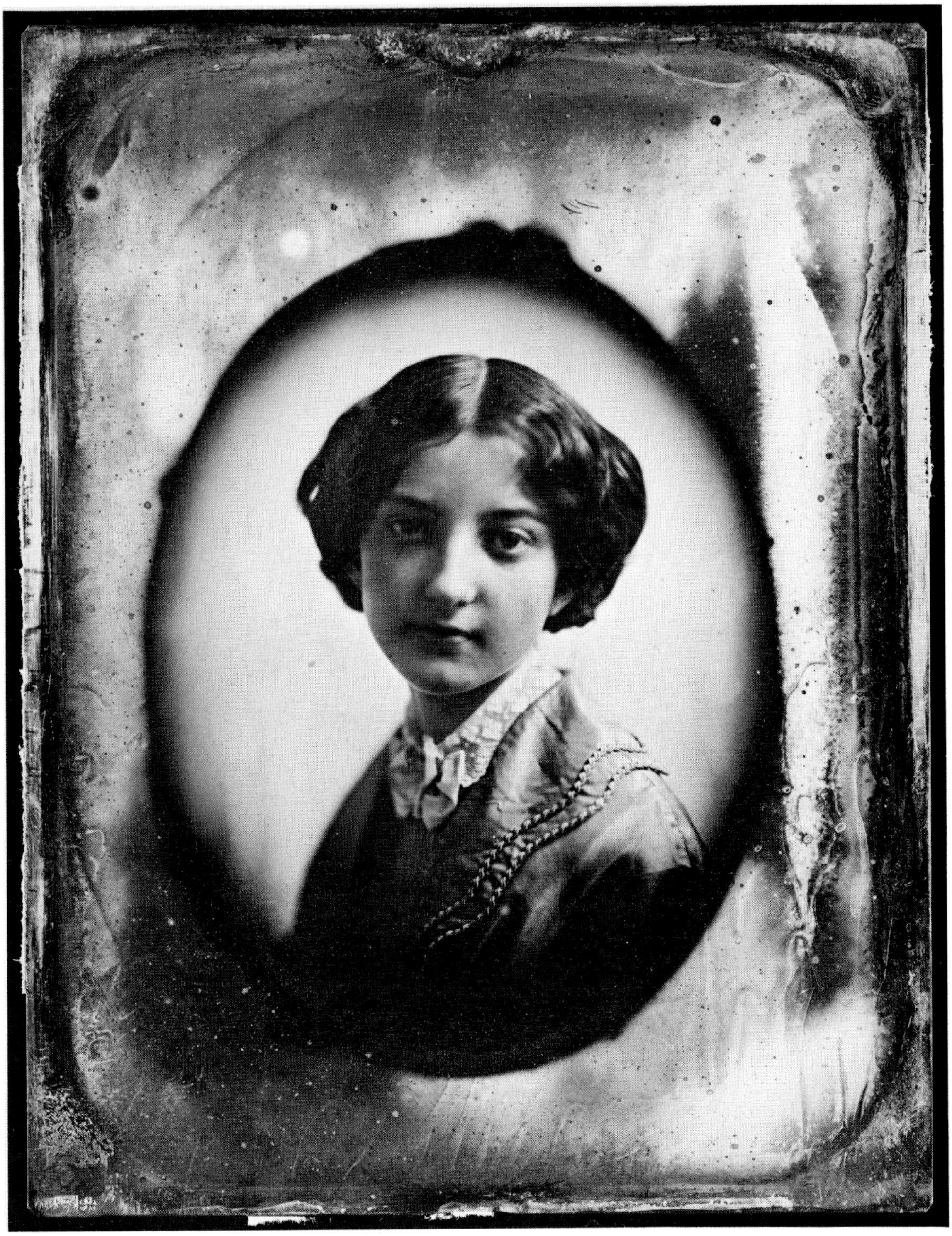

26. Miss Hodges of Salem

Whole plate. Hallmark: l.l.: Doublé J. P. Museum of Fine Arts, Boston. Gift of Edward Southworth Hawes in memory of his father, Josiah Johnson Hawes. 43.1394.

The pictorial value of this portrait of Miss Hodges of Salem lies as much in the capricious accidents of intervening years as to the first intentions of the artists. The plate had originally shown a bull's-eye medallion portrait of the young woman's bust (cf. Plate 37) with a Rembrandtesque backlighting and a "double elliptic" brass mat frame. Faint residual traces of this rectangular mat with four rounded corners can still be seen. Exactly when the mat was removed is uncertain. Surface tarnishing by oxidation and sulphurization, together with the slight imperfections along the edge of the oval medallion, create a soft painterly effect, unusual for the precisely defined daguerreotype likeness. The resulting atmosphere is as captivating as the openness with which the young woman faces her audience.

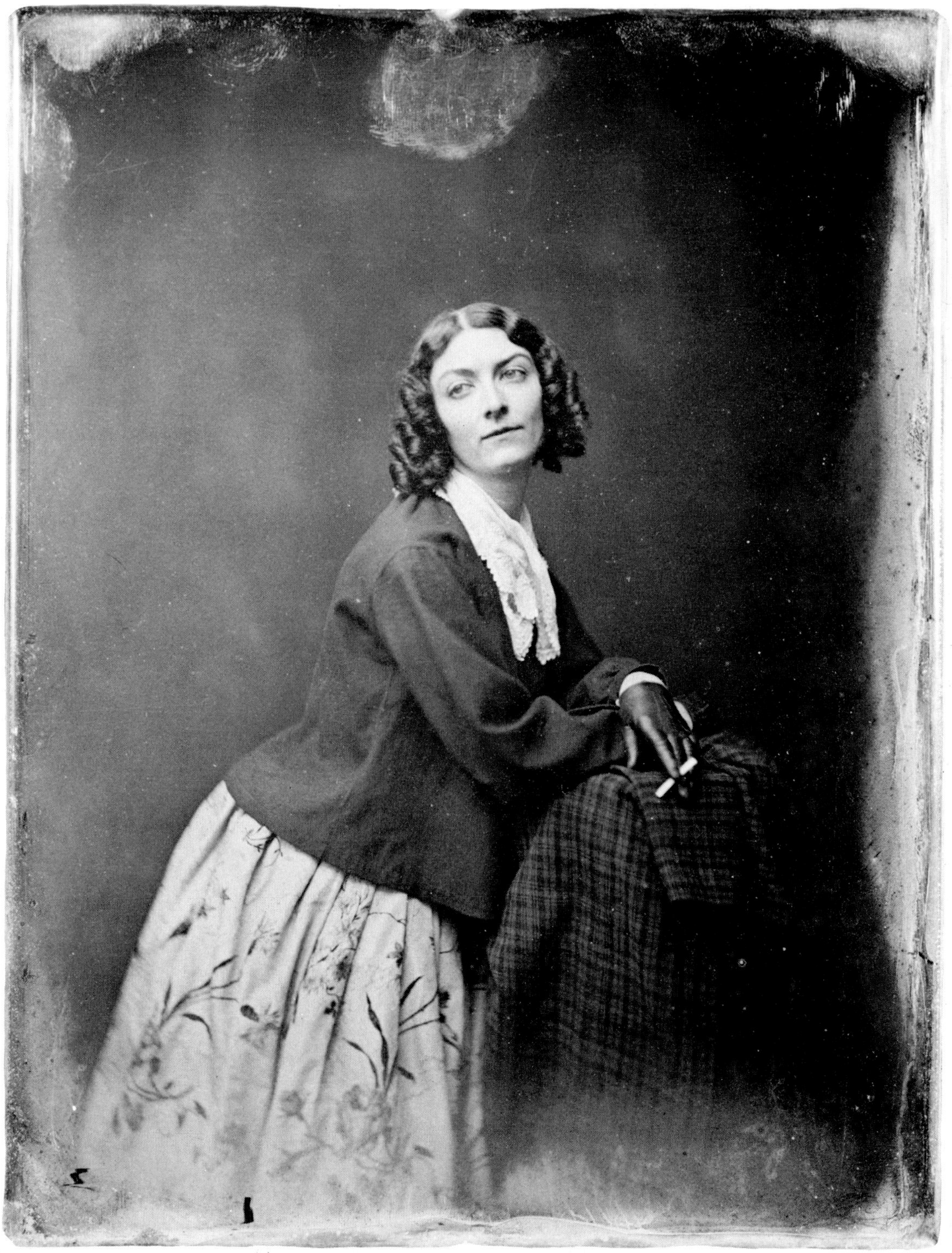

27. Lola Montez

Date: 1851. Whole plate. Hallmark: l.r.: Doublé J. P. Metropolitan Museum of Art. Gift of I. N. Phelps Stokes and the Hawes family. 37.14.41.

Marie Delores Eliza Rosanna Gilbert (1818–1861), daughter of a British army officer, was born in Ireland and raised in India and Europe. Later billing herself as "Lola Montez, Spanish Dancer," she became the most notorious of 19th-century courtesans. Her adventures and affairs with such notables as King Ludwig I of Bavaria became the subject of world-wide gossip. According to the French critic Arsène Houssaye, "Lola Montez showed the strumpet's way to success." She believed in total social equality and independence for women and demonstrated her beliefs whenever and wherever she could. Posing as a sophisticated decadent, she faced Southworth & Hawes's eminently proper camera with a completely improper cigarette in her hand. Her decision to wear walking gloves for an interior portrait was a further indication of her impropriety.

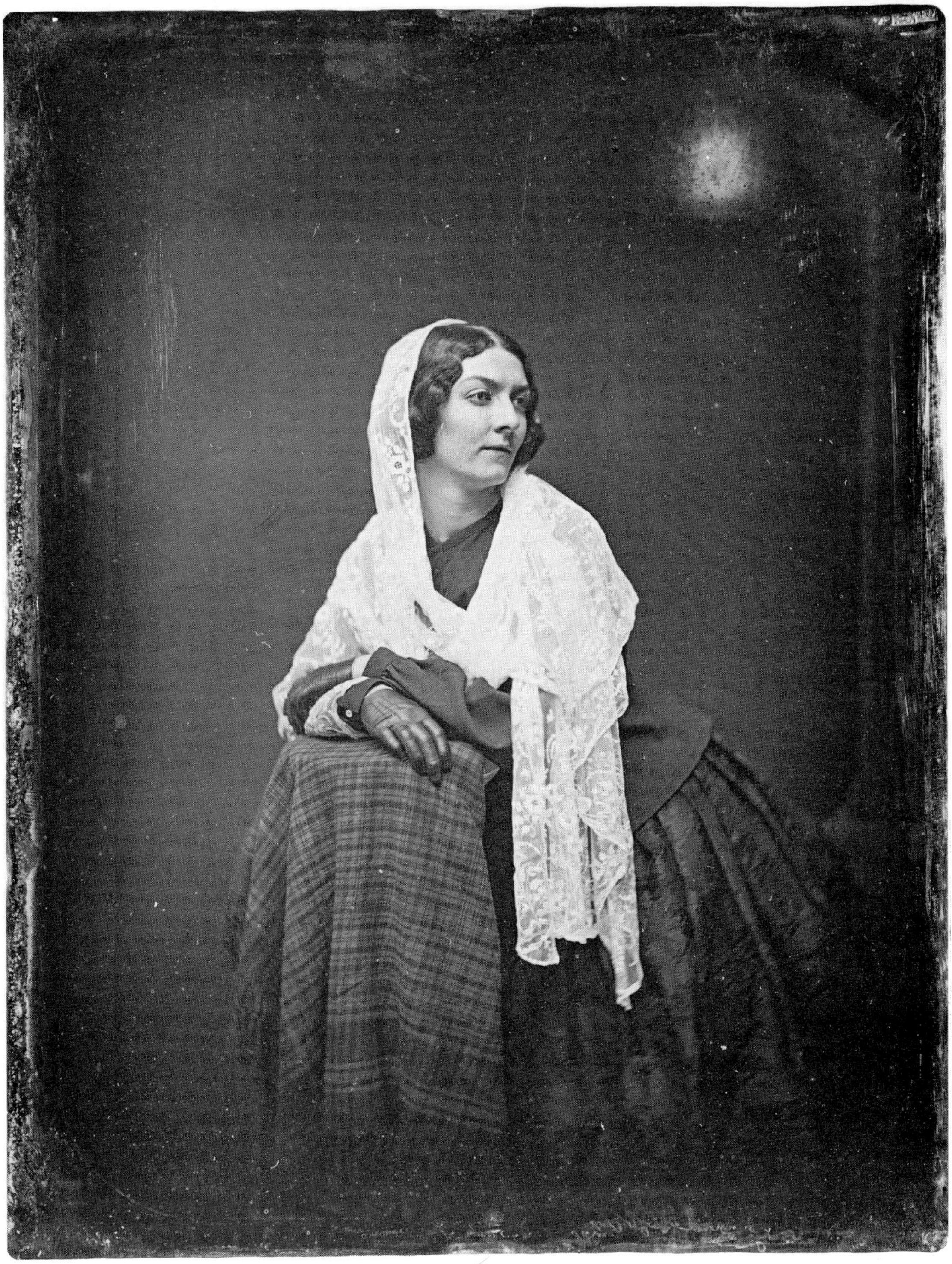

28. Lola Montez

Date: 1851. Whole plate. Hallmark: u.r.: Doublé J. P. Museum of Fine Arts, Boston. Gift of Edward Southworth Hawes in memory of his father, Josiah Johnson Hawes. 43.1396.

In a pose more demure than that of the preceding portrait, Montez presents herself as the actress and *demi-mondaine* who was also worldly-wise and independent minded. Still wearing her outdoor gloves, she lacks only her famous riding crop with which "she had made most of her conquests and reached her heights [and] which was a scepter in her hands." Most likely, she posed for this portrait as well as the previous one in 1851, the year she arrived in America as an actress and international celebrity. When her beauty began to fade, she abandoned her notorious life-style to become a religious convert and social worker in New York. She died using the family name of Eliza Gilbert and, unknown to the world, was buried at Greenwood Cemetery.

[Darling, Amanda. *Lola Montez.* New York: Stein & Day, 1961, passim. Houssaye, Arsène. *Man About Paris: The Confessions of Arsène Houssaye,* trans. and ed. Henry Knepler. New York: William Morrow & Co., 1970, p. 78.]

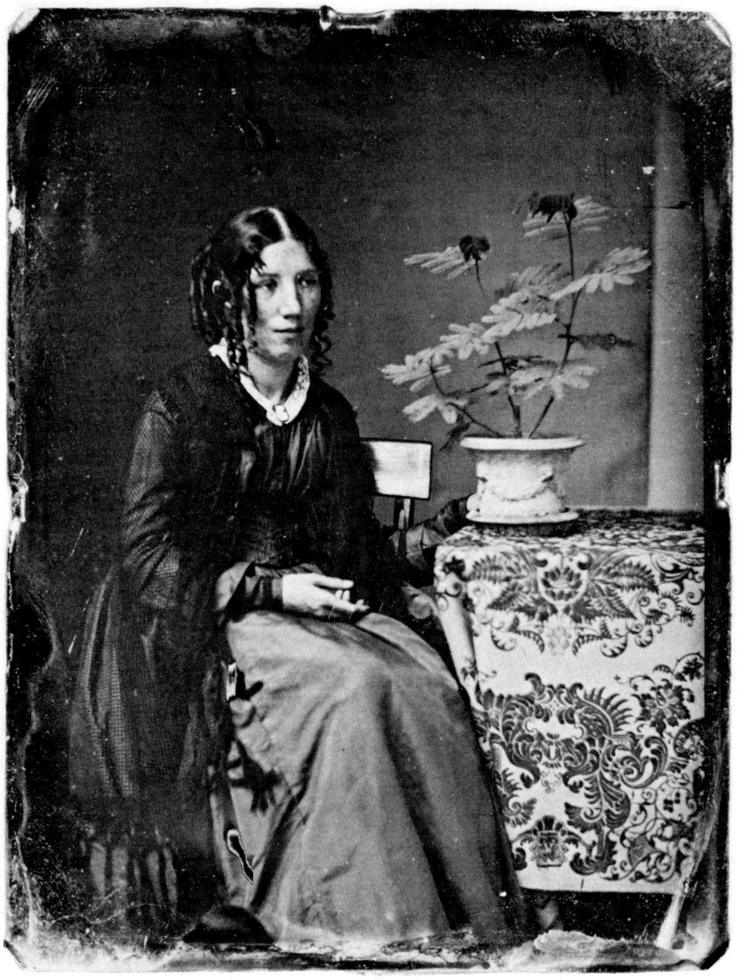

29. Harriet Elizabeth Beecher Stowe

Date: c. 1850. Quarter plate. Hallmark: u.r.: Scovills. Metropolitan Museum of Art. Gift of I. N. Phelps Stokes and the Hawes family. 37.14.40.

Accompanying her husband from Ohio to his new teaching job at Bowdoin College in Maine in 1850, Harriet Elizabeth Beecher Stowe (1811–1896) stopped in Boston to visit her brother Henry Ward Beecher. She found him a sympathetic supporter of her strong feelings against human slavery and received encouragement to express her thoughts in writing. Two years later, in 1852, she published *Uncle Tom's Cabin* which sold 300,000 copies in the first year and was ultimately translated into twenty-three languages. Shy and retiring, Mrs. Stowe quietly pursued the cause of abolition in numerous magazine and newspaper articles, while building a literary career that spanned over fifty years and produced many biographies and children's stories.

The date of Mrs. Stowe's visit coincides with Albert Southworth's visit to California, thereby indicating that Josiah Hawes was responsible for this sensitive portrait. The creative genius in Hawes's placement of Mrs. Stowe's demure figure next to the fragile plant rivals that of the daring pose of Lola Montez holding a cigarette in her hand (Plate 27).

[James Edward T., ed. *Notable American Women 1607–1950: A Biographical Dictionary.* Cambridge, Massachusetts: Harvard University Press, Belknap Press, 1971, vol. III, pp. 393–402. Symposium brochure, *Portraits of a 19th-Century Family.* Hartford, Connecticut: The Stowe-Day Foundation, October 3–4, 1975.]

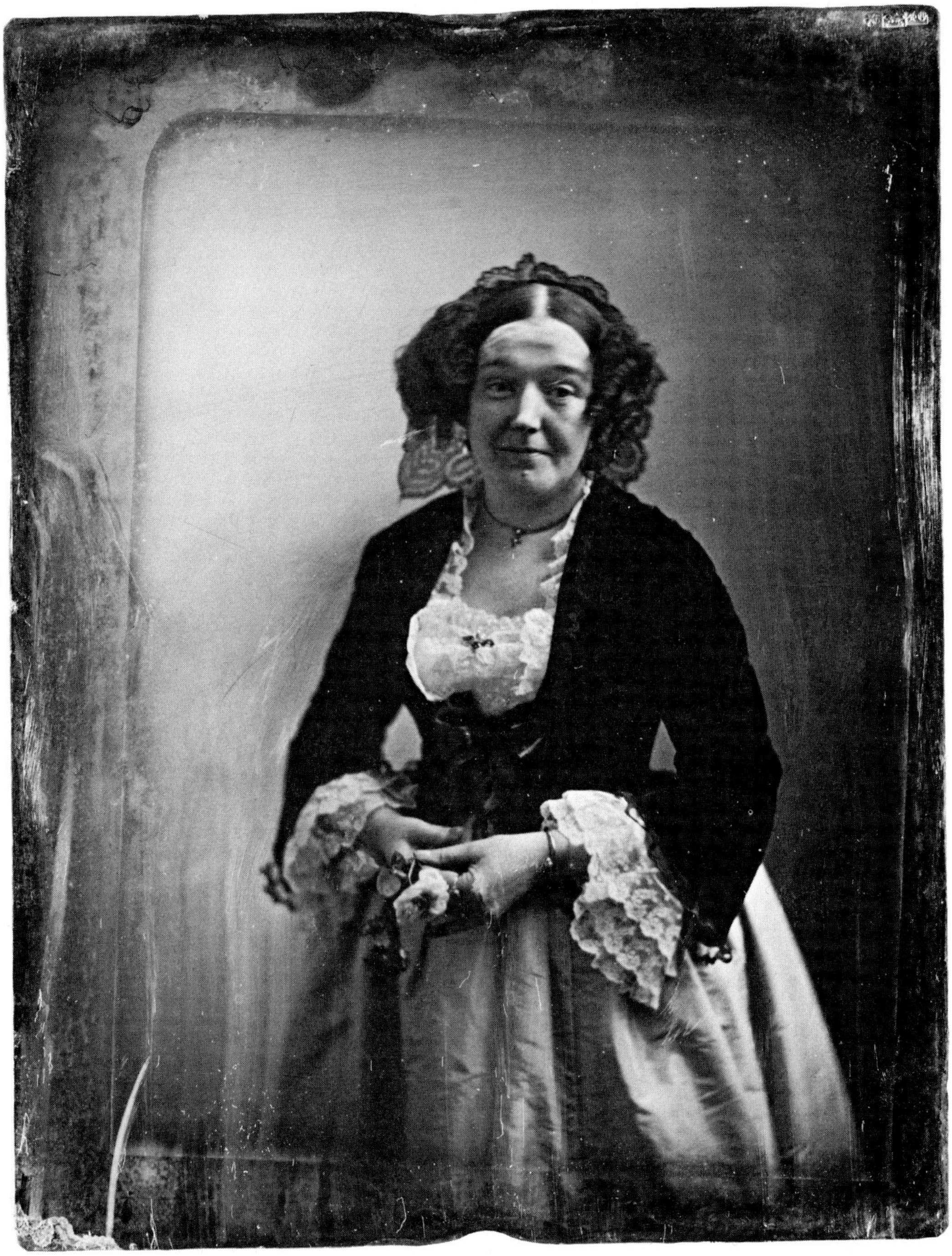

30. MRS. JAMES R. VINCENT

Date: c. 1854. Whole plate. Hallmark: u.r.: Doublé J. P. Museum of Fine Arts, Boston. Gift of Edward Southworth Hawes in memory of his father, Josiah Johnson Hawes. 43.1409.

This portrait shares little in common with the more famous works which employ dramatic lighting, intriguing composition or commanding poses. Its simplicity, however, embodies the qualities that Southworth thought mandatory for a good portrait:

> What is to be done is obliged to be done quickly. The whole character of the sitter is to be read at first sight; the whole likeness . . . is to be seen at first, in each and all its details, and in their unity and combinations.

Mrs. Vincent (1817–1887) had been on the stage for twelve years in her native England before she accompanied her actor husband to America in 1846. Settled in Boston, she became a member of the Old National Theater before joining the Boston Museum Stock Company in 1852. During the course of her thirty-five-year career she became a Boston institution, giving thousands of performances to her adoring audiences.

[Cf. Newhall, Beaumont, *The Daguerreotype in America,* 3rd revised ed., New York: Dover, 1976, pl. 55, for a variant pose of Mrs. Vincent by Southworth & Hawes. Russell, Foster W. *Mount Auburn Biographies,* p. 169. Southworth, Albert Sands, "An Address," *Philadelphia Photographer,* VIII (October 1871), p. 321.]

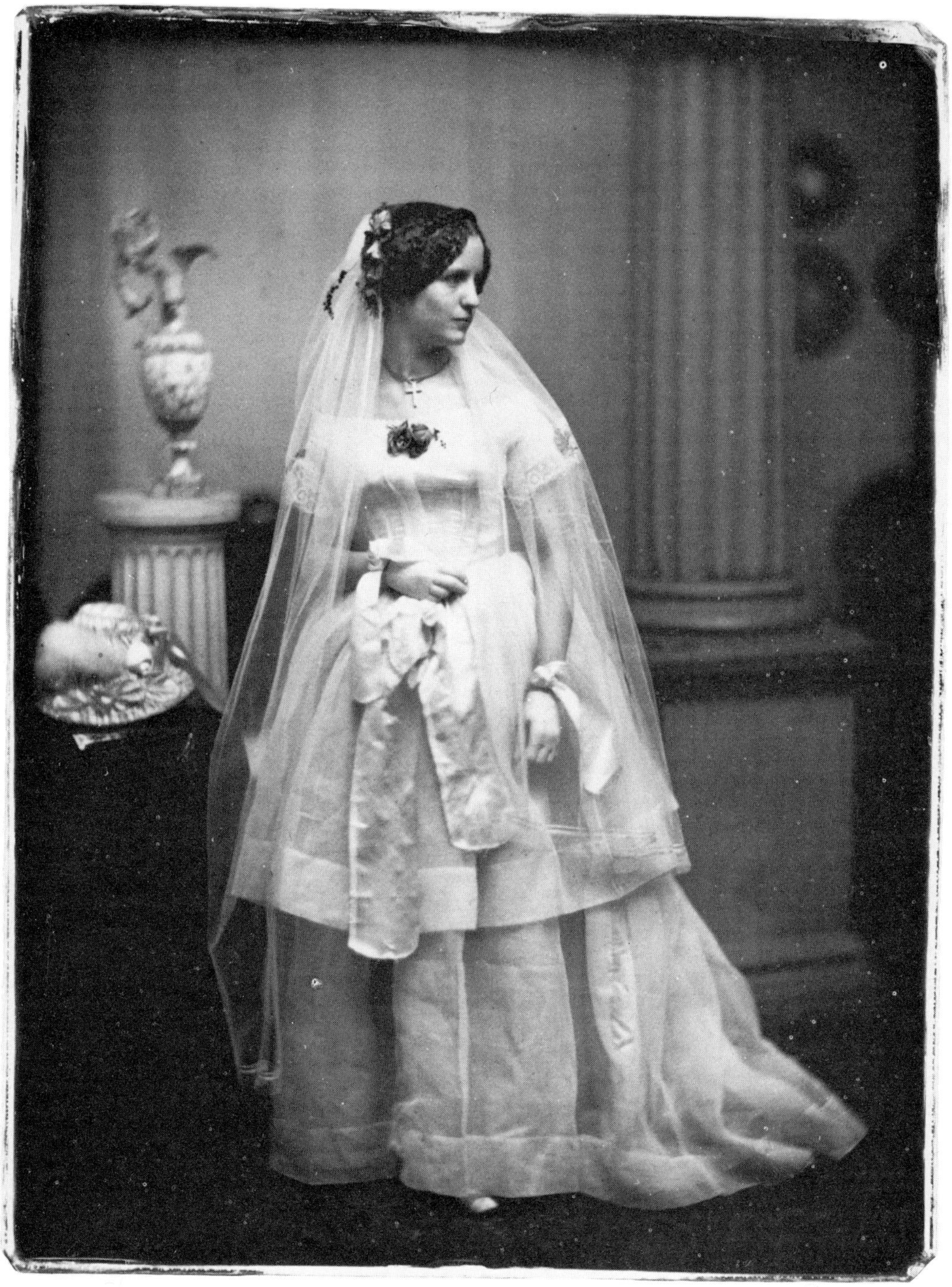

31. UNIDENTIFIED BRIDE

Whole plate, stereo daguerreotype. Hallmark: l.r.: 40. International Museum of Photography at George Eastman House. Southworth & Hawes Collection. 74:193:251.

Southworth & Hawes made a number of bridal portraits that were placed in their Grand Parlor and Gallery Stereoscope. The following poem was apparently inspired by such a stereographic presentation.

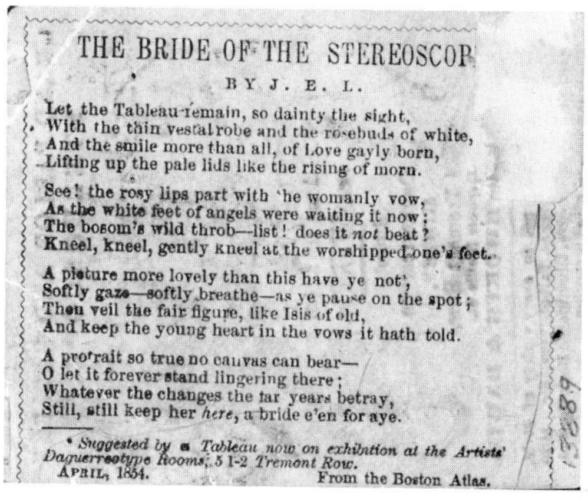

THE BRIDE OF THE STEREOSCOP

BY J. E. L.

Let the Tableau remain, so dainty the sight,
With the thin vestal robe and the rosebuds of white,
And the smile more than all, of Love gayly born,
Lifting up the pale lids like the rising of morn.

See! the rosy lips part with the womanly vow,
As the white feet of angels were waiting it now;
The bosom's wild throb—list! does it *not* beat?
Kneel, kneel, gently kneel at the worshipped one's feet.

A picture more lovely than this have ye not,
Softly gaze—softly breathe—as ye pause on the spot;
Then veil the fair figure, like Isis of old,
And keep the young heart in the vows it hath told.

A portrait so true no canvas can bear—
O let it forever stand lingering there;
Whatever the changes the far years betray,
Still, still keep her *here*, a bride e'en for aye.

* *Suggested by a Tableau now on exhibition at the Artists' Daguerreotype Rooms, 5 1-2 Tremont Row.*
APRIL, 1854. From the Boston Atlas.

RIGHT: Reverse of Season Ticket to Southworth & Hawes Studio for viewing of the Grand Parlor and Gallery Stereoscope, April 1854. Southworth & Hawes Collection, IMP/GEH.

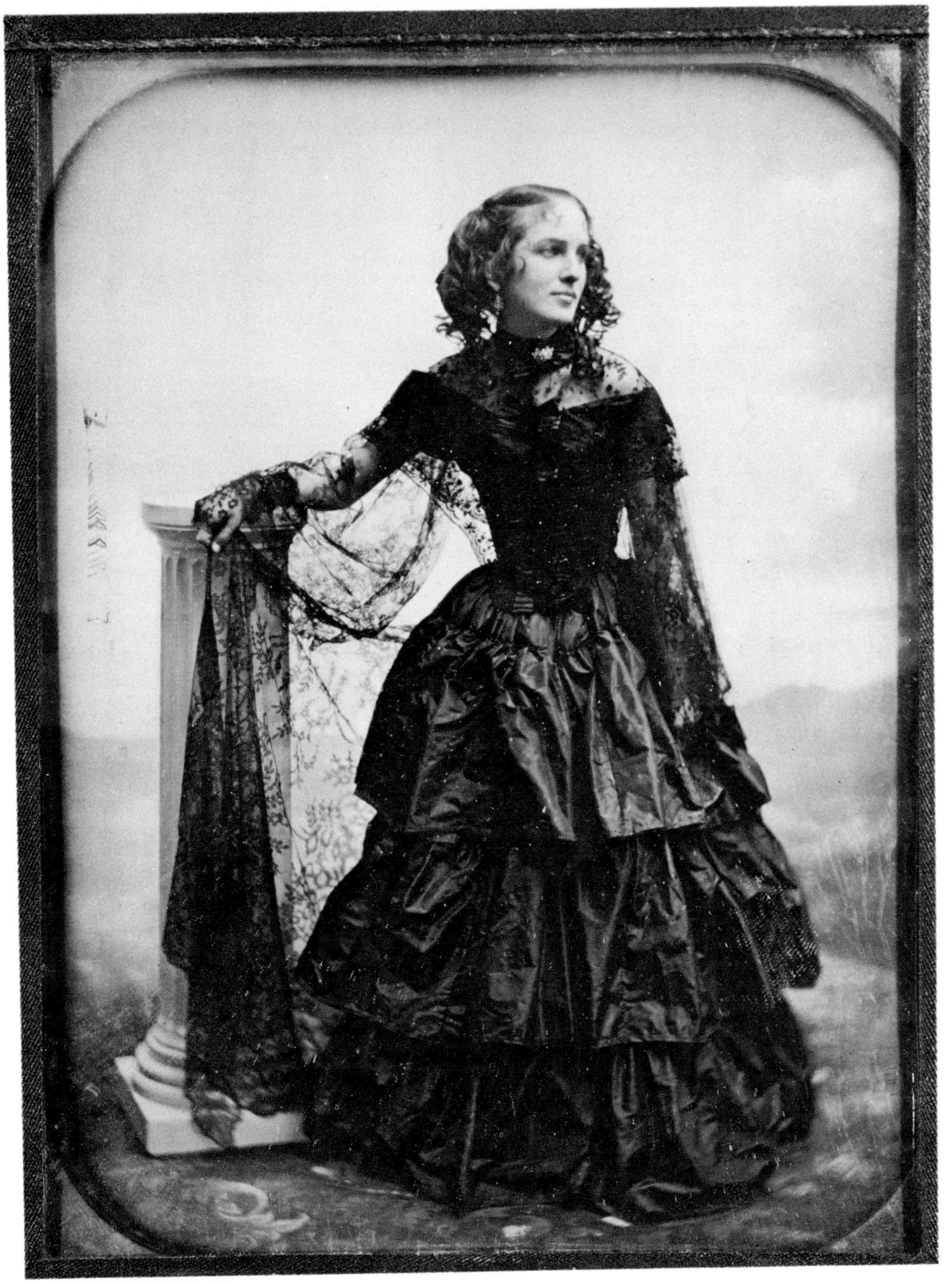

32. Unidentified "Boston Beauty"

Whole plate, hand-colored. Hallmark: l.r.: S & F in lozenge. Metropolitan Museum of Art. Gift of I. N. Phelps Stokes and the Hawes family. 37.14.4

One of the most repeated poses in 19th-century portraiture of young women was to show the full-length standing figure, gazing with abstracted melancholy off to the side with a hand resting on a miniature Doric column. Commonly found in many American daguerreotypes, French calotypes and especially British carte-de-visites, this pose becomes unique in the hands of Southworth & Hawes. Their portrait of this "Boston Beauty" would have been little more than a pretty likeness of an attractive and elegantly dressed female were it not for the spectacularly colored sunset behind her. Ranging from the brightest crimson to a brilliant yellow, Nancy Southworth Hawes's hand-applied hues of the skyscape remain one of the most sumptuous daguerreian backgrounds. The conventional portrait pose is totally transformed by the scale and the sensitively colored surface which is redolent of a contemporary fashion plate.

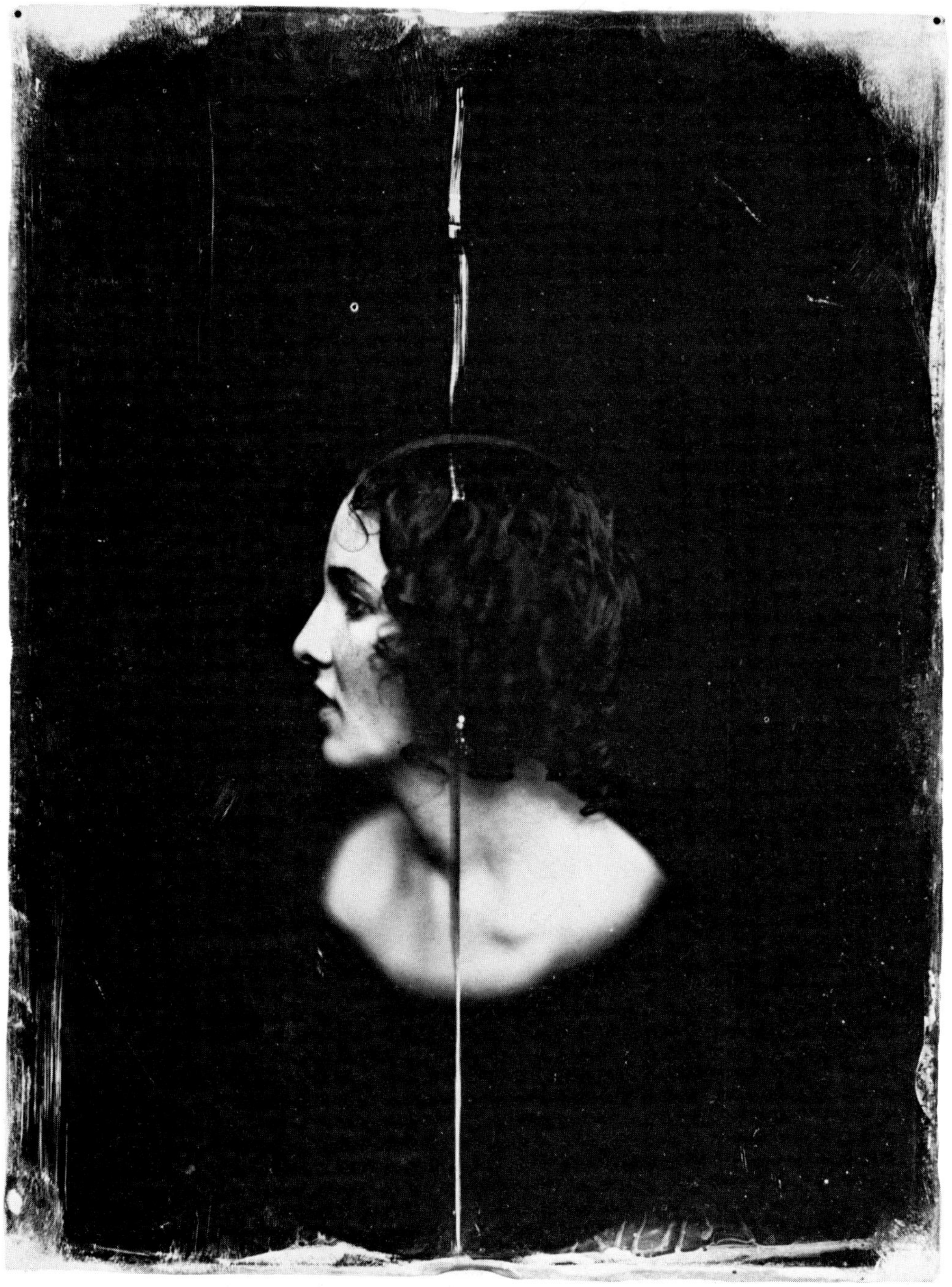

33. Unidentified Female

Whole plate, hand-colored. Hallmark: l.l.: Christofle. International Museum of Photography at George Eastman House. Southworth & Hawes Collection. 74:193:49

In Poe's story, "The Oval Portrait," the protagonist is brought from his slumberous state by a painting hanging opposite his bed. "The portrait, I have already said, was that of a young girl. It was a mere head and shoulders, done in what is technically termed a vignette manner; much in the style of the favorite heads of Sully. The arms, the bosom, and even the ends of the radiant hair melted imperceptibly into the vague yet deep shadow which formed the background of the whole. The frame was oval, richly gilded and filigreed in *Moresque*. . . . I had found the spell of the picture in an absolute *life-likeness* of expression, which, at first startling, finally confounded, subdued, and appalled me." Markings on this plate indicate that it once was indeed presented beneath an oval, probably brass, mat, thereby further enhancing its similarity to what had been a popular, formal motif in mid-19th-century portraiture. A similarity in the subject's features in this portrait and the preceding one (Plate 32) would indicate that both daguerreotypes are of the same woman.

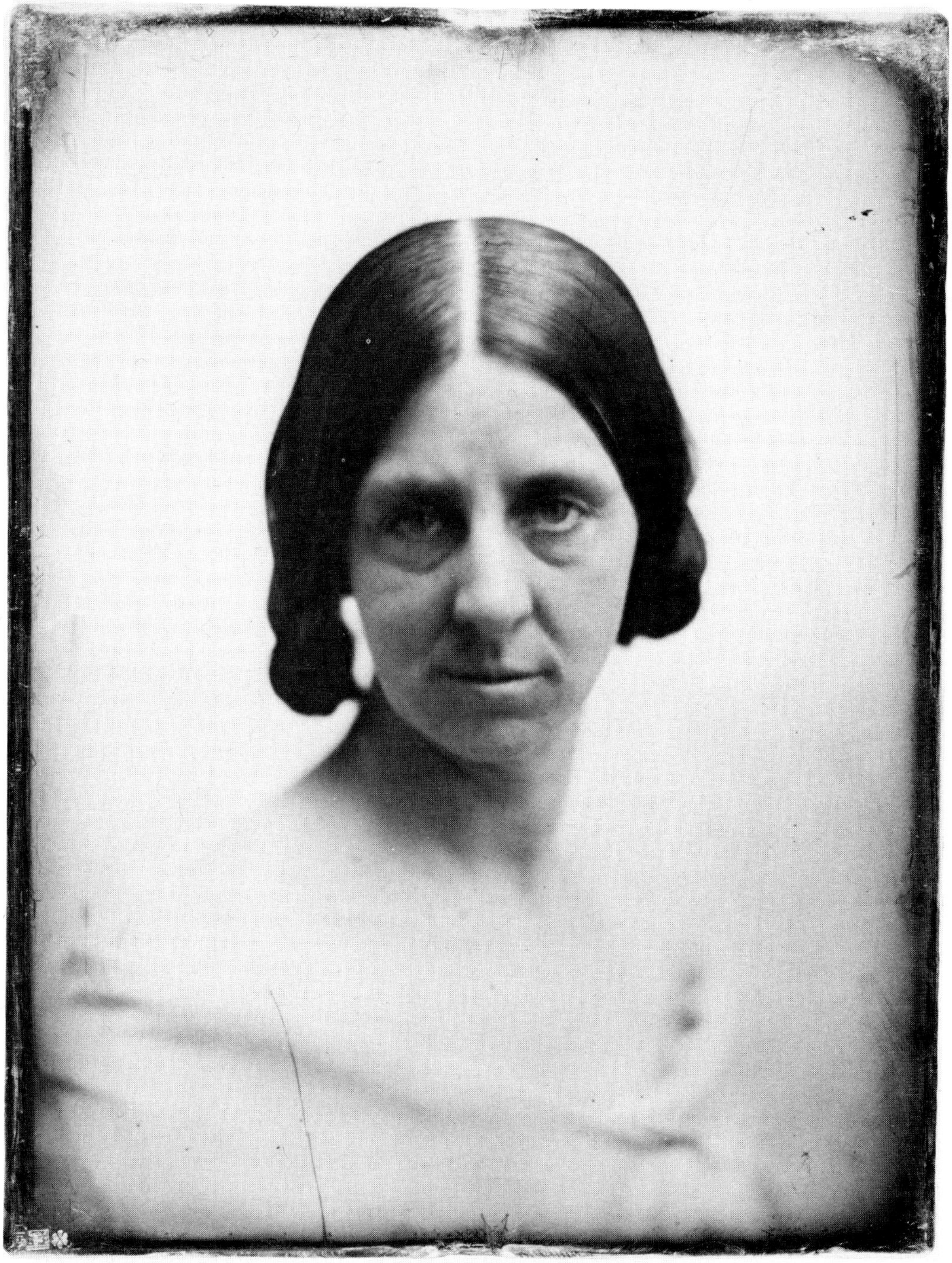

34. Unidentified Female

Whole plate, hand-colored. Hallmark: l.l.: Doublé J. P. International Museum of Photography at George Eastman House. Southworth & Hawes Collection. 74:193:15

Although J. A. Whipple of Boston is the undisputed inventor of the vignetted or "crayon" daguerreotype, there is some confusion as to who took out the patent. Snelling cites M. A. Root as the patentee and Humphrey claims it was Whipple. There is no record indicating that Southworth & Hawes ever negotiated for the rights to the invention, but the vignetted daguerreotype portrait is one of the main features of the partners' work.

A semicircular or a ring-shaped paper mask placed in front of the lens and moved during the exposure to destroy its own definition leaves only the center of the plate clearly delineated. The mask can thus be used to show the head or the bust of a sitter in a nebulous ambience of mercurial whiteness if the paper and background are white, or of silvered black if they are dark. This paper mask is positioned between the camera and the sitter at a point which allows for the desired amount of the sitter's body to be seen. In this portrait, a semicircular shape, probably white, was used partially during the exposure. Southworth & Hawes also experimented with variations of white and black vignetting masks with the opposite backgrounds (cf. Plates 33, 35, 36, 56).

[Snelling, Henry H. *The History and Practice of the Art of Photography. . . .* New York: G. P. Putnam, 1849, p. 120. Humphrey, S. D. *American Hand Book of the Daguerreotype. . .*, 5th ed. New York: S. D. Humphrey, 1858, pp. 170–171.]

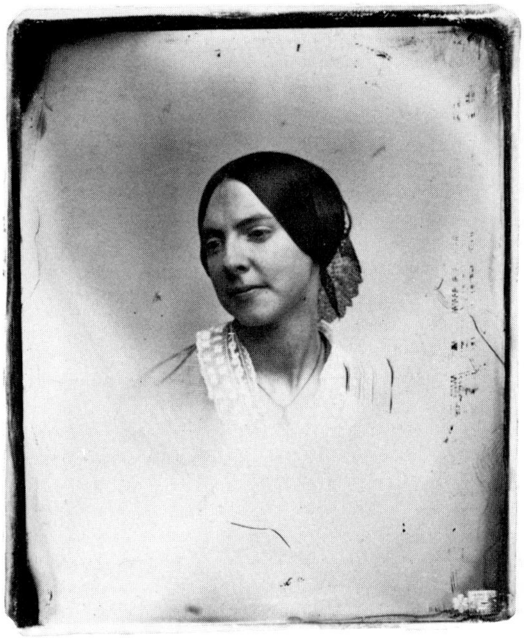
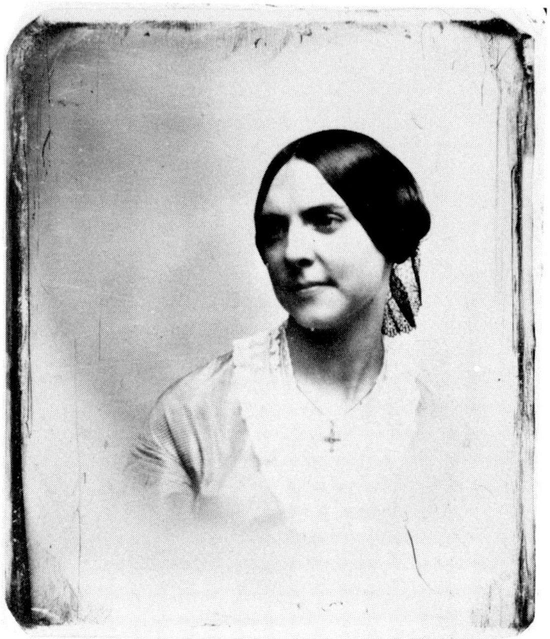
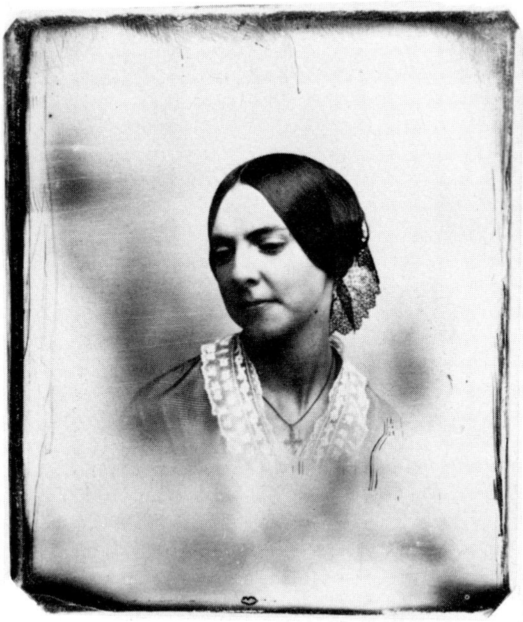
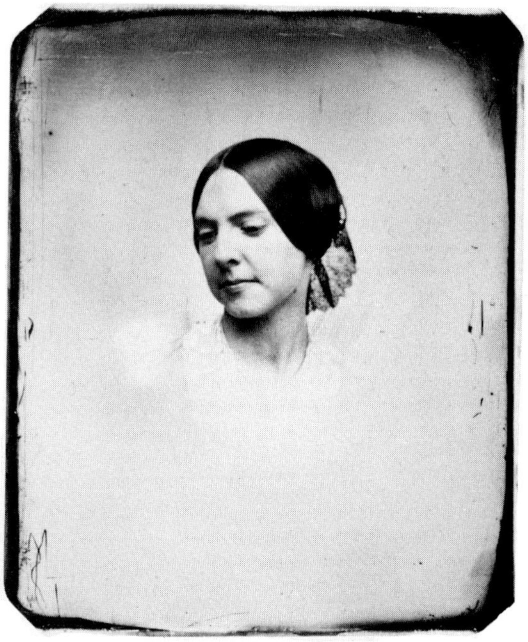

35a–d. Unidentified Female

a. Sixth plate. Hallmark: l.r.: Doublé J. P. International Museum of Photography at George Eastman House. Southworth & Hawes Collection. 74:193:783.

b–d. Sixth plate. Hallmark: none. International Museum of Photography at George Eastman House. Southworth & Hawes Collection. 74:193:480. 74:193:317. 74:193:329.

These four sixth-plate vignetted portraits of the same unidentified woman show variant poses and expressions recorded at a single sitting. Root, who may have held the patent for the "crayon" style of portraiture (cf. Plate 34), stated:

> A vignette portrait, i.e. the head and shoulders in the crayon style, I generally find more pleasing to the true artist and connoisseur, than either full-length or half figures. The apparent size of the head can be augmented by placing it somewhat above the middle of the plate; and as the image is produced by the centre of the lenses, there is less liability to distortion in it . . .a vignette portrait may be rendered more truthful, life-like, and artistically effective, than one wherein the head surmounts a half or a full-length figure.

[Root, Marcus Aurelius. *The Camera and the Pencil*, pp. 108–109.]

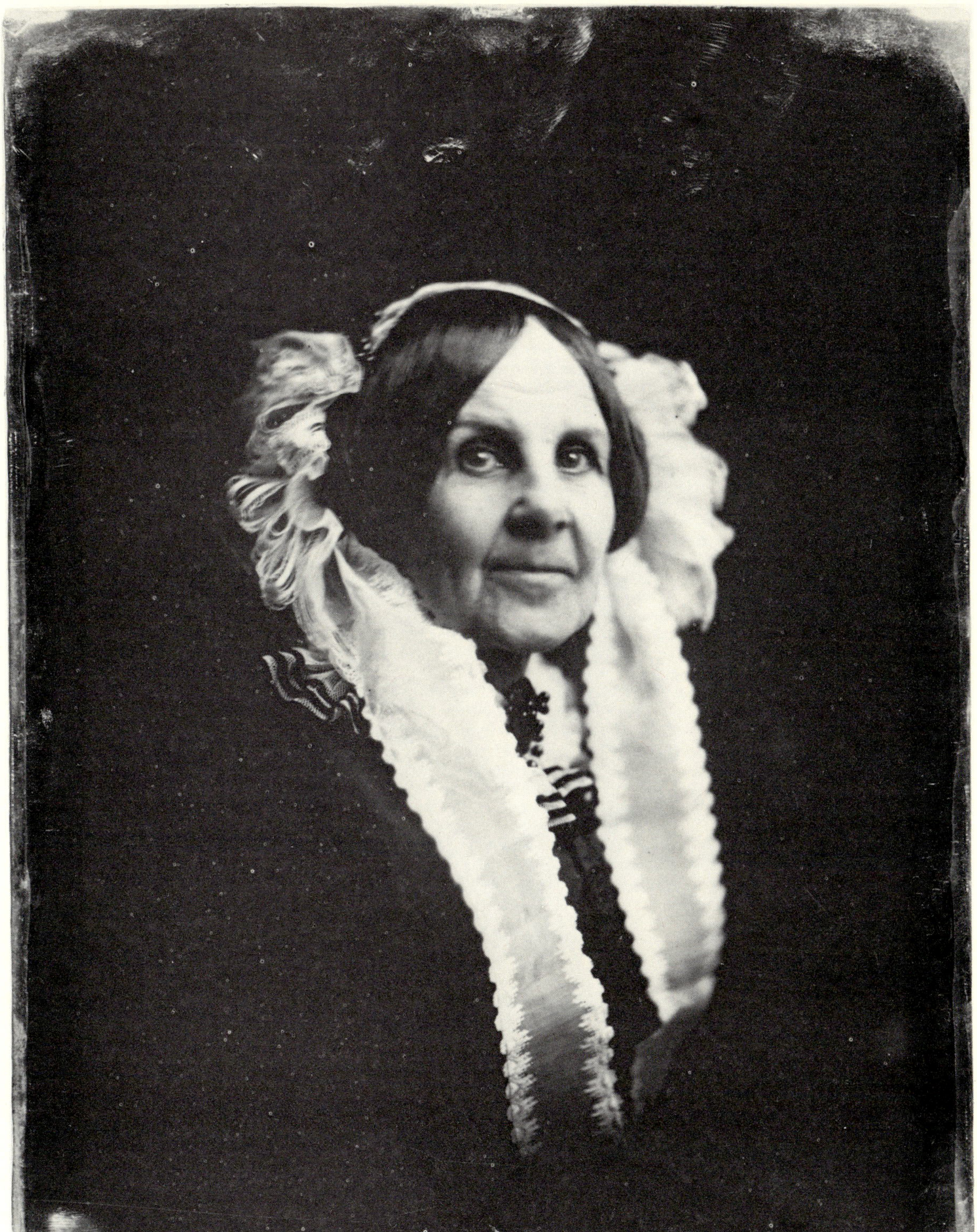

36. UNIDENTIFIED FEMALE

Whole plate. Hallmark: u.l.: S & F in lozenge. International Museum of Photography at George Eastman House. Southworth & Hawes Collection. 74:193:163.

This is another variation of the vignetted or "crayon" portrait style, this time with the unidentified sitter thrown into a deep relief by dramatic side-lighting. The theatricality of the face and its bold projection are heightened by the partially solarized white bonnet and its ribbons. The use of a dark mask to vignette the face against a black background results in showing the sitter against an ambiguously receding space.

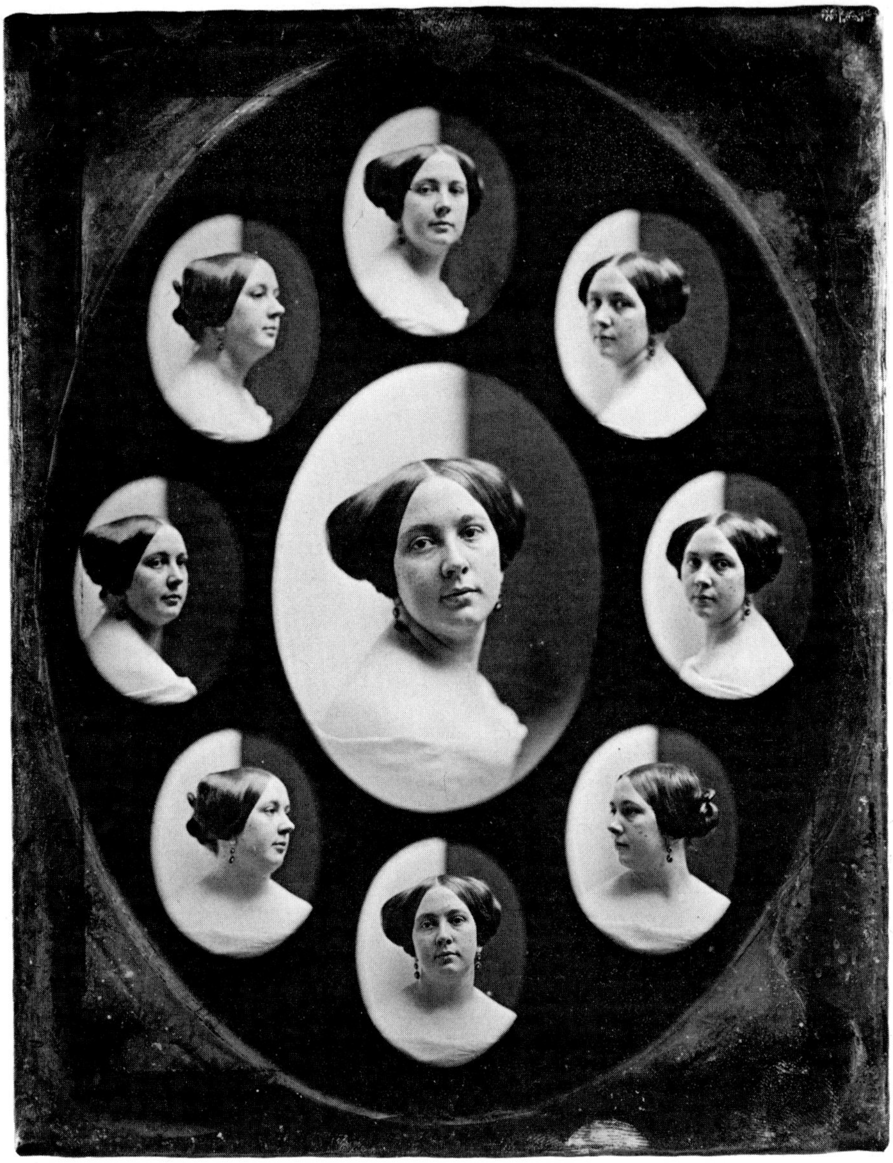

37. Unidentified Female, Medallion Daguerreotype

Whole plate. Hallmark: u.r.: Doublé J. P. Museum of Fine Arts, Boston. Gift of Edward Southworth Hawes in memory of his father, Josiah Johnson Hawes. 43.1405.

Related to the vignetted portrait style, yet very different in effect, the "medallion" portrait was technically the most difficult of the styles available in the 1850s. Southworth & Hawes's extant work contains only two examples of this technique, this particular portrait being the more outstanding of the two. (The other one is in the Metropolitan Museum collection: 39.22.4.) W. A. Pratt explained the technique:

Cut an oval opening in the centre of a piece of Bristol board, the size of the plate on which you wish to operate, and surround the edges with other openings—of any form your fancy may dictate—to resemble lacework . . . place the Bristol board over the [coated plate], and let it remain during its exposure in the camera, and over the mercury . . . it is necessary to have a large oval cut in a white screen . . . to correspond with the oval on the plate. This is to stand between the sitter and camera. . . .

Using the sliding plate-holder Southworth had patented in 1855, Southworth & Hawes further exploited this medallion (or hard-edged vignetting) style by continuing the process for eight sequential exposures of different, rotating poses of the unidentified subject. As Southworth explained,

I am thus enabled to take four impressions upon different portions of the same plate. These may be miniatures of the same person taken, as before stated, for the purpose of selecting the best for a locket; or they may be different views of the same face taken upon the same plate for the purpose of preserving them together; or they may be daguerreotypes of different persons. . . . It is evident, however, that it may be so arranged as to take any desired number—as six or eight, for example—without departing from the principle of my invention.

The sitter's face is presented as a visual charting of the lunar cycle by the arrangement of the face from "new" to "full" in various quarters and careful bisecting of the black and white background. Other photographers worked in this idiom, most notably Abraham Bogardus of New York, but none reached the level of perfection Southworth & Hawes achieved in this pictorial conceit and technical tour-de-force.

[(Pratt, W. A.) (Letter) *The Photographic Art-Journal,* I, 3 (March 1851), p. 190. Patent Specifications, for U. S. Patent No. 12,700, dated April 10, 1855, U. S. Patent Office, Washington, D. C. and entitled "Daguerreotype Camera Attachment."]

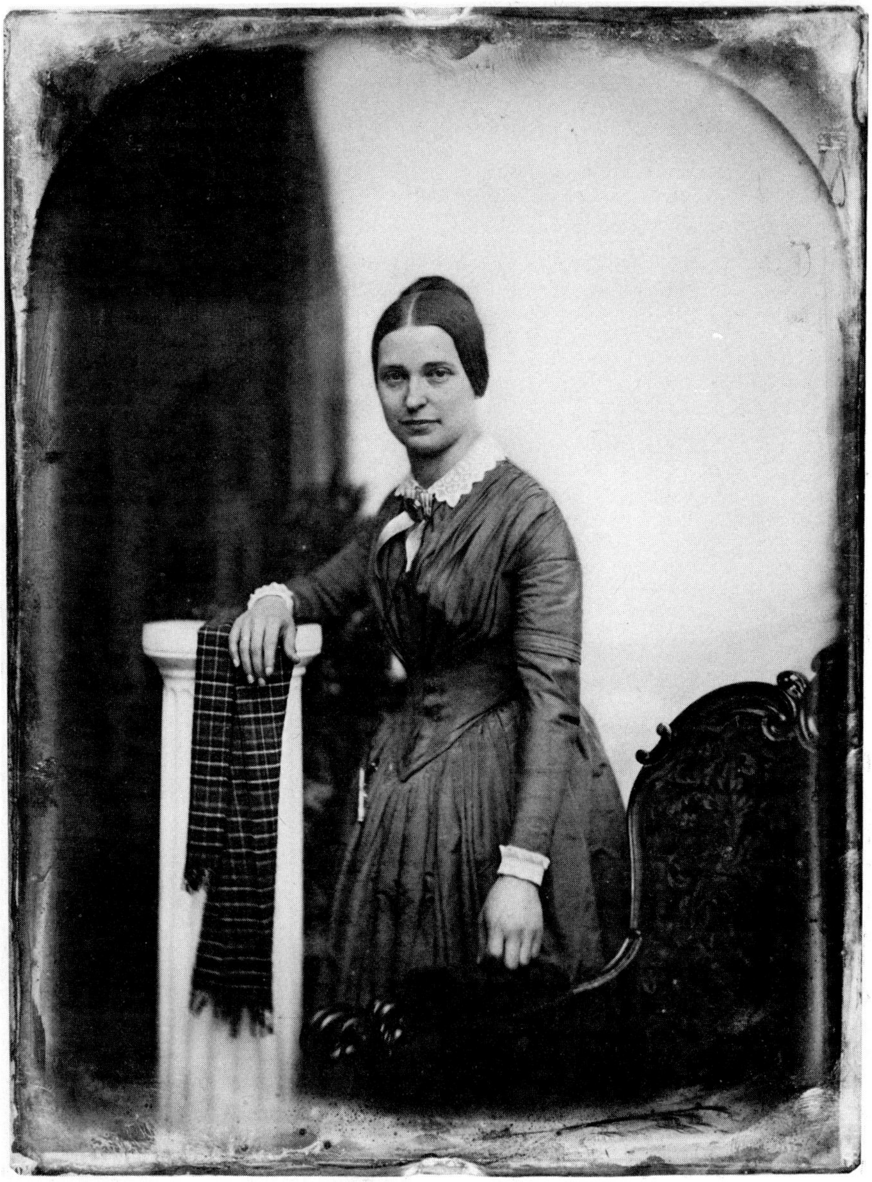

38. Unidentified Female

Whole plate, hand-colored. Hallmark: l.l.: 40; l.r.: star. International Museum of Photography at George Eastman House. Southworth & Hawes Collection. 74:193:155.

Many of the same motifs and gestures found in the portraits of the bride (Plate 31) and the "Boston Beauty" (Plate 32) are incorporated into this portrait. The classical column, the background drapery and the studio chair are all standard props for the mid-19th-century portraitist. Two aspects, however, of the portrait are quite unconventional and striking. First, there is the background of the woman and chair, vividly hand-colored with chrome yellow. The area detaches itself from the pictorial plane and floats above and in front of the sitter. Secondly, the woman's direct and pathological stare at the camera's lens completely destroys the pretentiousness and artificiality of the staging. Likewise, the swatch of a plaid scarf appears incongruous with the Greco-Roman column, diminishing its classicizing import.

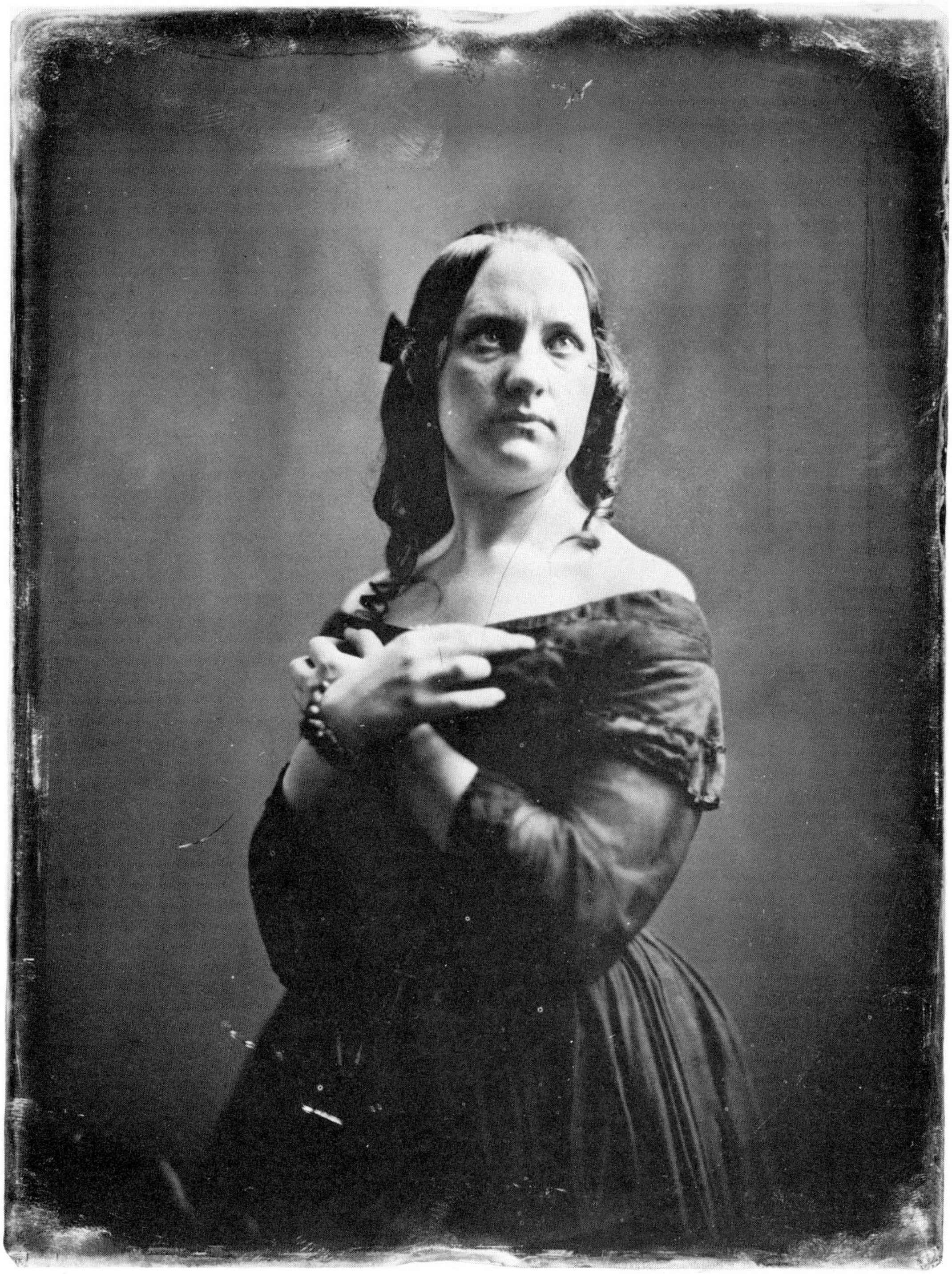

39. UNIDENTIFIED FEMALE

Whole plate. Hallmark: l.l.: 40; l.r.: star. International Museum of Photography at George Eastman House. Southworth & Hawes Collection. 74:193:119.

40. UNIDENTIFIED FEMALE

Whole plate. Hallmark: l.r.: S & F in lozenge. Museum of Fine Arts, Boston. Gift of Edward Southworth Hawes in memory of his father, Josiah Johnson Hawes. 43:1494.

Some 19th-century portrait manuals recommend that the photographer pose his professional subjects in mental guises and physical poses reflective of their calling whether they be politicians, orators or actors. The subject will then project a truthful expression of his personality. Heeding this advice, Root had an otherwise uninspiring Shakespearean actor "throw himself" into the persona of Othello and only then was able to capture a distinct expression. Southworth & Hawes likewise did not shy away from incorporating either Victorian histrionics or quaint costumes into their portraits. Unfortunately, the identities of these two apparent actresses and the specific roles they portray are unknown. Comparisons may be suggested with the portrait of Mrs. Vincent (cf. Plate 30).

[Rodgers, H. J. *Twenty-Three Years Under a Sky-Light . . .* Hartford: H. J. Rodgers, 1872, p. 89. Root, Marcus Aurelius. *The Camera and the Pencil,* p. 162.]

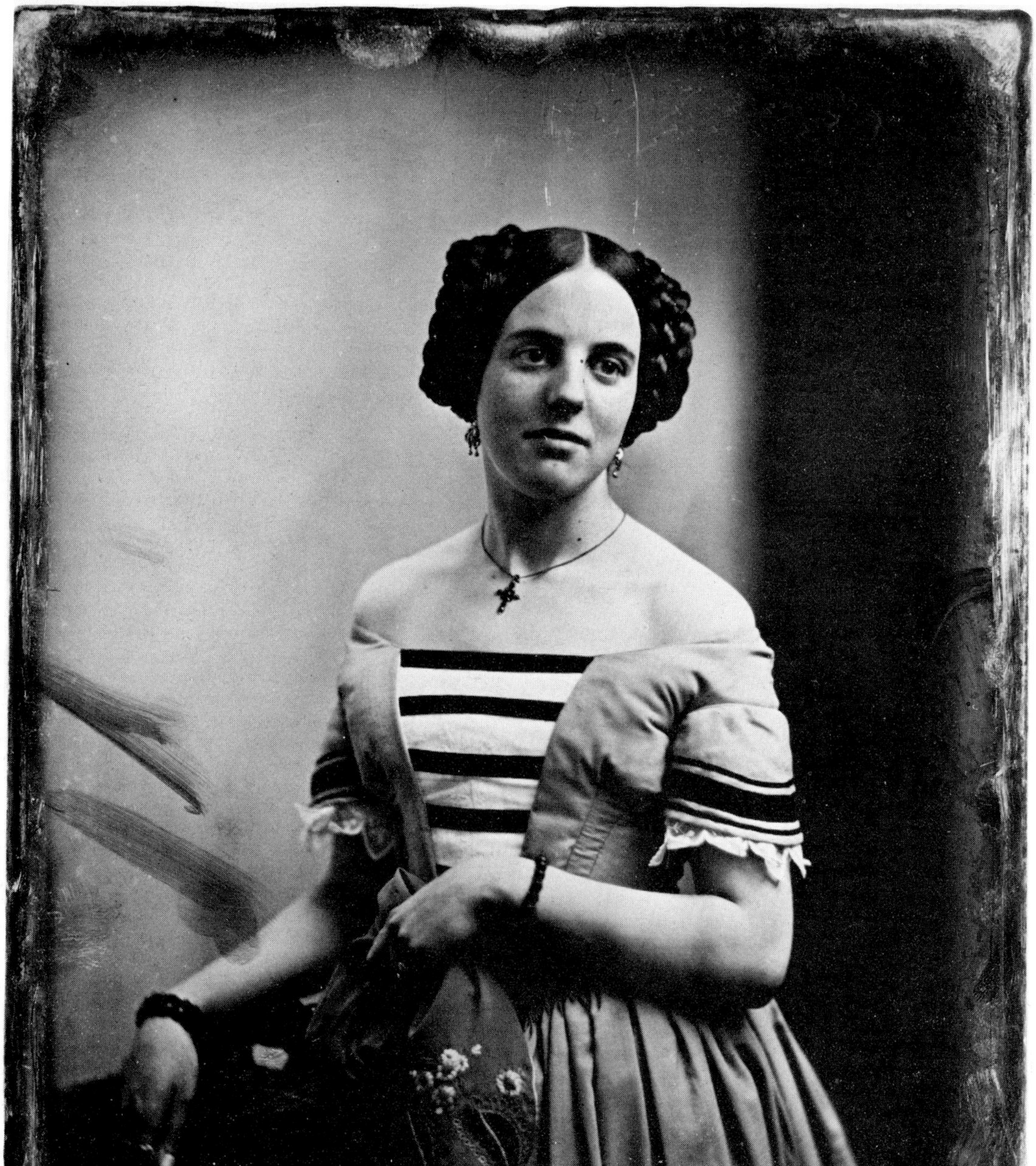

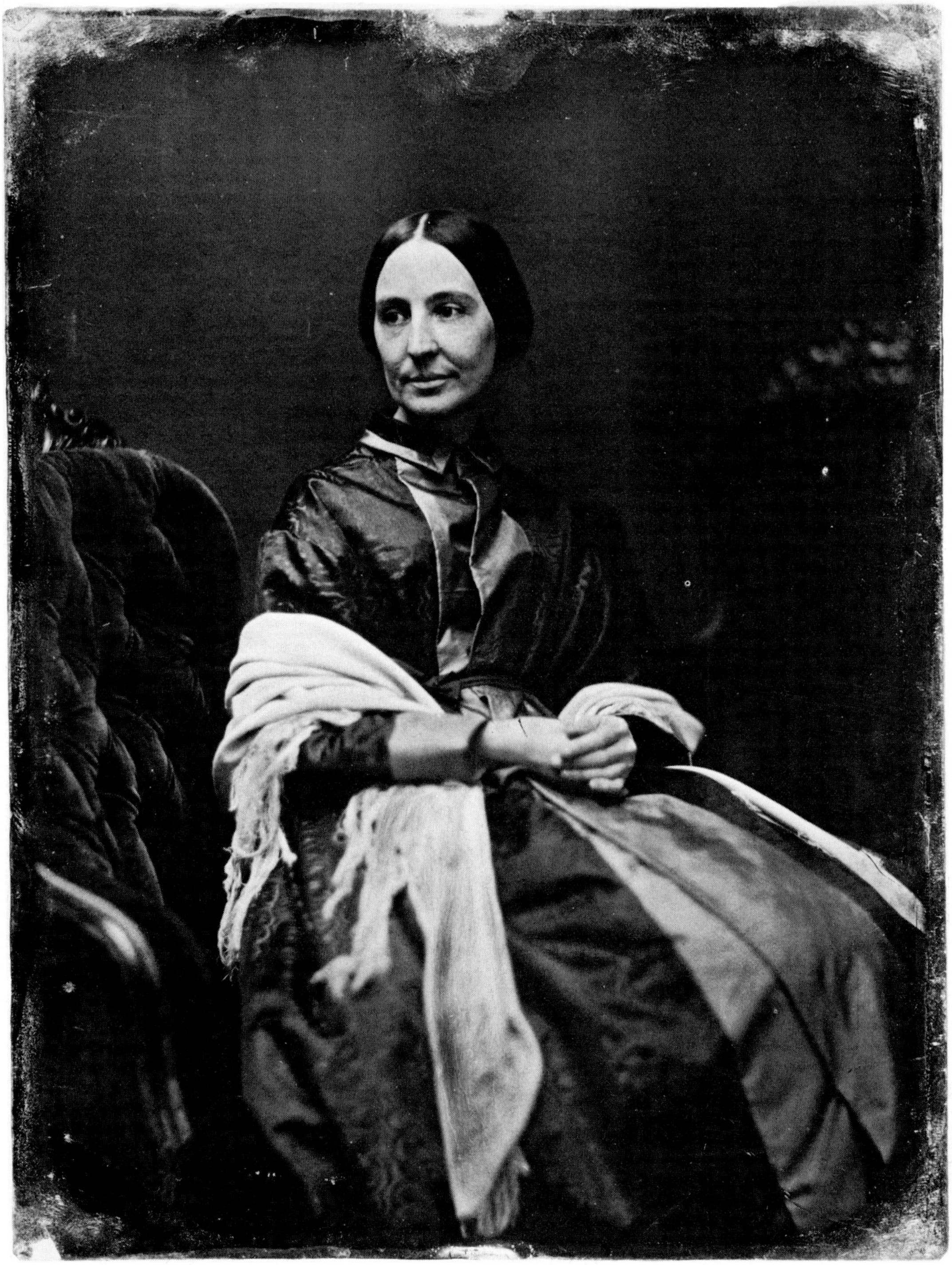

41. UNIDENTIFIED FEMALE

Whole plate. Hallmark: u.l.: S & F in lozenge. International Museum of Photography at George Eastman House. Southworth & Hawes Collection. 74:193:172.

42. UNIDENTIFIED FEMALE

Whole plate. Hallmark: l.r.: S & F in lozenge. International Museum of Photography at George Eastman House. Southworth & Hawes Collection. 74:193:78.

The posing and lighting effects in these images reflect the conventional academic formulas developed in the portraits by Joshua Reynolds and Bachrach. One daguerreotype manual of the period recommends the following:

The posture of the person sitting for the portrait should be easy and unconstrained; the feet and hands neither projecting too much nor drawn too far back; the eyes should be directed a little sideways above the camera, and fixed upon some object there, but never upon the apparatus. . . . Stout persons should be placed at a certain distance from the apparatus, turning towards it a little sidewise; whilst people of slender make should be made to sit full in front, and nearer the apparatus. . . . The hands should rest easy on the lap, neither too high nor too low; or one hand may be placed on the table, the other holding a book or some other object . . . . In the case of ladies, a shawl or boa, or similar article of dress, thrown lightly over the shoulders, and arranged in a manner to hide some defect, and to properly distribute light and shadow, will mostly tend to produce a pleasant impression.

[Haley, W. S. *The Daguerreotype Operator, A Practical Work. . . .* New York: W. S. Haley, 1854, pp. 45–46.]

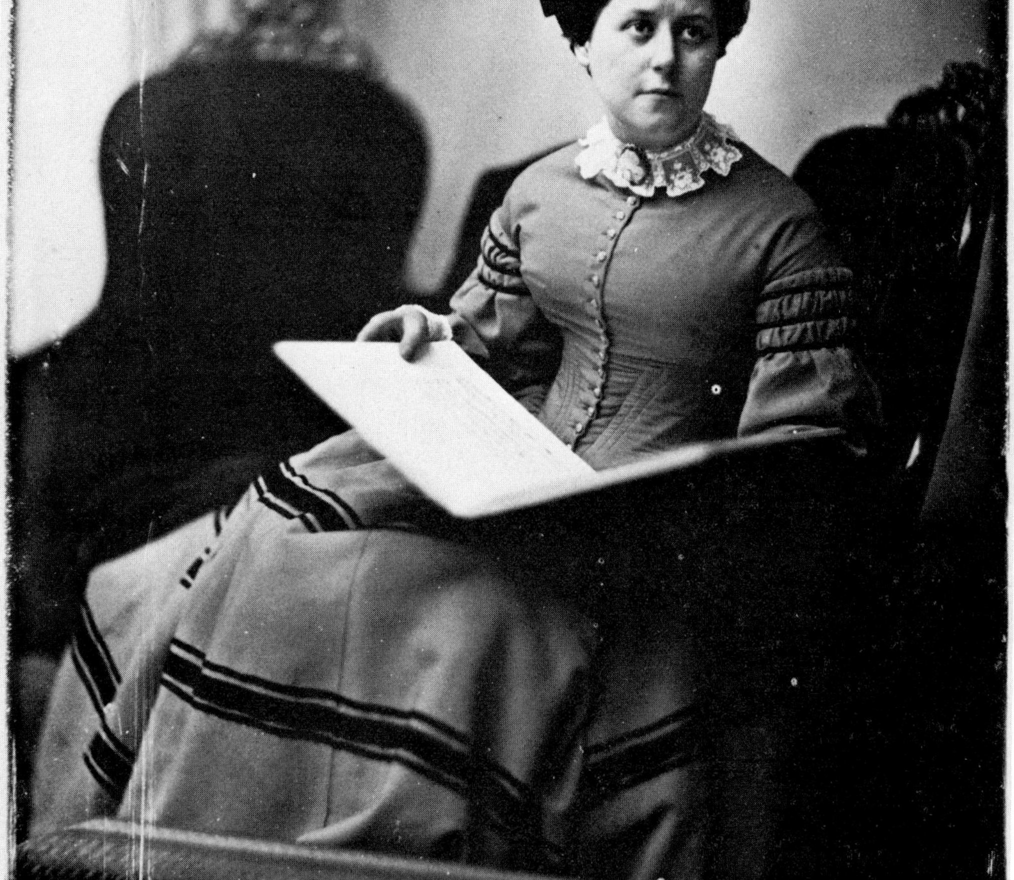

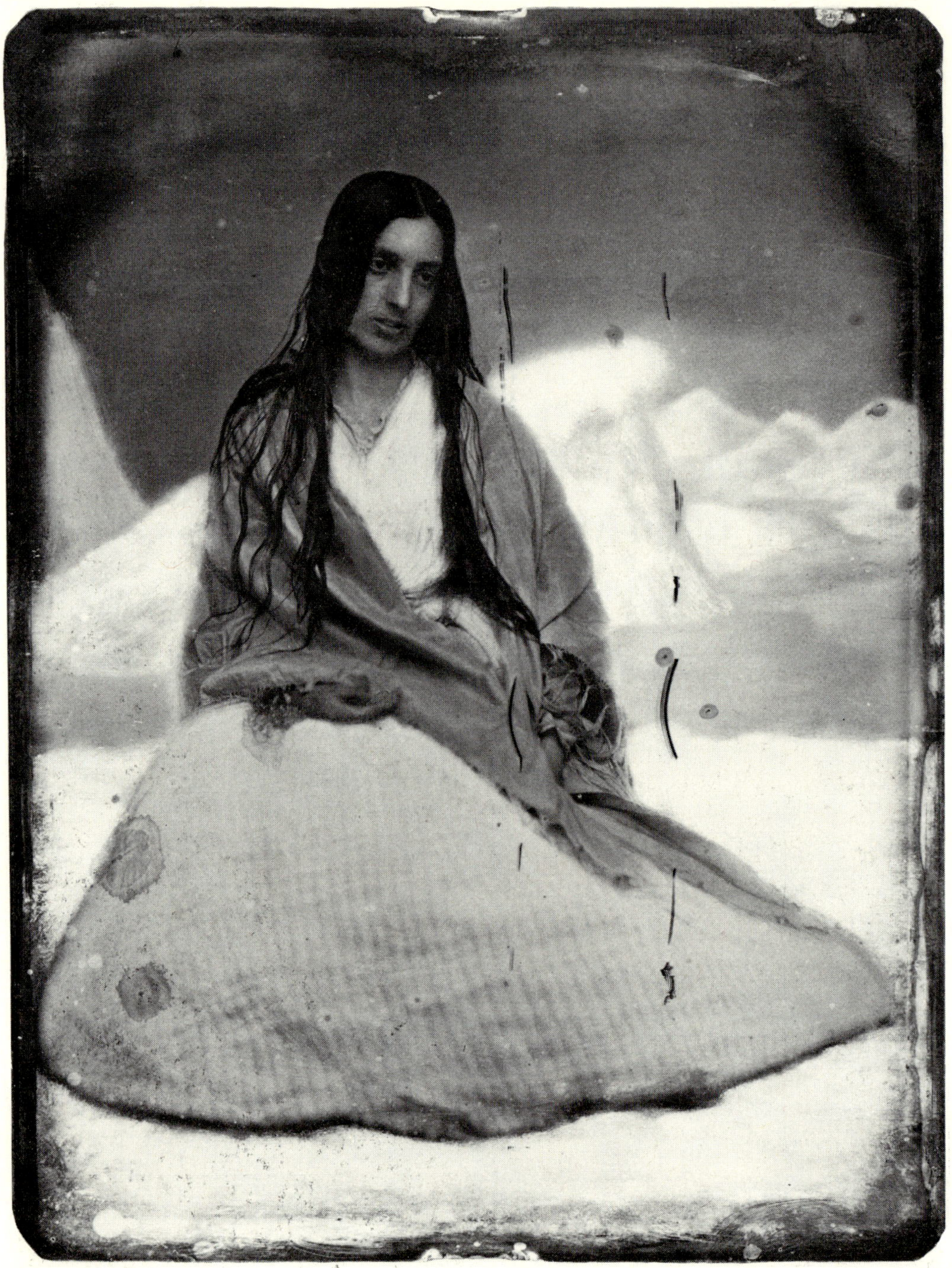

43. UNIDENTIFIED FEMALE

Half plate, hand-colored. Hallmark: u.r.: Scovills. International Museum of Photography at George Eastman House. Southworth & Hawes Collection. 74:193:954.

Bizarre and uncommon, this image provokes more questions than the visual data can satisfy. A gypsy, a vagabond, or perhaps an American Indian woman—certainly not a member of Southworth & Hawes's usual Boston clientele—is seated upon a simulated ice floe against the painted backdrop of icebergs. Nor is the hand-coloring technique of the entire plate consistent with Nancy's usual delicate and subtle style. Instead, thick pigments of unharmonious and acrid colors are roughly applied. The provenance, however, would indicate that the image is by Southworth & Hawes. This atypical portrait, together with that of the East Indian sailor (cf. Plate 22), are fascinating exceptions to the main body of the two partners' work.

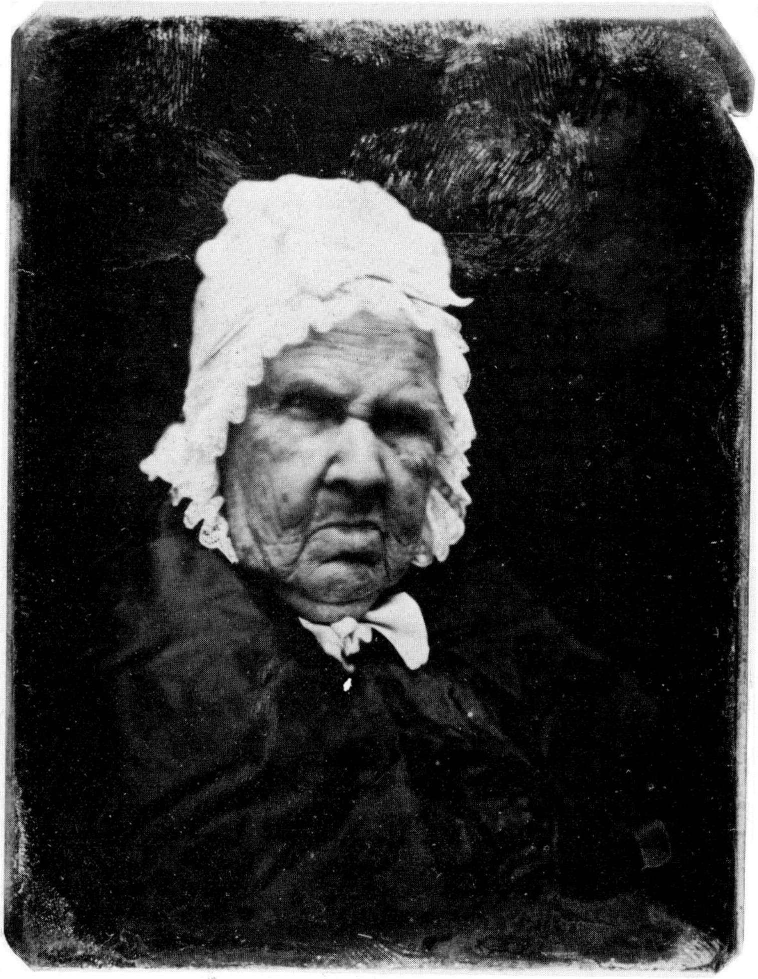

44. Unidentified Female

Quarter plate. Hallmark: none. Museum of Fine Arts, Boston. Gift of Edward Southworth Hawes in memory of his father, Josiah Johnson Hawes. 43.1437.

This eloquent portrait of human expression corroborates Southworth's statement:

> . . .the genius and spirit of poetry must possess the artist, so that he can ever elevate his characters in portraiture far above common nature. He must have power to embody the beauties and perfections of his subjects, and at the same time make clear resemblance and identity.

The portrayal of old age recalls Walt Whitman's first edition of *Leaves of Grass* (1855), containing two similar images of age: "Old age superbly rising! O welcome, ineffable grace of dying days!" ("Song of Myself"), and "Women sit or move to and fro, some old, some young,/ The young are beautiful—but the old are more beautiful than the/ Young." ("By the Roadside").

This portrait recalls Paul Strand's early 20th-century portrait of an old woman, a parallelism which underlines the constancy of a direct and pure photographic vision. Both portraits are, as Stieglitz said of Strand's work, "brutally direct . . . devoid of trickery."

[Southworth, A.S. "On the Use of the Camera," *The Photographic News* [London], XVIII, 809 (6 March 1874), p. 110. (Stieglitz, Alfred.) "Our Illustrations," *Camera Work,* 49/50 (1917).]

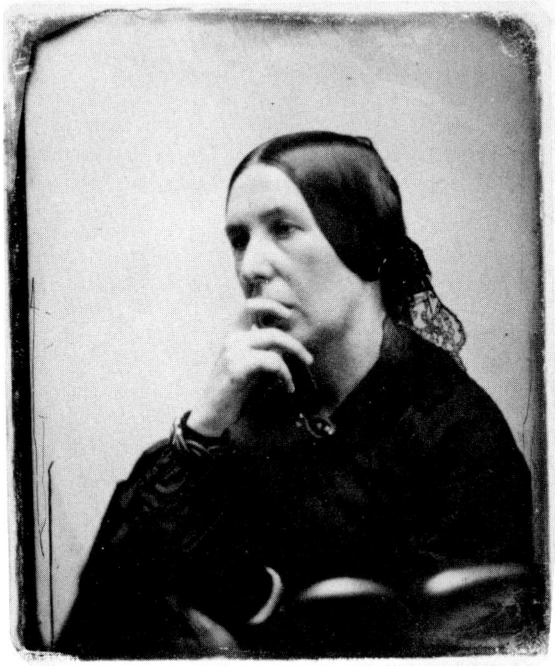

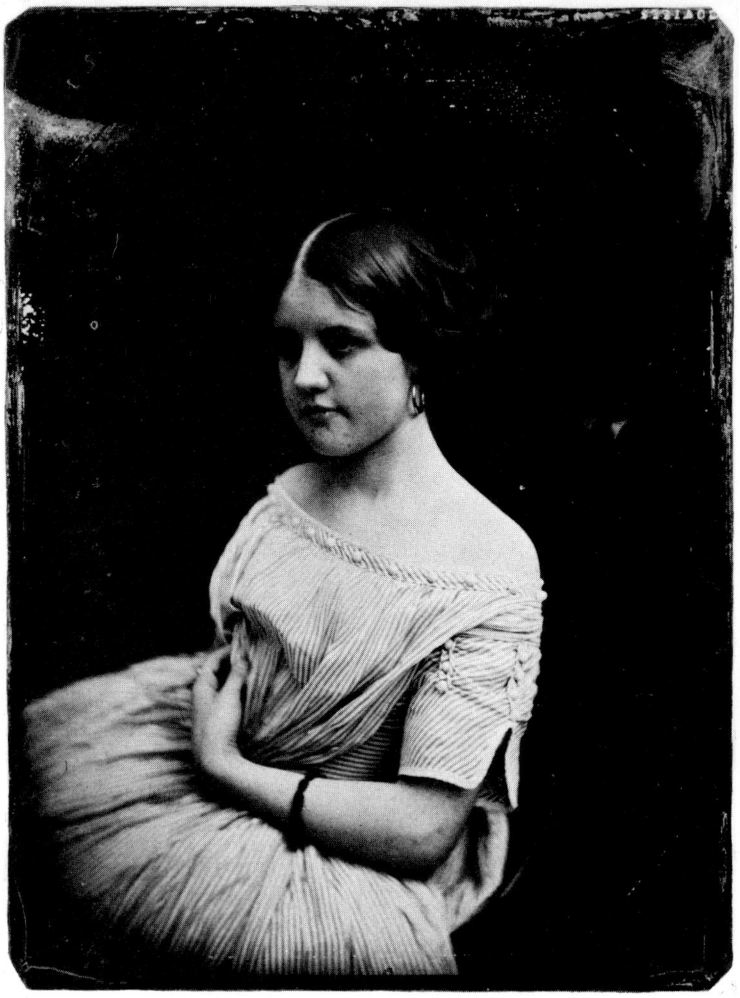

45. Unidentified Female

Sixth plate. Hallmark: l.r.: H. B. H. / eagle / 40. International Museum of Photography at George Eastman House. Southworth & Hawes Collection. 74:193:291.

46. Unidentified Female

Quarter plate, hand-colored. Hallmark: u.r.: Scovills. International Museum of Photography at George Eastman House. Southworth & Hawes Collection. 74:193:738.

47. Unidentified Female

Whole plate, hand-colored. Hallmark: u.r.: Doublé J. P. International Museum of Photography at George Eastman House. Southworth & Hawes Collection. 74:193:149.

These sensitive interpretations of three dissimilar subjects —a middle-aged woman, quite possibly Nancy Southworth Hawes, another ''Boston Beauty'' (cf. Plate 32), and a young girl—provide unique solutions to the problem of using the hand as an expressive means. The positioning of the three pairs of hands ranges from artificial to automatic to demure (cf. Plates 47, 45, 46 respectively).

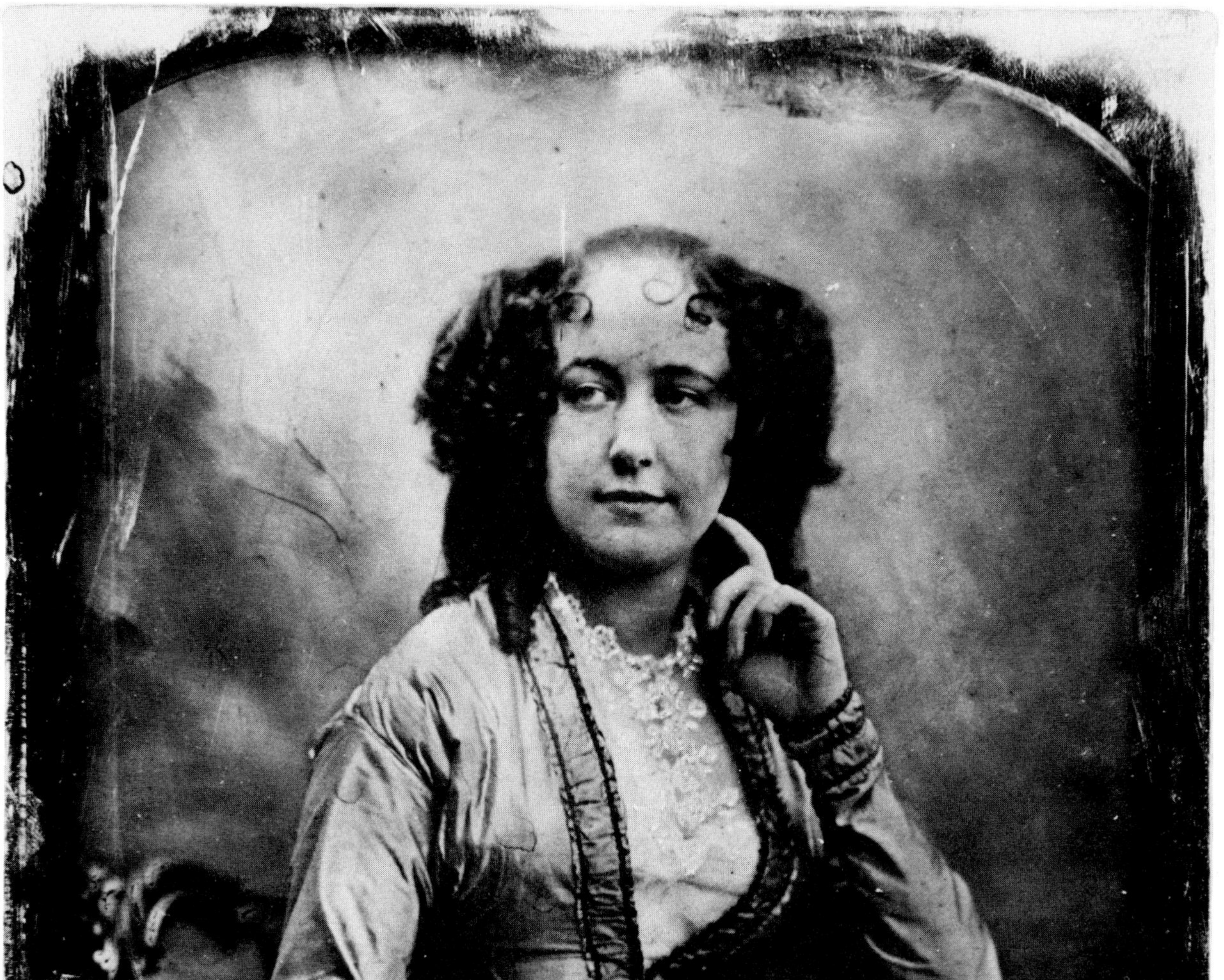

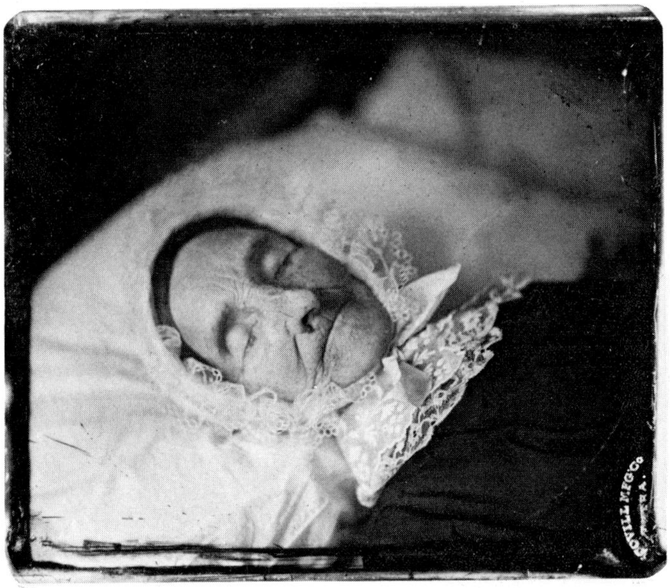

48. UNIDENTIFIED FEMALE, DECEASED

Sixth plate. Hallmark: l.l.: Scovill Extra. International Museum of Photography at George Eastman House. Southworth & Hawes Collection. 74:193:640.

This portrait of a deceased woman recalls two stanzas from a poem popular in the early 1850s called "The Daguerreotype" by Mrs. L. G. Abell.

A mother's life! a mother's life! what
  pictured words are those!
What frequent scenes of tenderness and
  beauty they disclose!
The patient toil, the watchful love, the
  anxious, sleepless eye,
All, all in colors beautiful, and all too bright
  to die.

A mother's death! a mother's death! how
  desolate that home
That only knows its blessings by the losses
  that have come!
They only learn to know the worth, the
  value of her love,
When its guardian influence is withdrawn
  to a better world above.

[*The Photographic Art-Journal,* V, 5 (May 1853), pp. 303-304.]

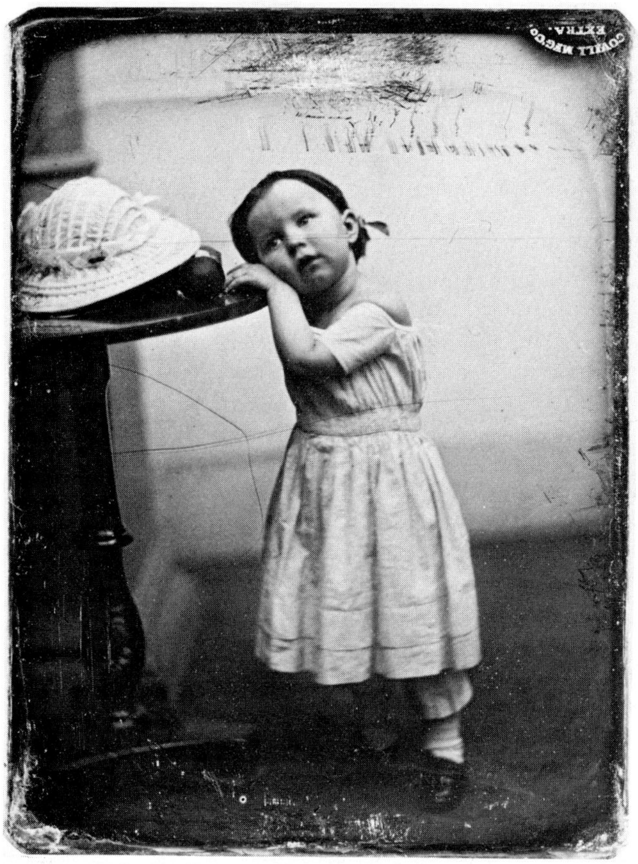

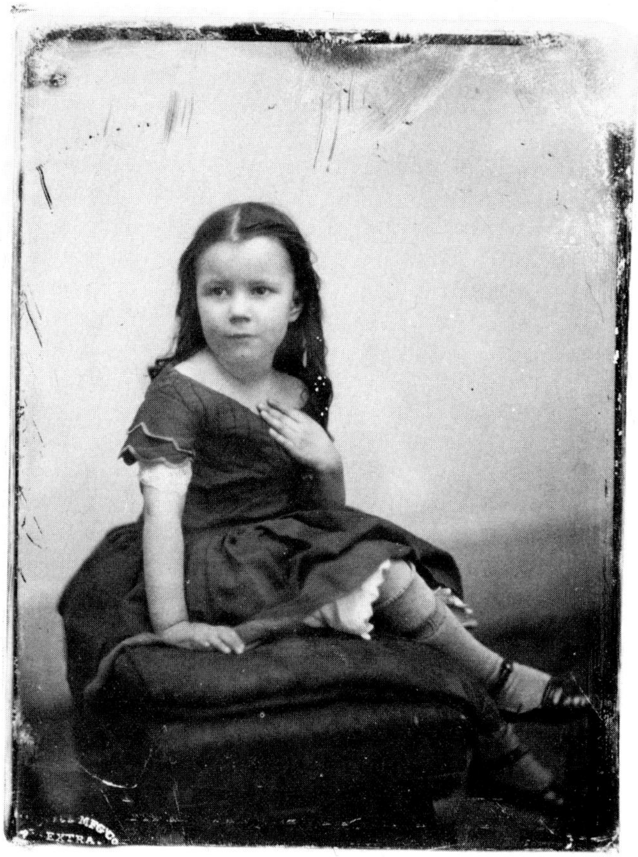

49. ALICE MARY HAWES

Quarter plate. Hallmark: u.r.: Scovill Extra. Museum of Fine Arts, Boston. Gift of Edward Southworth Hawes in memory of his father, Josiah Johnson Hawes. 43.1414.

50. ALICE MARY HAWES
OR MARION AUGUSTA HAWES

Quarter plate. Hallmark: l.l.: Scovill Extra. International Museum of Photography at George Eastman House. Southworth & Hawes Collection. 74:193:703.

Late in his life, Southworth would comment on how to pose and take portraits of infants and young children. These images, the first of Alice Mary Hawes (1850–1938), the second of Alice or her sister Marion Augusta Hawes (1855–1941), are early illustrations of his later prescriptions:

> . . . the whole figure may be prettily taken if they can be kept quiet four or five seconds. As a good rule, let the frock be very low in the neck, with short waist, not tight, yet fitting the form, reaching to the foot; the sleeves very loose, ornamented with narrow lace. The skirt should be of woolen fabric, not too full, reaching about half-way from the knee to the ankle . . . . If the child is taken half-reclining, the bottom part of the dress can easily be arranged to show parts of the bottom of the skirts, and the feet and ankles, and all be in good keeping and taste.

[Southworth, Albert Sands. "On the Use of the Camera," p. 110.]

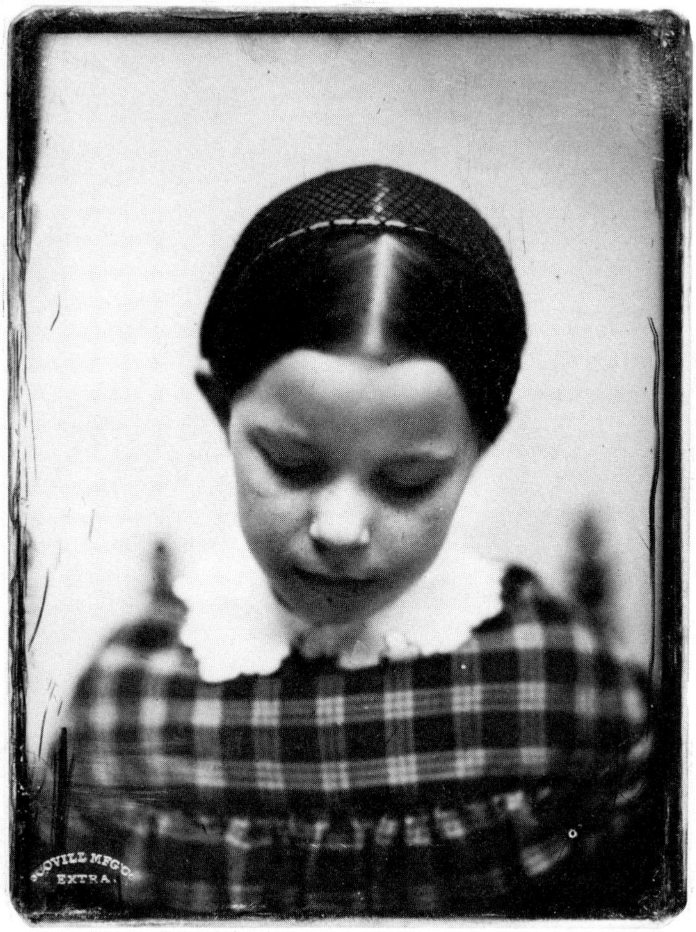

51. Alice Mary Hawes or
Marion Augusta Hawes

Quarter plate. Hallmark: l.l.: Scovill Extra. International Museum of Photography at George Eastman House. Southworth & Hawes Collection. 74:193:823.

52. Unidentified Child

Sixth plate. Hallmark: l.l.: Scovill Extra. International Museum of Photography at George Eastman House. Southworth & Hawes Collection. 74:193:304.

53. Unidentified Child

Quarter plate, hand-colored. Hallmark: l.l.: Scovills. International Museum of Photography at George Eastman House. Southworth & Hawes Collection. 74:193:387.

"The Baby in Daguerreotype"
By Mrs. Anna L. Snelling

What! put *her* in daguerreotype,
And victimize the pet!
Those ruby lips, so cherry-ripe,
On lifeless silver set!

The frisking, laughing, bouncing thing,
So full of life and glee—
A restless bird upon the wing—
A sunbeam on the sea!

Put shadows on that forehead fair—
That look of quick surprise—
And give a dull unmeaning stare
To those blue laughing eyes!

Now, do you think a chance you've caught?
Out with the colors quick;
She's screaming at the very thought
Of such a shabby trick.

Now she is still—fly to the stand;
The smiling features trace!
In vain—up goes a tiny hand,
And covers half her face.

Give up the task—let childhood be
Nature's own blooming rose!
You cannot catch the spirit free,
Which only childhood knows.

Earth's shadows o'er that brow will pass,
Then paint her at your will;
When time shall make her wish, alas!
She were a baby still.

While not the most consummate of poets, Mrs. Snelling, wife of the photographer, author and editor Henry H. Snelling, does accurately portray a Victorian sentimentality towards children and their photographs.

[*The Photographic Art-Journal,* I, 2 (February 1851), p. 126.]

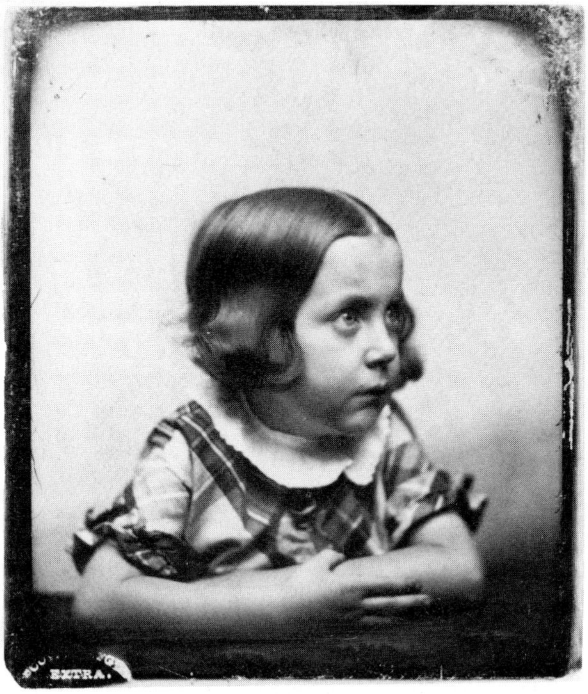
EXTRA.

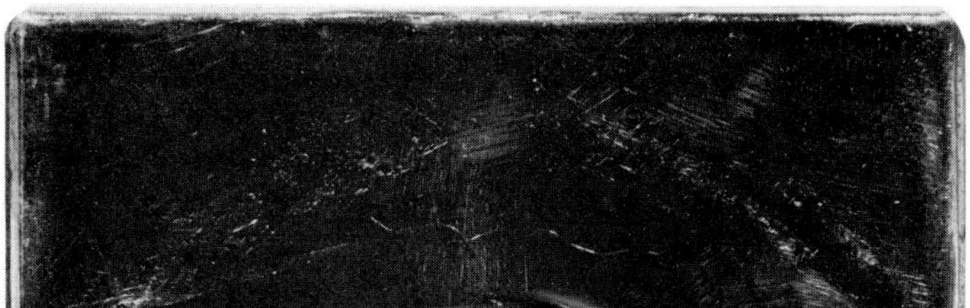

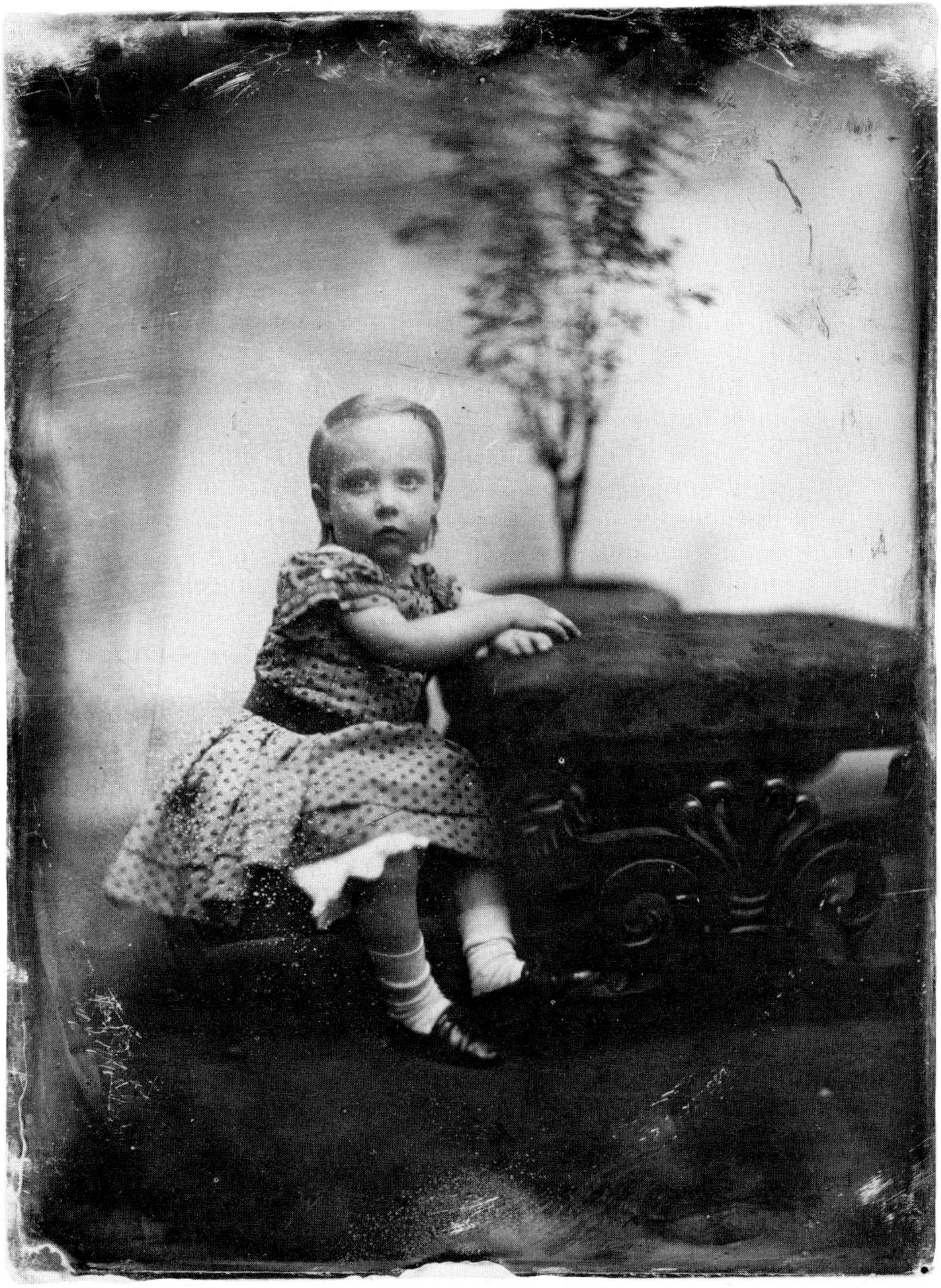

54. Unidentified Child

Whole plate. Hallmark: u.r.: Christofle. International Museum of Photography at George Eastman House. Southworth & Hawes Collection. 74:193:123.

Among the whole-plate portraits of eccentrically posed children, this image particularly stands out because of its ambiguous background of wind-blown tree and mottled sky. In 1846 an unidentified New York reviewer at a daguerreotype exhibition stated: "our attention has been particularly called to those [daguerreotypes] of Messrs. Southworth and Hawes of No. 5½ *Tremont Row, Boston* . . . . Their miniatures of children are remarkably bold and clear, and the expression of countenance very pleasant. The variety of artistic arrangement, of attitude and drapery are also very striking, while the size of some of them is very considerably larger than any we have seen executed in this country." Whether this reviewer was referring to mammoth-plate portraits of children or simply to a collection of whole plates is unclear. His next reference is to a picture of "Mr. Tucker of the Tremont House" (cf. Plate 17) whose mammoth-plate portrait has come down to us. No oversized portraits of children, however, are extant.

[*New York Daily Times,* 15 October 1846, p. 2.]

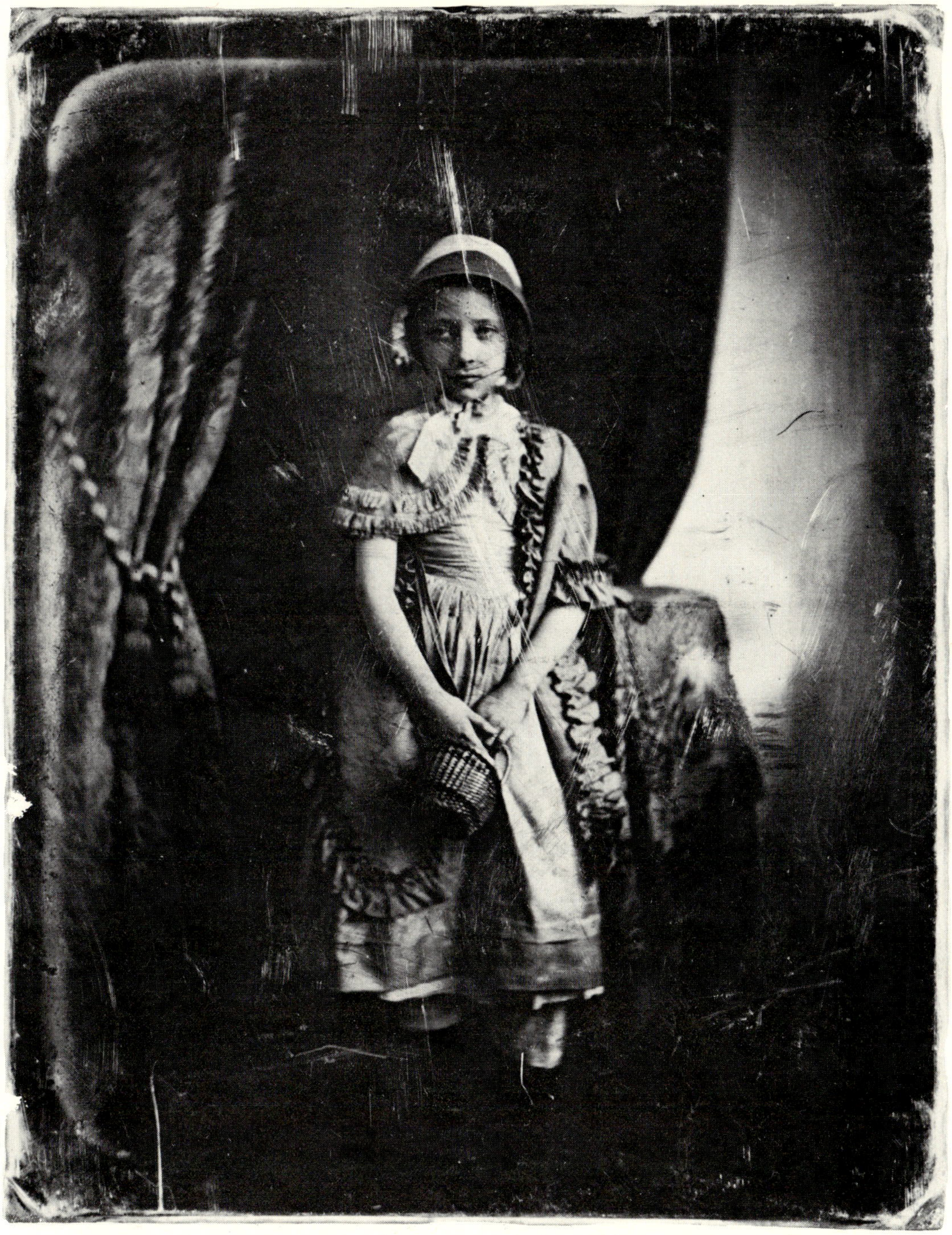

55. Unidentified Child

Undersized whole plate (5⅞″ x 7½″). Hallmark: none. International Museum of Photography at George Eastman House. Southworth & Hawes Collection. 74:193:499.

The selective use of decorative or symbolic costumes was common to many daguerreotypists of the period, but seldom was a figure posed in an outdoor outfit in such an obvious studio setting. Again, the provenance alone attributes this portrait to Southworth & Hawes. The unusual plate size and the presentation style of the subject lead one to question their authorship. Yet, the image shares certain elements with the other portraits by Southworth & Hawes: the catatonic stare of the sitter into the camera (cf. Plate 38), the placement of the full-length figure in the pictorial space (cf. Plate 22), and the anecdotal qualities and artifice of the staging (cf. Plates 54, 57). Possibly, the unusual plate size could have resulted from the trimming of the original full plate.

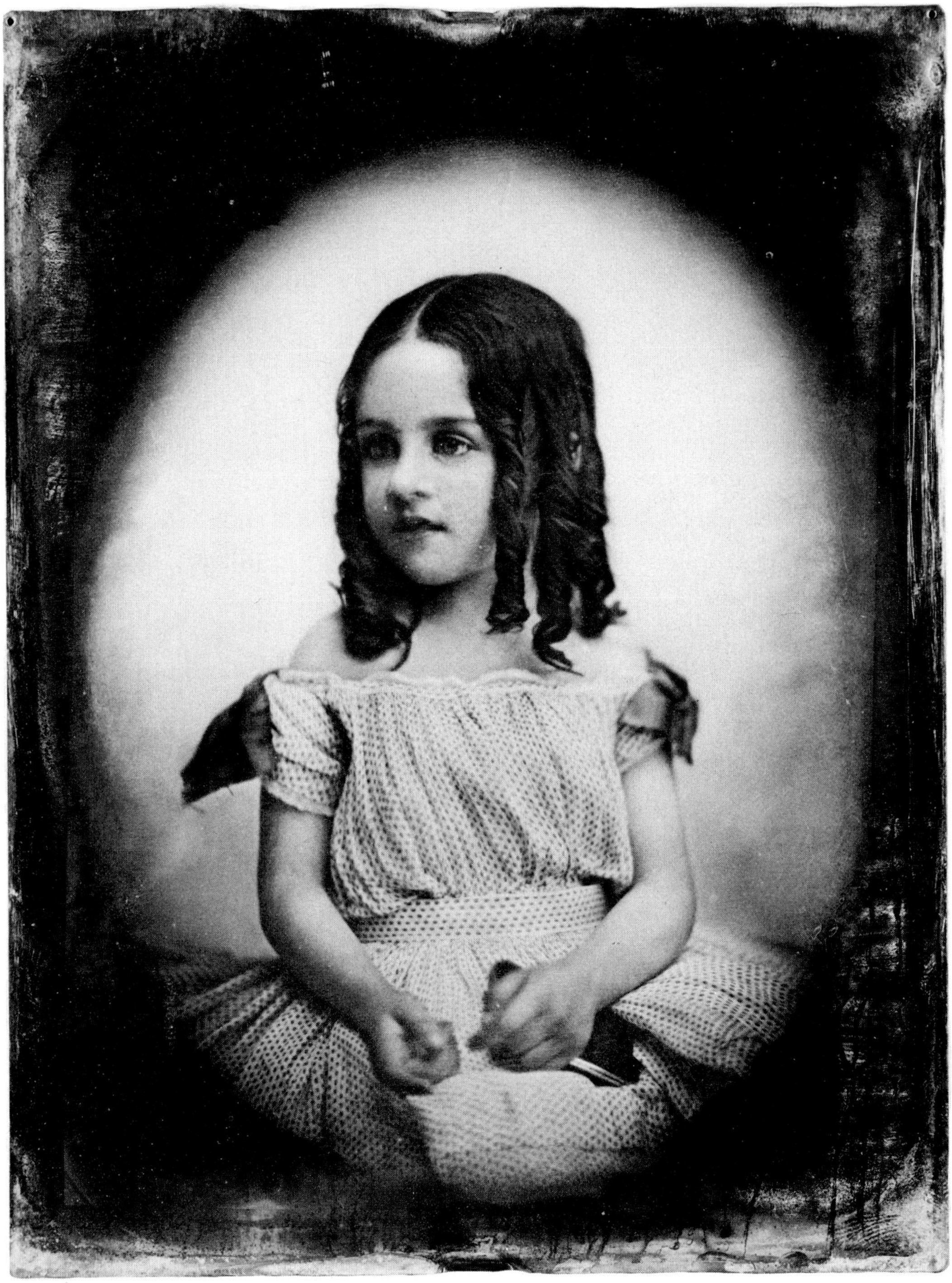

56. Unidentified Child

Whole plate, hand-colored. Hallmark: u.r.: Christofle. Museum of Fine Arts, Boston. Gift of Edward Southworth Hawes in memory of his father, Josiah Johnson Hawes. 43.1487.

A typical example of Southworth & Hawes's portraits of children, this image exhibits the effects achieved by the use of a dark vignetting mask between the camera and the sitter posed against a light background.

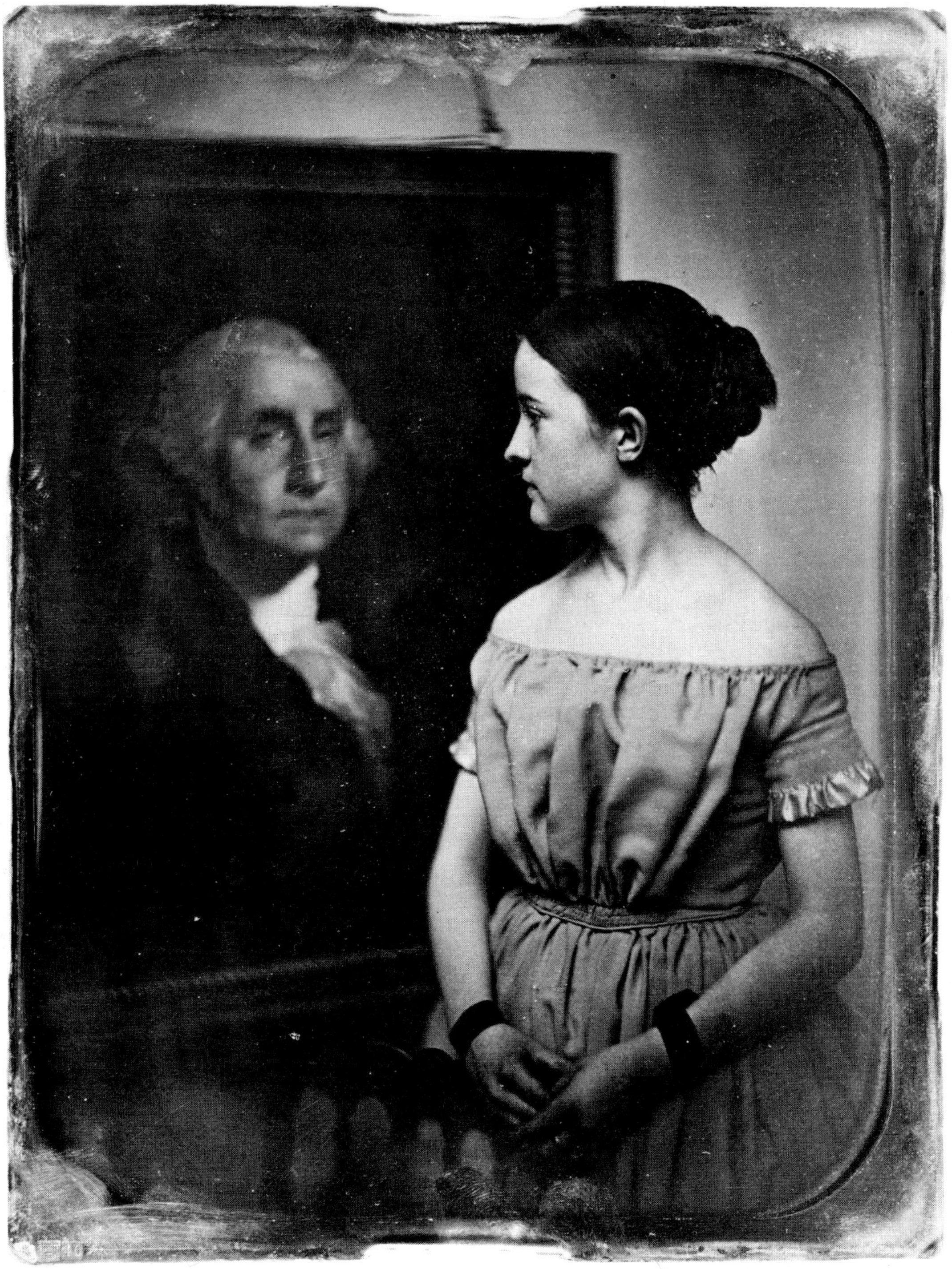

57. UNIDENTIFIED CHILD

Whole plate. Hallmark: l.l.: Doublé J. P. Metropolitan Museum of Art. Gift of I. N. Phelps Stokes and the Hawes family. 37.14.53.

Rather captivating and interpretive, this portrait of a young woman reflecting over Stuart's painting of George Washington (cf. Plate 106) exemplifies one of Snelling's "Hints and Suggestions":

A very pleasing effect is given to portraits, by introducing, behind the sitter, an engraving or other picture—if a painting, avoid those in which warm and glowing tints predominate. The subject of these pictures may be applicable to the taste or occupation of the person whose portrait you are taking. This adds much to the interest of the picture, which is otherwise frequently dull, cold and inanimate.

While Southworth & Hawes achieved dramatic portraits without such conventions, their use of the prescribed visual trope reveals their desire to go beyond a mere likeness. The enigmatic turning of the girl's head away from the camera relates her personally to what would otherwise have been an ordinary stage prop, thus adding a suggestive dimension to her personality.

[Snelling, Henry H. *The History and Practice of the Art of Photography,* p. 41.]

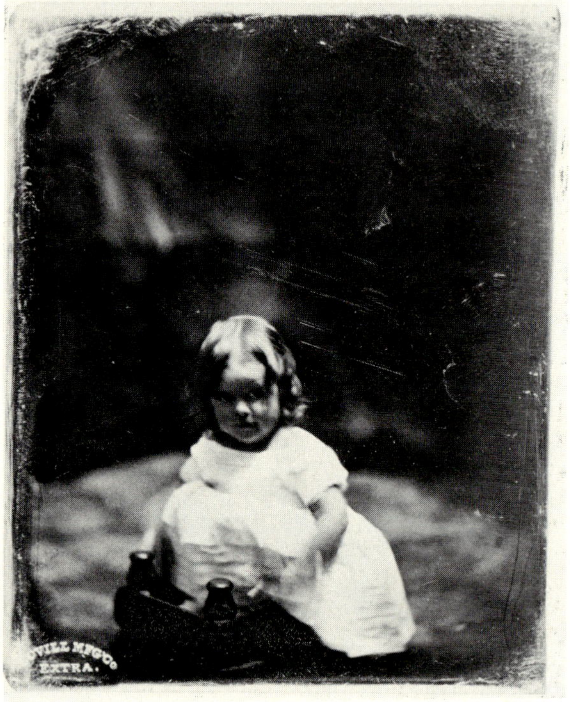

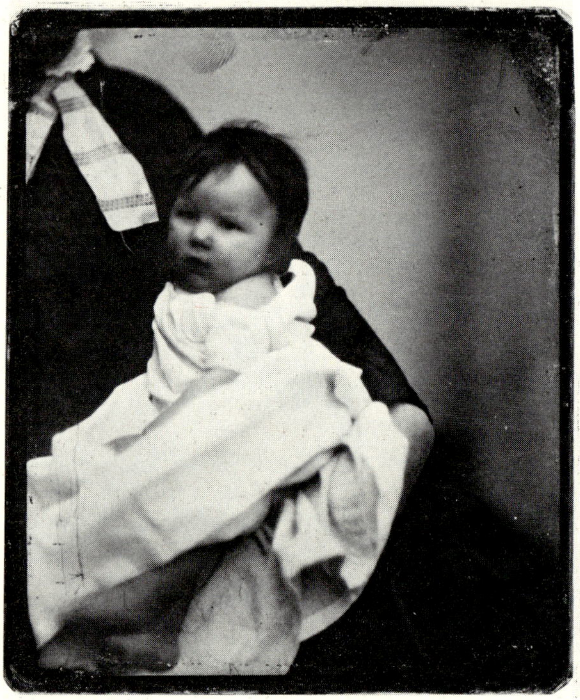

58. UNIDENTIFIED CHILD

Sixth plate. Hallmark: l.l.: Scovill Extra. International Museum of Photography at George Eastman House. Southworth & Hawes Collection. 74:193:1122.

59. UNIDENTIFIED CHILD

Sixth plate. Hallmark: u.l.: star. International Museum of Photography at George Eastman House. Southworth & Hawes Collection. 74:193:671.

These "snaps" of young children, one bathed in mottled sunlight and the other cradled in the arms of an unseen adult, are wonderfully informal and evocative (cf. Plate 63). An essayist writing in the 1850s proclaimed, "Childhood, we repeat, in its innocence and joyousness, reflects its own light and happiness upon others, like a Claude Lorrain glass, which imparts to all objects its own beautiful tints." Both the author and the photographers seem to have shared a romantic approach to the child as a poetic symbol.

[(Saunders, Fred.) *Mosaics.* New York: Charles Scribner, 1859, p. 90.]

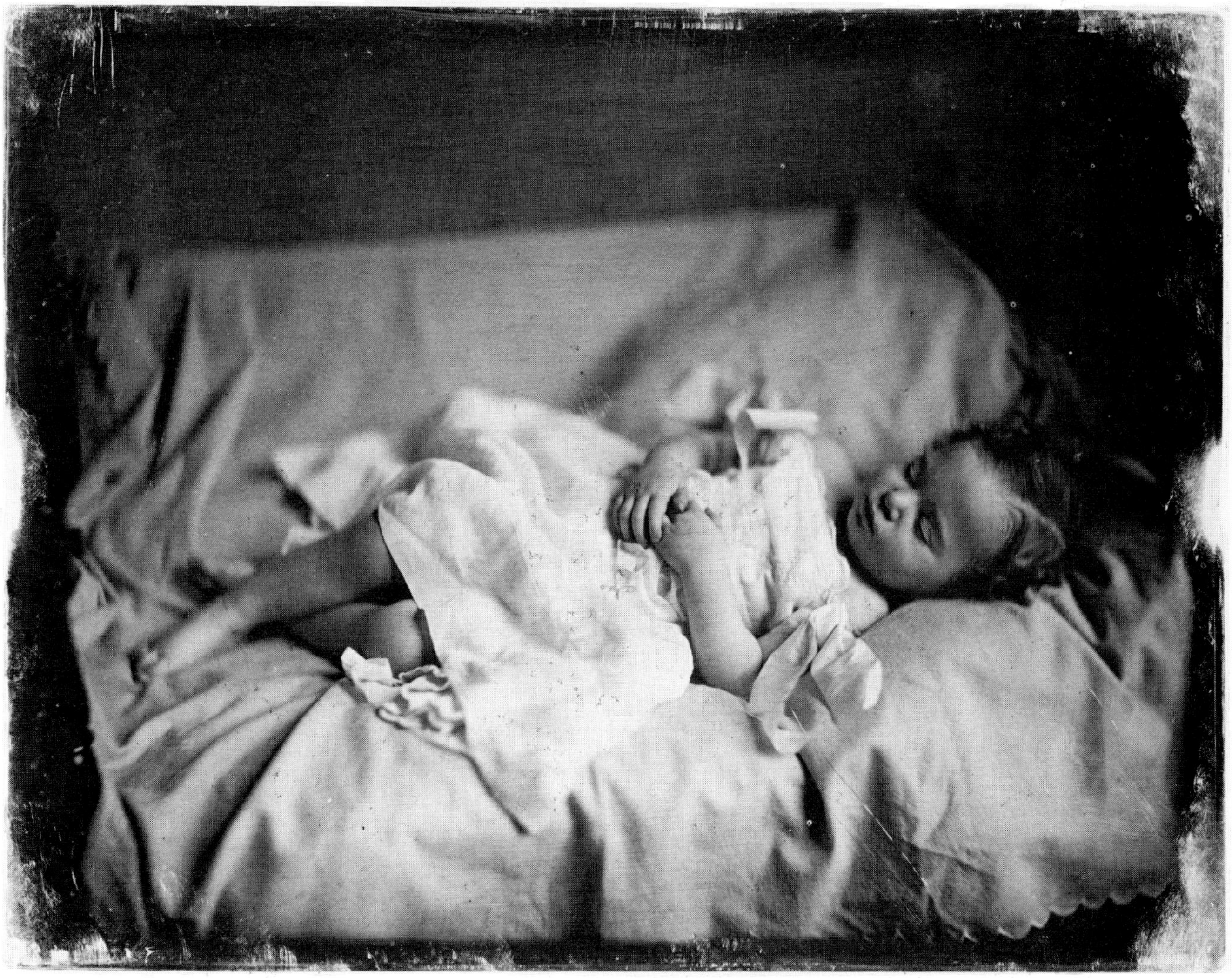

60. UNIDENTIFIED CHILD,
DECEASED

Whole plate. Hallmark: l.l.: S & F in lozenge. International Museum of Photography at George Eastman House. Southworth & Hawes Collection. 74:193:130.

Funerary portraits or post-mortems of children, as Rudisill points out in his *Mirror Image,* were tremendously popular during the mid-19th century. Often, the deceased child was portrayed as if sleeping quite naturally. An 1855 article states:

All the likenesses taken after death will of course only resemble the inanimate body, nor will there appear in the portrait anything like life itself, except indeed the sleeping infant, on whose face the playful smile of innocence sometimes steals even after death. This may be and is oft-times transferred to silver plate.

This portrait of an unidentified child bathed in light could easily be assumed a likeness taken when the child was fast asleep were it not for the subtle yet clearly emblematic inclusion of the rosary.

[*Photographic and Fine Art Journal,* VIII, 3 (March 1855), p. 80. Rudisill, Richard. *Mirror Image,* pp. 217–220.]

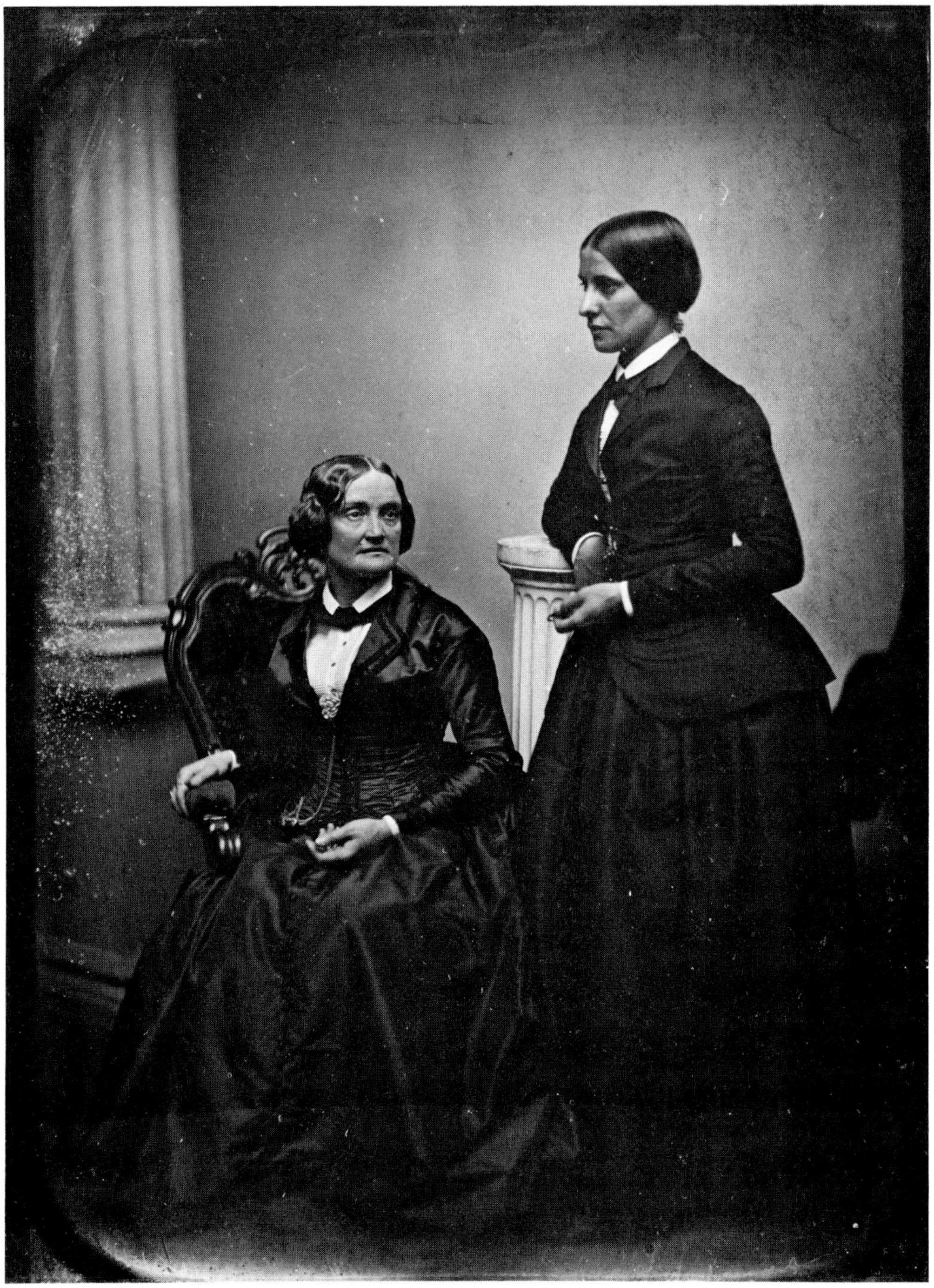

61. Charlotte Saunders Cushman and Unidentified Female

Whole plate. Hallmark: l.l.: Christofle. Metropolitan Museum of Art. Gift of I. N. Phelps Stokes and the Hawes family. 37.14.49.

Charlotte Saunders Cushman (1816–1876) has been remembered as one of America's greatest actresses of the last century, an equal to Rachel or Bernhardt. Forced to give up a promising career in singing, she turned from the operatic to the dramatic stage at the age of nineteen. Over the next forty years, traveling extensively between America and Europe, she became celebrated for her vivid performances.

The identity of the standing woman is uncertain. She has been previously identified as Miss Emma Stebbins (1815–1882), an American artist who became her friend and companion and, later, her biographer. The apparent age difference between the two women rules out this attribution. A second possibility is a certain Miss Hayes, a fellow actress and friend of Cushman's. No portrait of this person, however, has survived to substantiate this attribution. A third possibility is Cushman's life-long companion and maid, Sallie Mercer. Stebbins claimed that "Miss Cushman was struck by her serious, steady ways, her anxious forehead, but especially by her eyebrows; she believed in what she called 'conscientious eyebrows.' " The strong severe features of the standing figure and her dutiful attentive posture support Mercer as the most likely candidate.

[Clement, Clara Erskine. *Charlotte Cushman.* Boston: James R. Osgood, 1882, passim. Stebbins, Emma. *Charlotte Cushman: Her Letters and Memories of Her Life.* Boston: Houghton, Osgood, 1878, p. 37 and passim.]

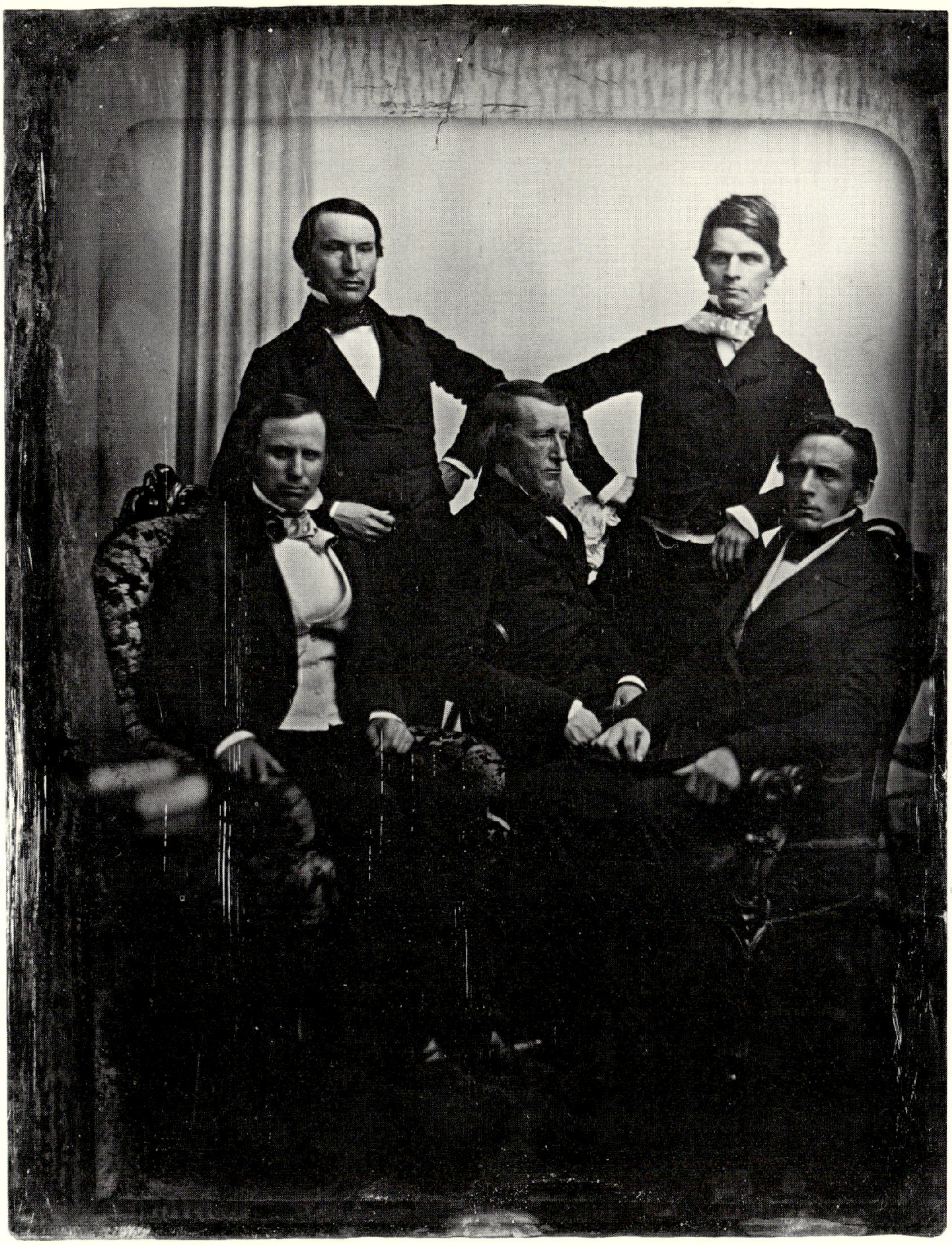

62. The Free-Soilers

Whole plate. Hallmark: none. Museum of Fine Arts, Boston. Gift of Edward Southworth Hawes in memory of his father, Josiah Johnson Hawes. 43.1406.

The Free-Soil Party was a minor political party opposing the extension of slavery into land acquired from Mexico in 1848. Representing seventeen states, the party members were less concerned with abolition as an ethical question than with the use of Blacks, either slave or free, as a labor source in the new territory. Support of the party dwindled after 1850 and in 1856 the scattered remains were absorbed into the newly forming Republican Party.

This group composition of five carefully balanced Massachusetts party representatives attests to Southworth & Hawes's consummate skill in handling body angles and postures of the sitters. Arranged in a loosely pyramidal group are, from left to right: Mr. Hopkins and Governor N. P. Banks (standing), Anson Burlingame, Henry Wilson and George S. Boutwell (seated).

[Business papers of Louis Holman, Boston, Massachusetts, S & H, IMP/GEH.]

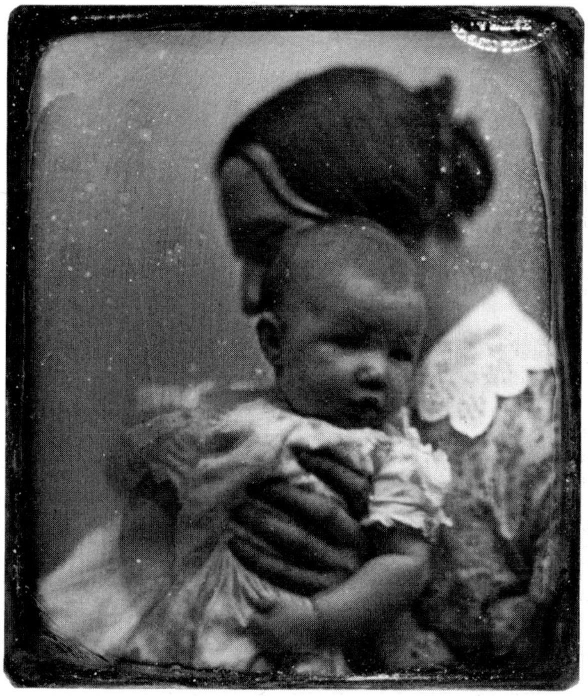

63. Mrs. Josiah Johnson Hawes Holding Alice Mary Hawes

Sixth plate. Hallmark: u.r.: Scovill Extra. Museum of Fine Arts, Boston. Gift of Edward Southworth Hawes in memory of his father, Josiah Johnson Hawes. 43.1421.

Although famed as expressive interpretations and for the individuality of the poses, few official portraits from the studio of Southworth & Hawes could be considered informal "snapshots" in the modern sense. A few family "snaps," however, have survived; their unposed quality appears exceptionally contemporary (cf. Plates 58, 59). Most likely taken by her husband, this portrait of Nancy Southworth Hawes (1820–1895) holding her infant daughter Alice Mary exudes the intimacy of a family portrait. Because of the technical difficulties of the daguerreotype process, few family "snaps," were taken and even fewer have survived. The family snapshot became popular only some thirty years later when the hand camera and fast films became available and the nuclear family was more socially valued.

[Halpern, Steven. "Souvenirs of Experience: The Victorian Studio Portrait and the Twentieth Century Snapshot," *Aperture*, XIX, 1 (1974), p. 64.]

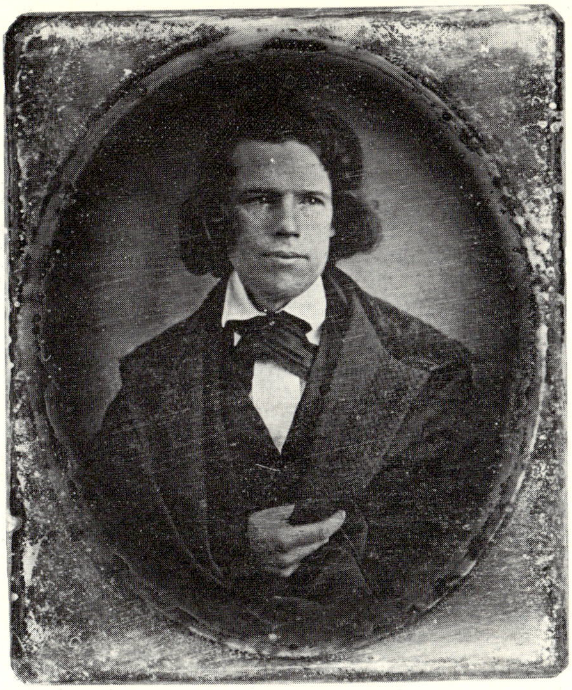

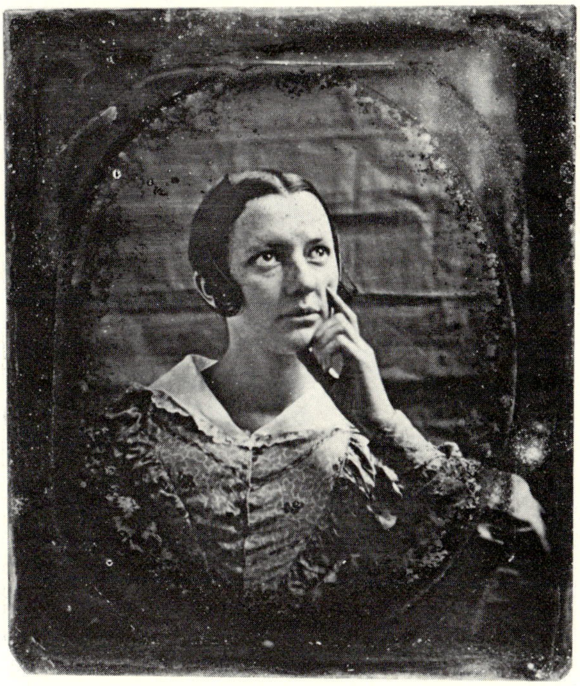

64a & b. JOSIAH JOHNSON HAWES AND NANCY SOUTHWORTH HAWES

Sixth plates, both in one case. Hallmarks: none. Museum of Fine Arts, Boston. Gift of Edward Southworth Hawes in memory of his father, Josiah Johnson Hawes. 43.1428 and 43.1427.

Josiah Johnson Hawes (1808–1901) probably met Nancy Southworth in the daguerreotype studio of her brother Albert Southworth when he joined the firm in 1843. In 1841 Nancy had come from Fairlee, Vermont, to assist with her brother's work; after her marriage to Hawes in 1849, she stayed to perform most of the hand-coloring work in the studio.

Throughout the summer and autumn seasons during the 1850s, Nancy would take the children back to her parents' farm in Vermont. From the frequent letters Josiah and Nancy exchanged during those months, it is obvious that they were devoted to one another. Reminiscent of conventional marriage portraits of the daguerreian era in its size and intimacy, this small double portrait shows the couple during the early years of their marriage.

[Letter, Albert Southworth, Cabotville, Massachusetts, to Nancy Southworth, location unknown (probably West Fairlee, Vermont), 29 November 1840, S & H, IMP/GEH. Letters, Josiah Johnson Hawes, Boston, and Nancy Hawes, West Fairlee, Vermont, 1850s, S & H, IMP/GEH.]

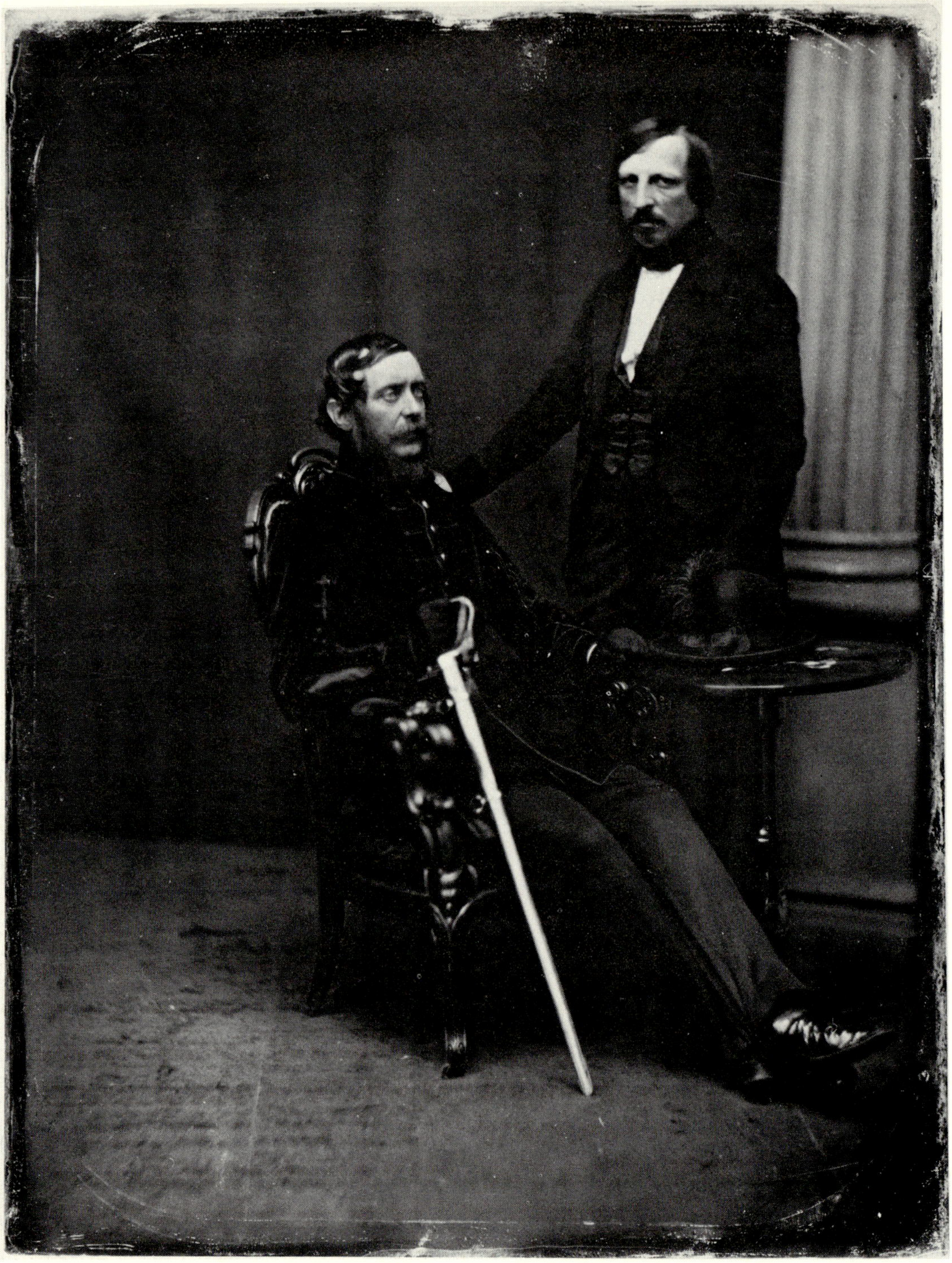

65. Louis Kossuth and His Secretary

Whole plate. Hallmark: none. International Museum of Photography at George Eastman House. Southworth & Hawes Collection. 74:193:263a.

Among the then-recognizable celebrities on view in Southworth & Hawes's Stereoscope was Louis Kossuth (1802–1894), seen here with his secretary. A longtime political activist in his native Hungary, Kossuth had been a popular hero since he was first arrested in 1837 for his liberal and extremely nationalistic views. He gained international fame when, as one of the foremost leaders of the revolution of 1849, he was forced to resign his post of governorship and flee the arrival of Russian troops. Seeking official support for Hungary, he first visited England, then came to America in 1851 where he was enthusiastically welcomed. Despite his personal magnetism and oratorical skills which made him the object of national reportage, he was unable to gain the support he desired for his native country. He soon returned to Europe and remained in Turin, Italy, until his death. Recognizing the popularity of the revolutionist, the Hungarian government allowed the return of his body which was then buried at Pest.

[Bancroft, Frederic. ''Louis Kossuth,'' *Harper's Weekly,* 31 March 1894, pp. 290, 295.]

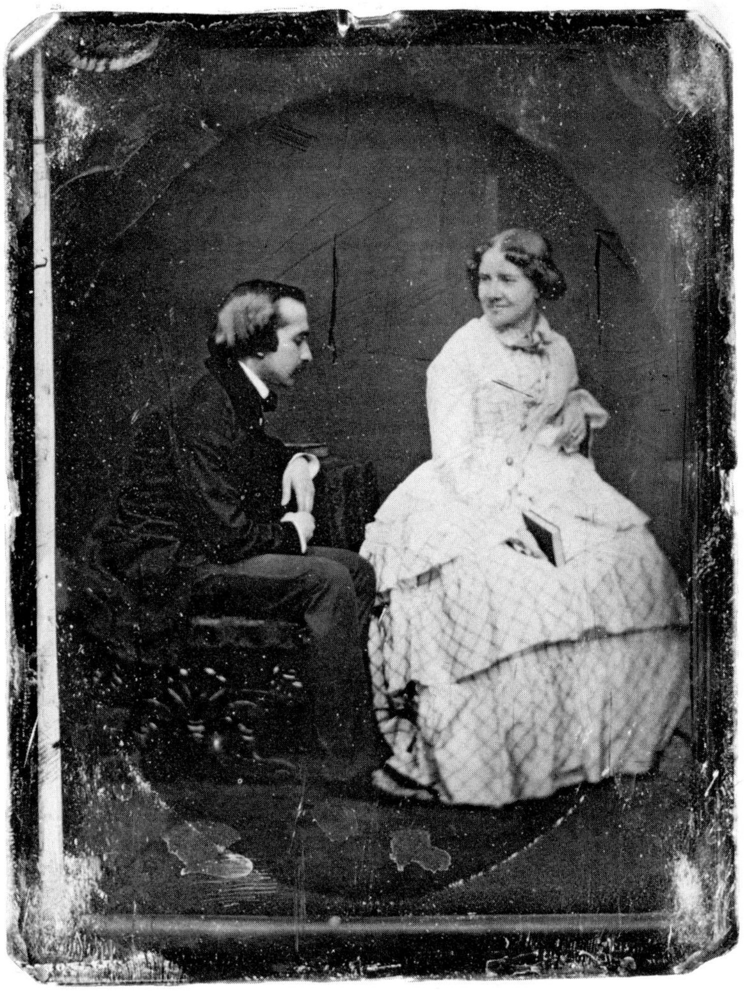

66. Jenny Lind and Otto Goldschmidt

Date: 1852. Quarter plate. Hallmark: l.l.: Scovills. Metropolitan Museum of Art. Gift of I. N. Phelps Stokes and the Hawes family. 37.14.46.

A week or two before their wedding, the "Swedish Nightingale" Jenny Lind (1820–1887) and her German fiancé Otto Goldschmidt (1829–1907) visited the Tremont Row studio for their wedding portrait. Nine years younger than his bride, Goldschmidt, a composer and pianist, had been introduced at the age of sixteen to Miss Lind by Chopin in Leipzig. He had long been solicitous of her well-being and for many years served as her accompanist. Their portrait was kept a secret by Southworth & Hawes until after their wedding on February 5, 1852, which took Boston and the cultural world by surprise.

[(Holman, Louis.) "Josiah Johnson Hawes: Daguerreotyper," *Within the Compass of a Print Shop,* November 1934, p. 6. Shultz, Gladys Denny. *Jenny Lind, the Swedish Nightingale.* Philadelphia and New York: J. B. Lippincott, 1962.]

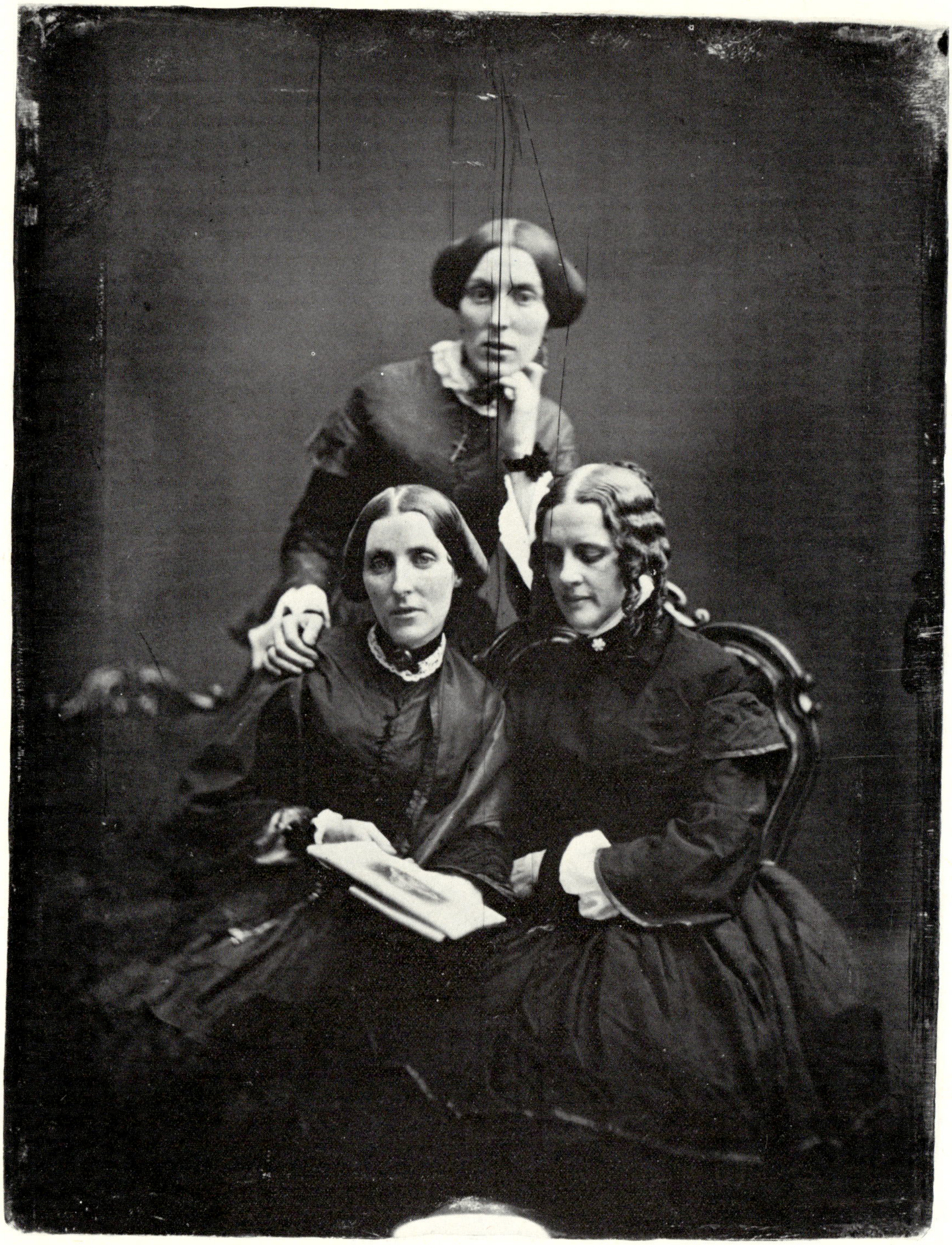

67. Unidentified Female Group

Half plate, hand-colored. Hallmark: none. International Museum of Photography at George Eastman House. Southworth & Hawes Collection. 74:193:1070.

Nineteenth-century group portraiture is replete with pyramidal compositions. Taking their cues from the Renaissance tradition of group compositions, photographers stressed such arrangements as being pleasing and suitable. Often, too, groups were positioned to convey an idea of interrelated activity—reading, looking at prints, etc. This graceful and serene portrait of three unidentified females shows how Southworth & Hawes can utilize the conventional pyramid formula to capture the supple and casual flow of female shapes and forms.

[Robinson, Henry Peach. *Pictorial Effect in Photography.* London: Piper & Carter, 1869 (New York edition 1881), chapter 14, ''Pyramidal Forms.'']

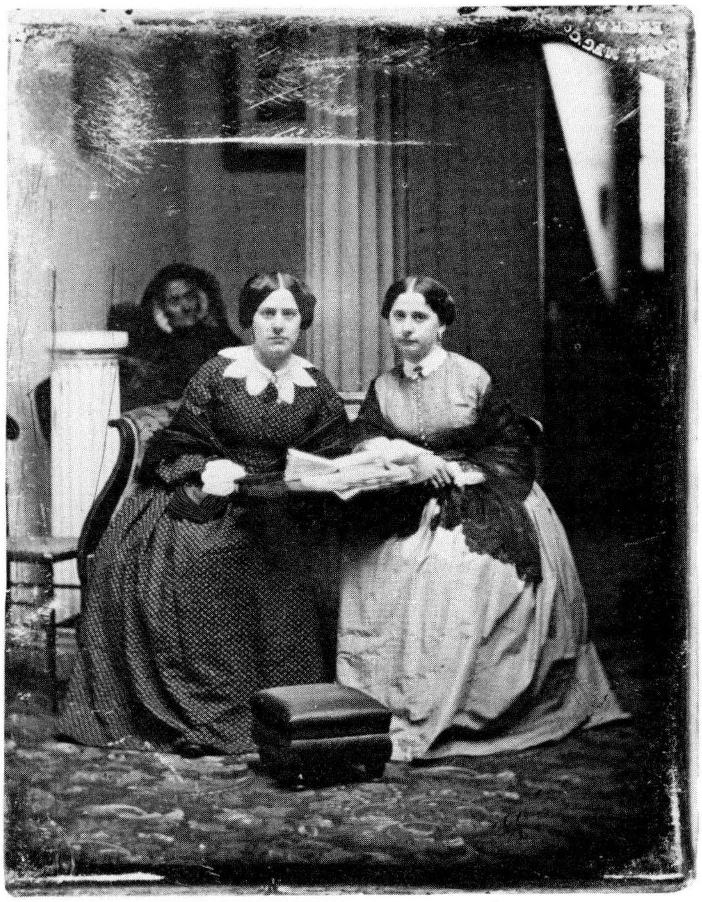

68. Unidentified Female Group

Sixth plate. Hallmark: u.r.: Scovill Extra. International Museum of Photography at George Eastman House. Southworth & Hawes Collection. 74:193:1109.

This small double portrait could be interpreted as a triple portrait, an uncommon document of 19th-century social propriety. From the shadows of the background, as haunting as a specter, appears the older chaperon of the two young women. It is quite probable that the two women wished to include their guide and protector in this portrait, but not necessarily on an equal basis. Much as the fluted columns between which she sits, the chaperon is more of a pictorial symbol than a corporeal presence. This same background, especially the large column and triangular section of the window bay, appears again in a larger group portrait of unidentified women (cf. Plate 80).

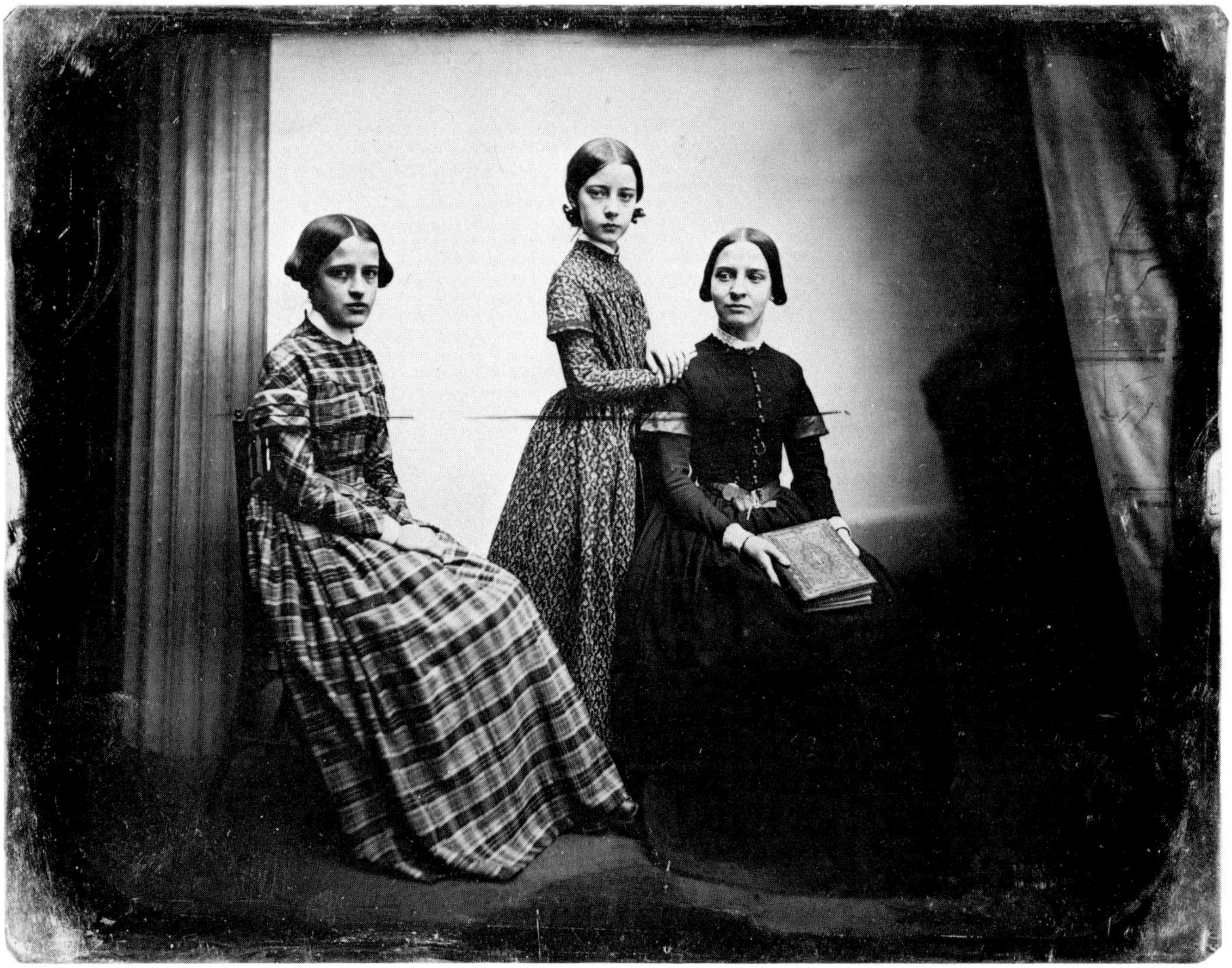

69. Unidentified Female Group

Whole plate. Hallmark: u.r.: star; l.r.: 40. International Museum of Photography at George Eastman House. Southworth & Hawes Collection. 74:193:502.

70. Unidentified Female Group

Whole plate. Hallmark: u.l.: 40; u.r.: star. International Museum of Photography at George Eastman House. Southworth & Hawes Collection. 74:193:1131.

Although the subjects remain the same, these two portraits are substantially different. The loose arrangement of the three figures glancing to the left of the camera in the first portrait contrasts sharply with the compact grouping in the second portrait of the trio staring in different directions. The conventional studio space of the first portrait, as indicated by the column and drapery, differs from the ambiguous background space of the second. Yet, even with these drastic contrasts, both images make full use of pyramidal structures and, more importantly, convey the same infused expression of the three females. Reading from left to right, the psychological interpretations of the subjects are identical in both pictures despite the differences in composition: shy and recluse, coyly assertive, and proudly self-confident, respectively. Few daguerreotypes exhibit such skill and sensitivity in the handling of the subjects.

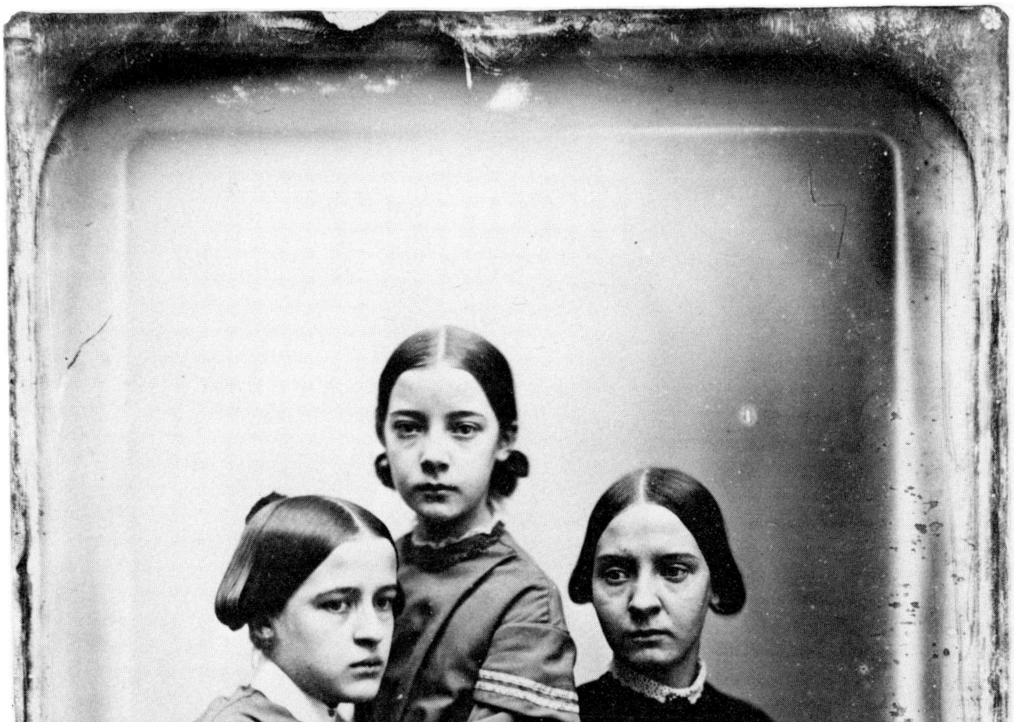

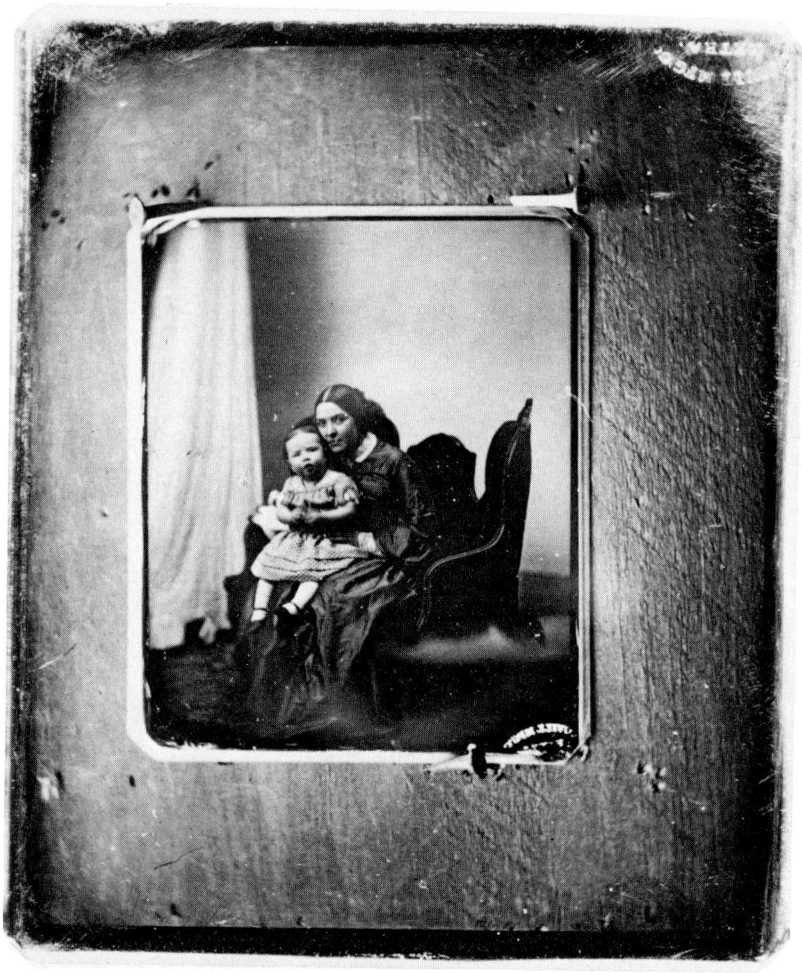

71. Unidentified Mother and Child

Sixth plate, copy. Hallmark: u.r.: Scovill Extra. International Museum of Photography at George Eastman House. Southworth & Hawes Collection. 74:193:337.

72. Unidentified Mother and Child

Whole plate. Hallmark: u.r.: 40. Metropolitan Museum of Art. Gift of Dr. Edward S. Hawes and Miss Marion Augusta Hawes. 39.22.1.

Grouped here are two portraits of mothers and children. The first is a copy daguerreotype of a mother with a child on her lap; the second is an idyllic, nearly saccharin genre scene of a child dozing in the security of his mother's lap after listening to a music box. The daguerreotype was a unique image, much like the contemporary Polaroid. With no negative to reproduce from, copies of the original daguerreotype had to be obtained through yet another daguerreotype. It is frequently difficult and often impossible to identify a daguerreotype copy of another daguerreotype. Sometimes a degree of visual deterioration can be detected, as in the portrait of General Zachary Taylor (Plate 16). At other times, the mounting tacks holding up the plate for copy are visible, as in this portrait. Rarely, the image is an obvious enlarged detail from another picture (see illustration), as in the full-plate portrait of Doctor Adams in the IMP/GEH collection (74:193:11). Visual information, unfortunately, is most often insufficient for identifying copy daguerreotypes.

[Barnard, George N. "Copying Daguerreotypes," *The Photographic Art-Journal,* IV, 3 (September 1852), pp. 151–152.]

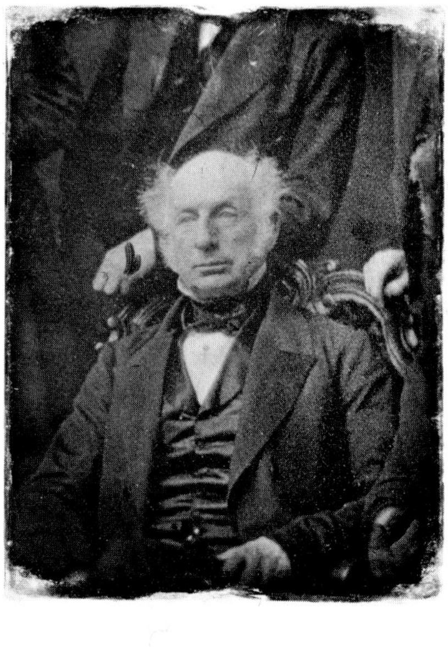

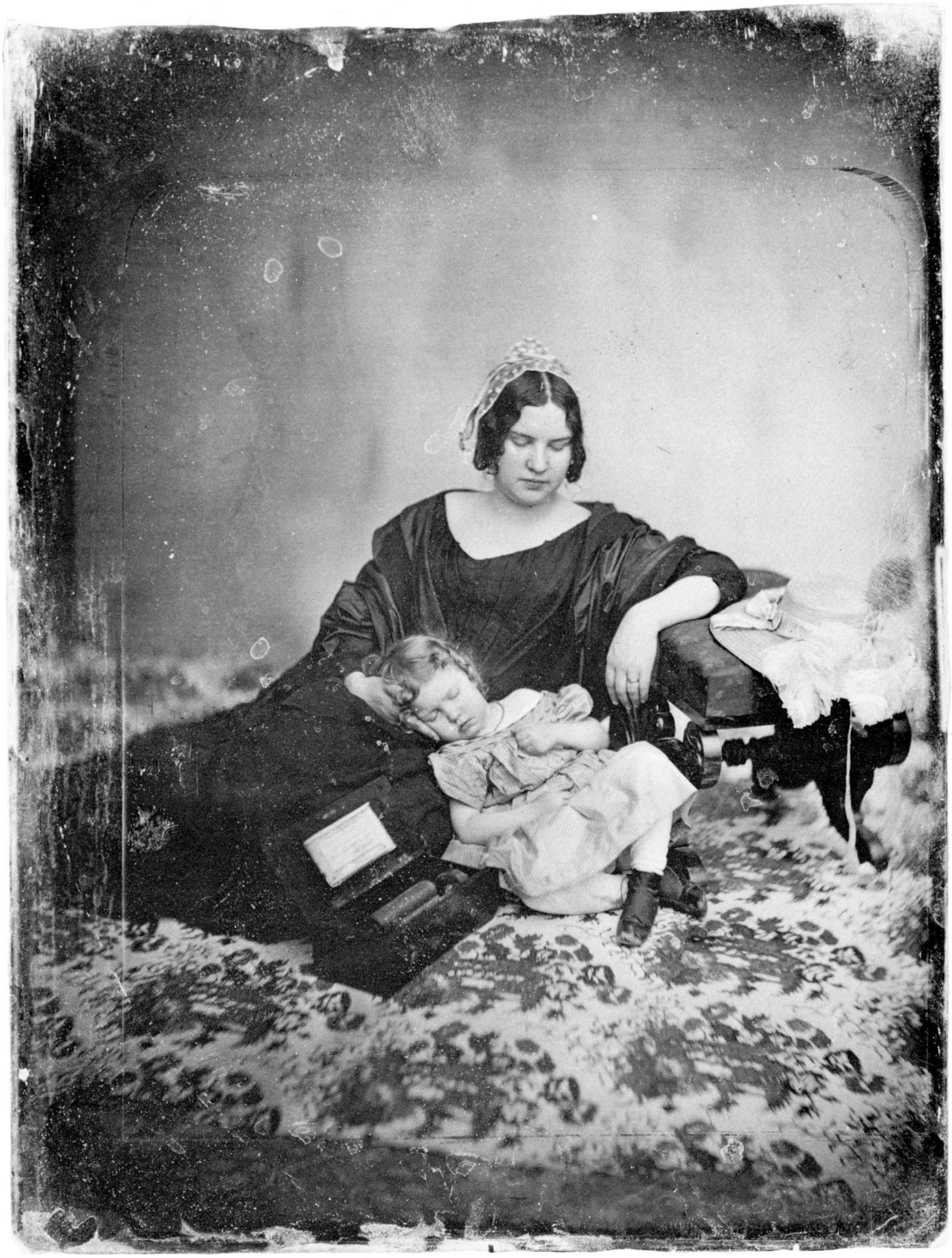

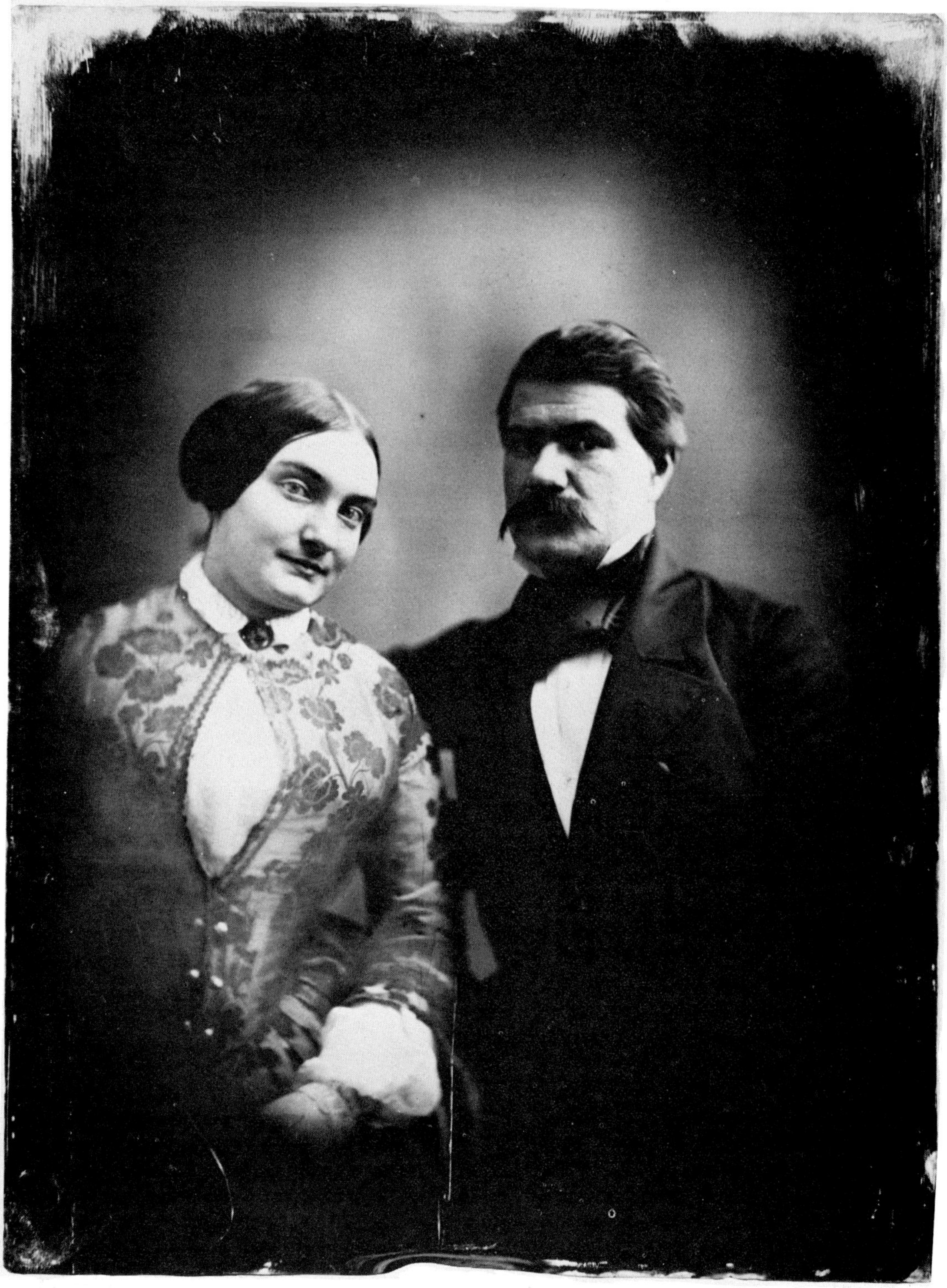

73. UNIDENTIFIED COUPLE

Whole plate, hand-colored. Hallmark: u.r.: Doublé J. P. International Museum of Photography at George Eastman House. Southworth & Hawes Collection. 74:193:9.

74. UNIDENTIFIED COUPLE

Whole plate. Hallmark: l.l.: Doublé J. P. International Museum of Photography at George Eastman House. Southworth & Hawes Collection. 74:193:189.

Quite modern in feeling, these two restrained portraits of couples exhibit the directness and simplicity characteristic of the daguerreotype portrait at its best. Similar to August Sander's portraits of couples taken during the second and third decades of this century, these two portraits of married couples display a minimum of artifice in posing and accoutrements. Each subject, allowed complete autonomy in presenting himself before the camera, contributes to a direct, forceful expression of the human record.

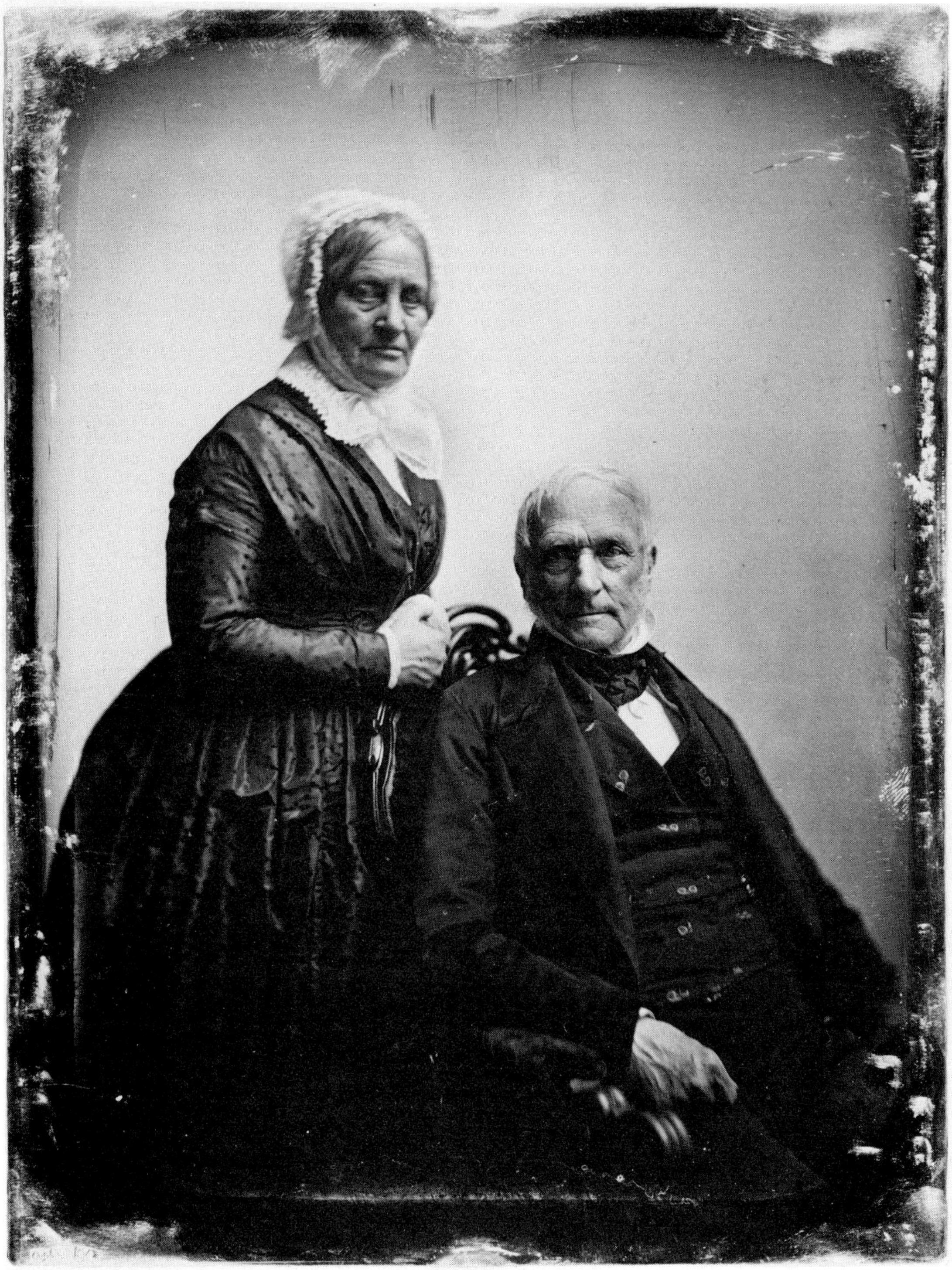

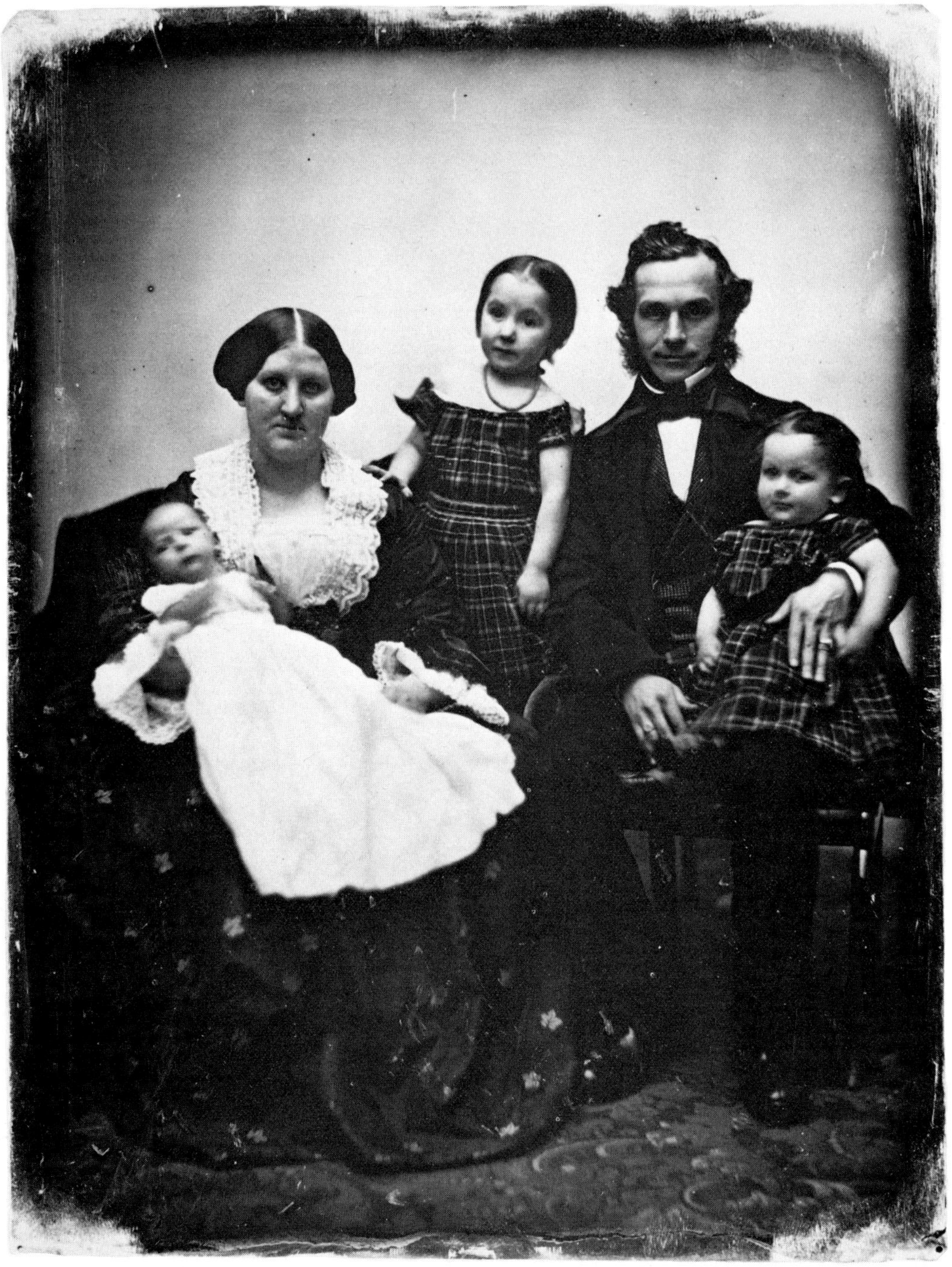

75. Unidentified Family Group

Whole plate. Hallmark: u.l.: Christofle. International Museum of Photography at George Eastman House. Southworth & Hawes Collection. 74:193:68.

76. Unidentified Family Group

Whole plate. Hallmark: u.r.: N⁰ 40. International Museum of Photography at George Eastman House. Southworth & Hawes Collection. 74:193:74.

Large family groups often posed difficult problems in figure arrangement, composition of the masses and interrelated facial expressions. While not equal to the aesthetic standards of contemporary group paintings, double or group daguerreotype portraits do often exude surprisingly modern qualities of directness and simple structure (cf. Plates 73, 74). Given so many figures to choreograph, Southworth & Hawes simply placed them in the general area of the studio facing the camera and allowed the subjects to compose themselves within certain limits. The fundamentally photogenic stare, directly into the lens, confronts the viewer and solidifies the sense of past presence of the subjects. One of the most basic rules of mid-19th-century portraiture was that "the eyes should . . . never [be directed] into, or on the instrument, as some direct; the latter generally gives a fixed, silly, staring, scowling or painful expression to the face." Paradoxically, with the exception of "silly," the description is consistent with many of the most evocative and captivating portraits made with the camera.

[Snelling, Henry H. *The History and Practice of the Art of Photography,* p. 41.]

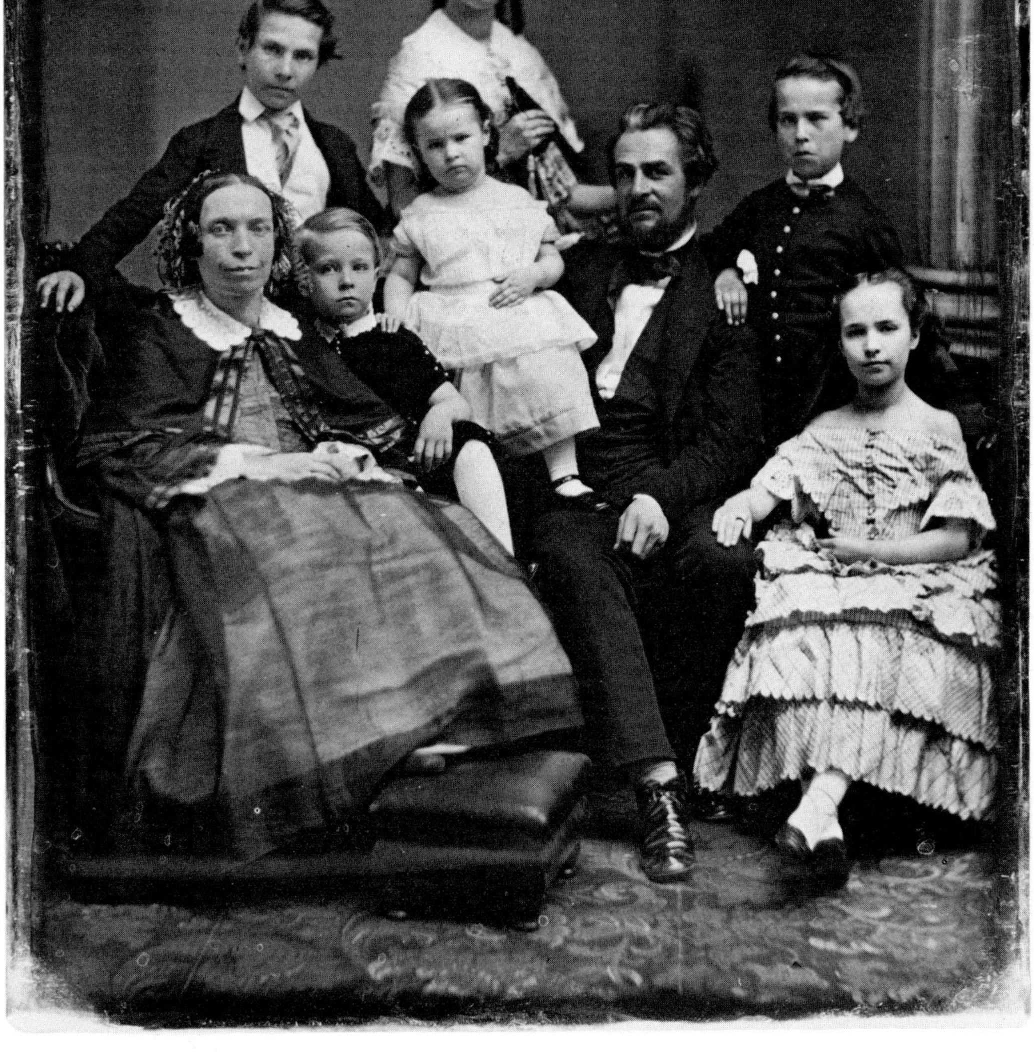

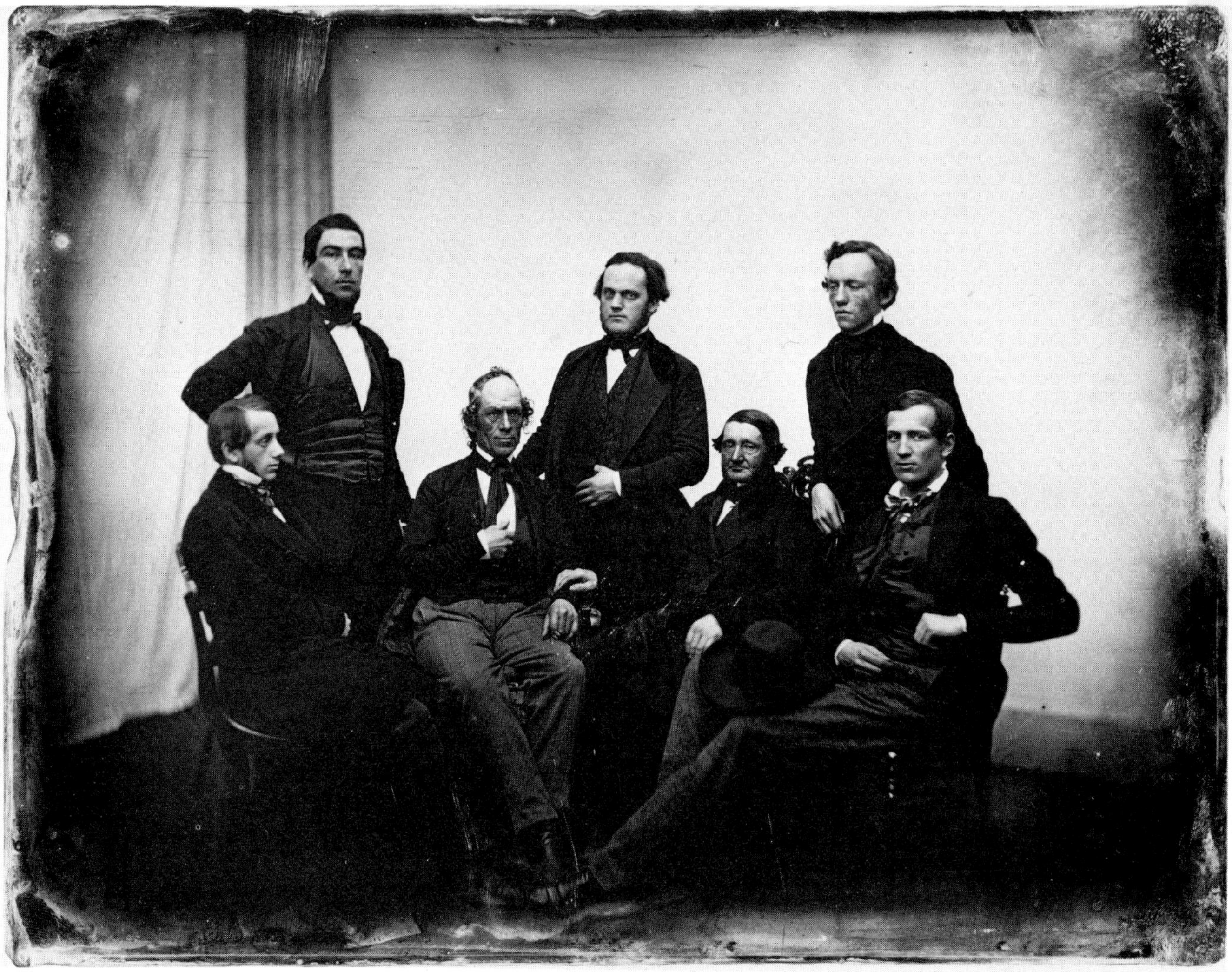

77. Unidentified Male Group

Whole plate. Hallmark: u.l.: star; l.l.: 40. Richard Parker Collection, Marblehead, Massachusetts.

Similar in some respects to the group portrait of Free-Soilers (Plate 62), this daguerreotype of seven gentlemen, associated by some unknown activity or belief, appears casual and hastily accomplished. Little, if any, attempt has been made to hide the seam of floor and wall, nor to diminish the disruptive effect of the white curtain. The singular inclusion of the classical column is nearly ludicrous in this context. A charming folk-art naiveté, however, characterizes this awkward group of figures.

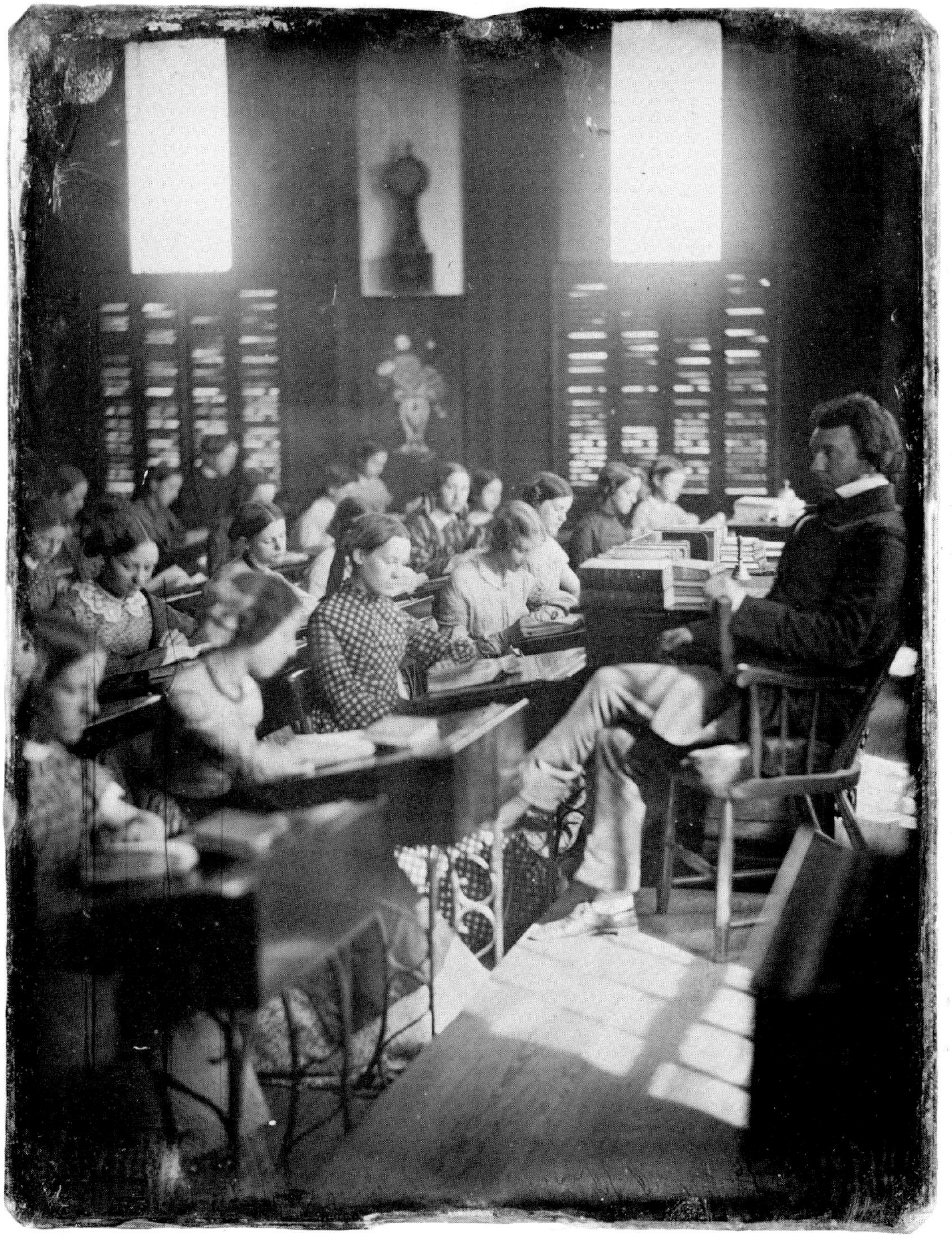

78. CLASSROOM IN THE EMERSON SCHOOL FOR GIRLS

Whole plate. Hallmark: l.r.: B. F. 40. Metropolitan Museum of Art. Gift of I. N. Phelps Stokes and the Hawes family. 37.14.22

Photographic manuals and literature of the period allow little possibility of creating a group portrait within a non-studio setting where only natural light is available. This daguerreotype is simply labeled "Emerson School, Interior." Records in the Boston libraries show no such place of education. Nevertheless, in this unique image, Southworth & Hawes have captured the look and the feel of a mid-19th-century classroom with the sensitivity and skill one commonly experiences in the quasi-genre, documentary photography of Lewis Hine.

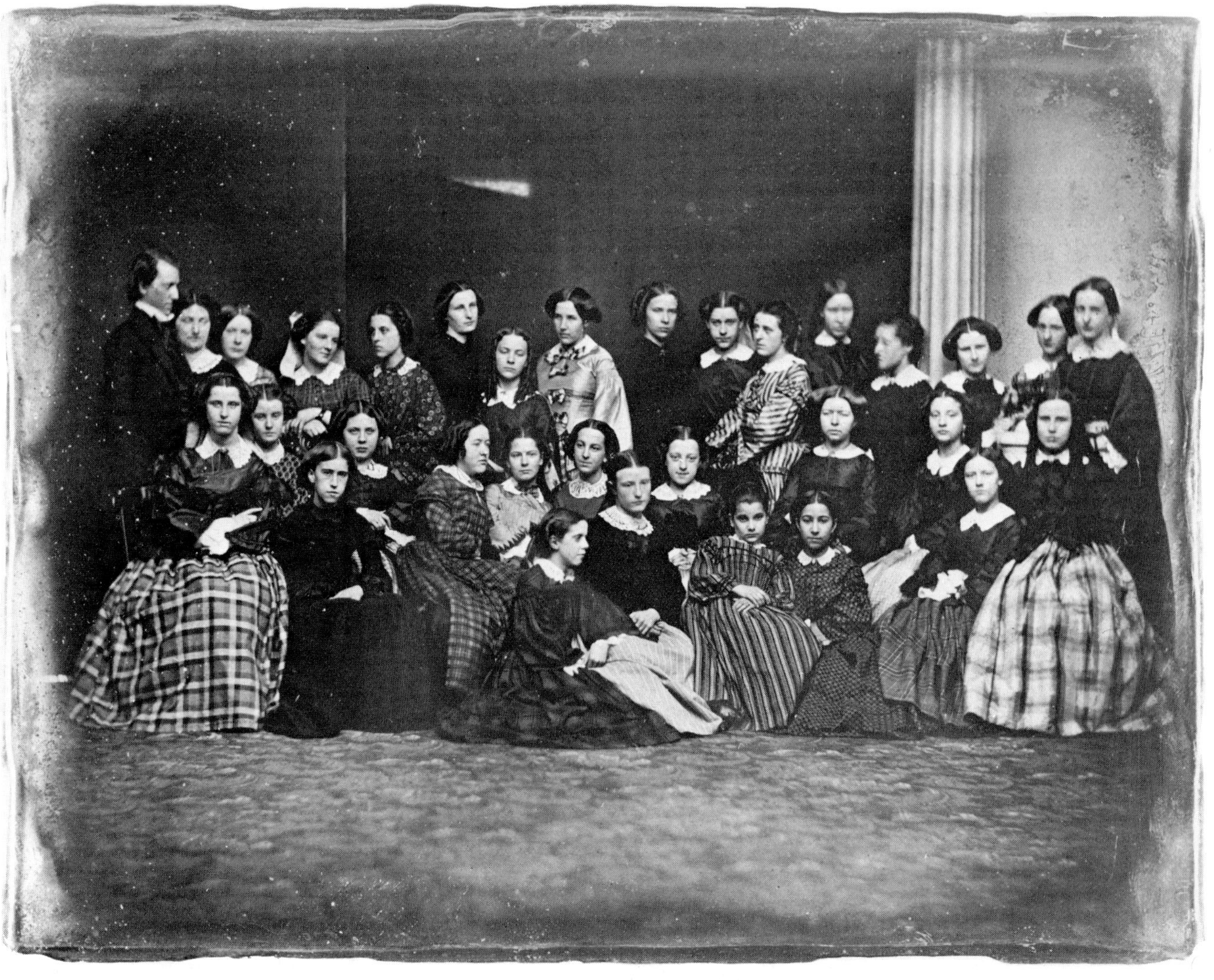

79. SCHOLARS OF THE EMERSON SCHOOL FOR GIRLS

Whole plate. Hallmark: l.r.: Doublé J. P. Metropolitan Museum of Art. Gift of I. N. Phelps Stokes and the Hawes family. 37.14.8.

In another photograph of the Emerson School, the class of female students sit and stand for their official class portrait in the Southworth & Hawes studio. The male teacher is seen standing at the far left. The background column and the design on the carpet definitely place the portrait setting at the Tremont Row studio. As a revealing and expressive portrait of over thirty figures, this full-plate daguerreotype group remains unrivaled. The subtle differences in facial expressions, gestures and angles of bodies and heads—especially within the seated students in the center of the group—make up a thesaurus of types and characters.

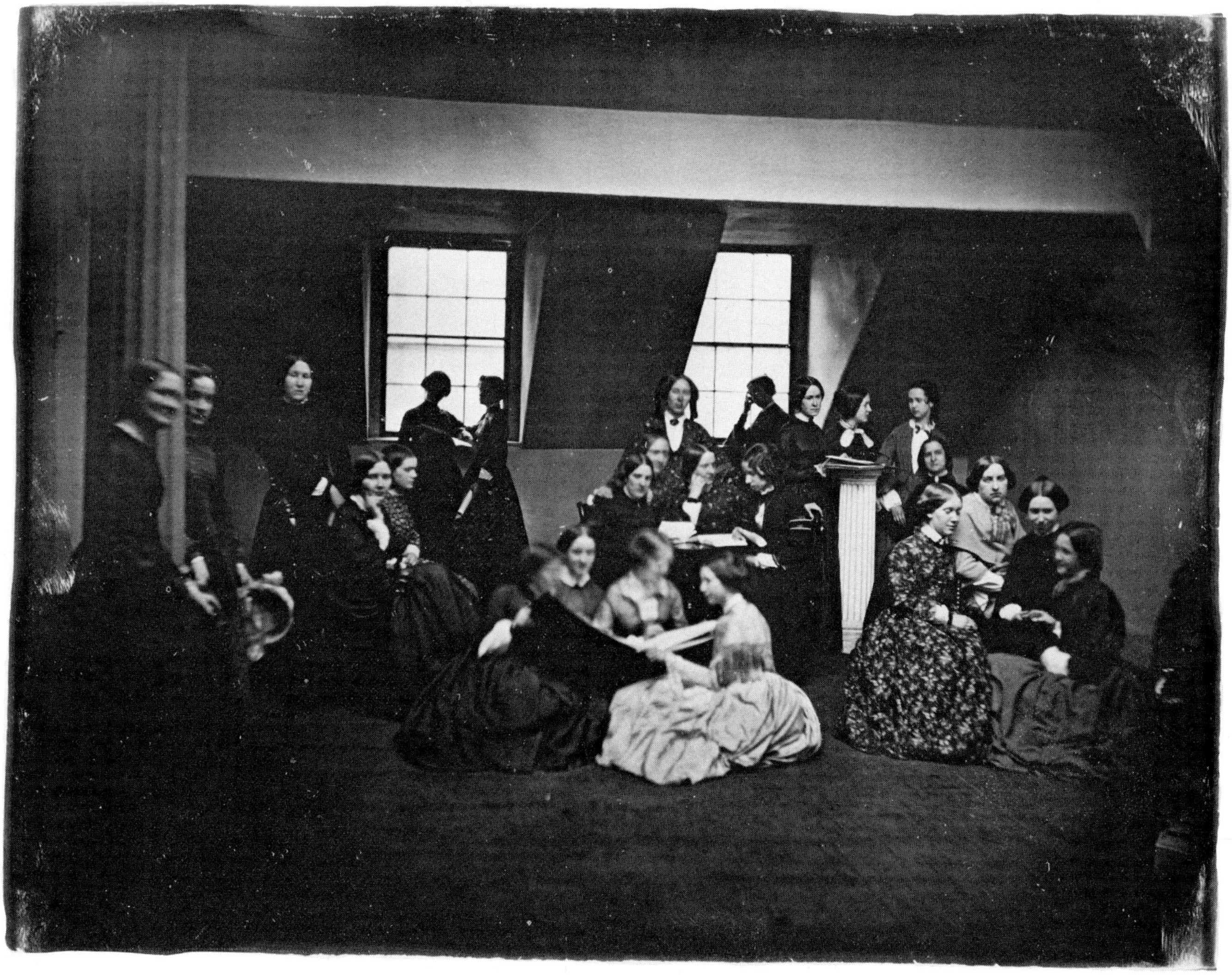

80. Unidentified Group of Females in the Southworth & Hawes Studio

Whole plate. Hallmark: l.r.: Doublé J. P. Metropolitan Museum of Art. Gift of I. N. Phelps Stokes and the Hawes Family. 37.14.56.

Twenty-five unidentified young women in the interior of the Southworth & Hawes studio are recorded in a seemingly haphazard confluence of bodies. As in the famous portrait of Chief Justice Lemuel Shaw (cf. Plate 10), this group portrait was probably achieved by an initial insight into the fortuitous and instantaneous harmonies of light and posture. Far from the first impression of a loosely articulated arrangement, the composition is based on a series of diagonals and pyramids. The right side of the group consists of a truncated pyramid of eighteen seated and standing figures; this construction, the left edge of which is so visually noticeable, contains two subordinate groupings of seated women at either corner of its base, both groupings being pyramidal or nearly so. Diagrammatic lines can be drawn between various figure groups to juxtapose the casual structure of the left side against the compact design of the right side. Discrete vignettes of different poses and expressions are woven throughout the image. Photographic history can offer few such magnificently orchestrated group portraits. Never had the complex problem of organizing a large body of figures been so successfully resolved before Rejlander's *Two Ways of Life* of 1857.

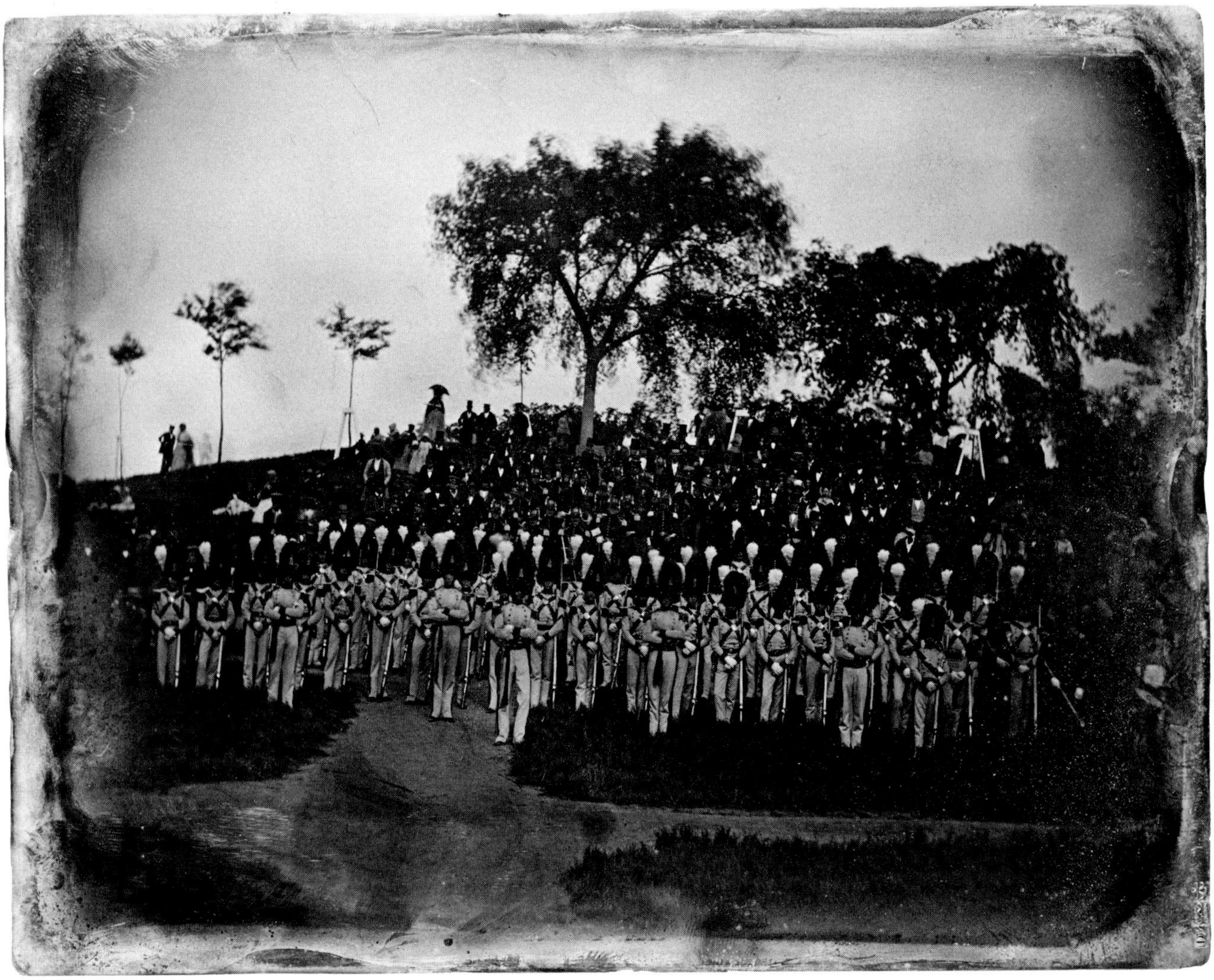

81. UNIDENTIFIED MUSTER ON THE BOSTON COMMON

Whole plate. Hallmark: l.r.: Doublé J. P. Society for the Preservation of New England Antiquities, Boston. Gift of Herbert Foster Otis. 1964.257d.

82. UNIDENTIFIED MUSTER ON THE BOSTON COMMON

Whole plate. Hallmark: l.r.: star. Richard Parker Collection, Marblehead, Massachusetts.

These two views of unidentified military musters in presentational formations upon the Boston Common are probably scenes of some holiday festivity or celebration and perhaps were exposed on the same day. Because daguerreotype group portraits of over ten figures are rare, these two panoramic portraits, together with the portraits of the young girls' school classes, are fairly unique to this early period of photography in America. Both muster portraits predict the use of the Kircut camera at the beginning of this century to document company picnics and the like with a sweeping, all-inclusive image. The small groups of observers atop the knoll in the one picture and the Bulfinch Capitol dome looming over the trees in the other are of equal visual interest. Although incidental to the image's content, both of these elements help balance the pictures precisely between portraiture and landscape with figures.

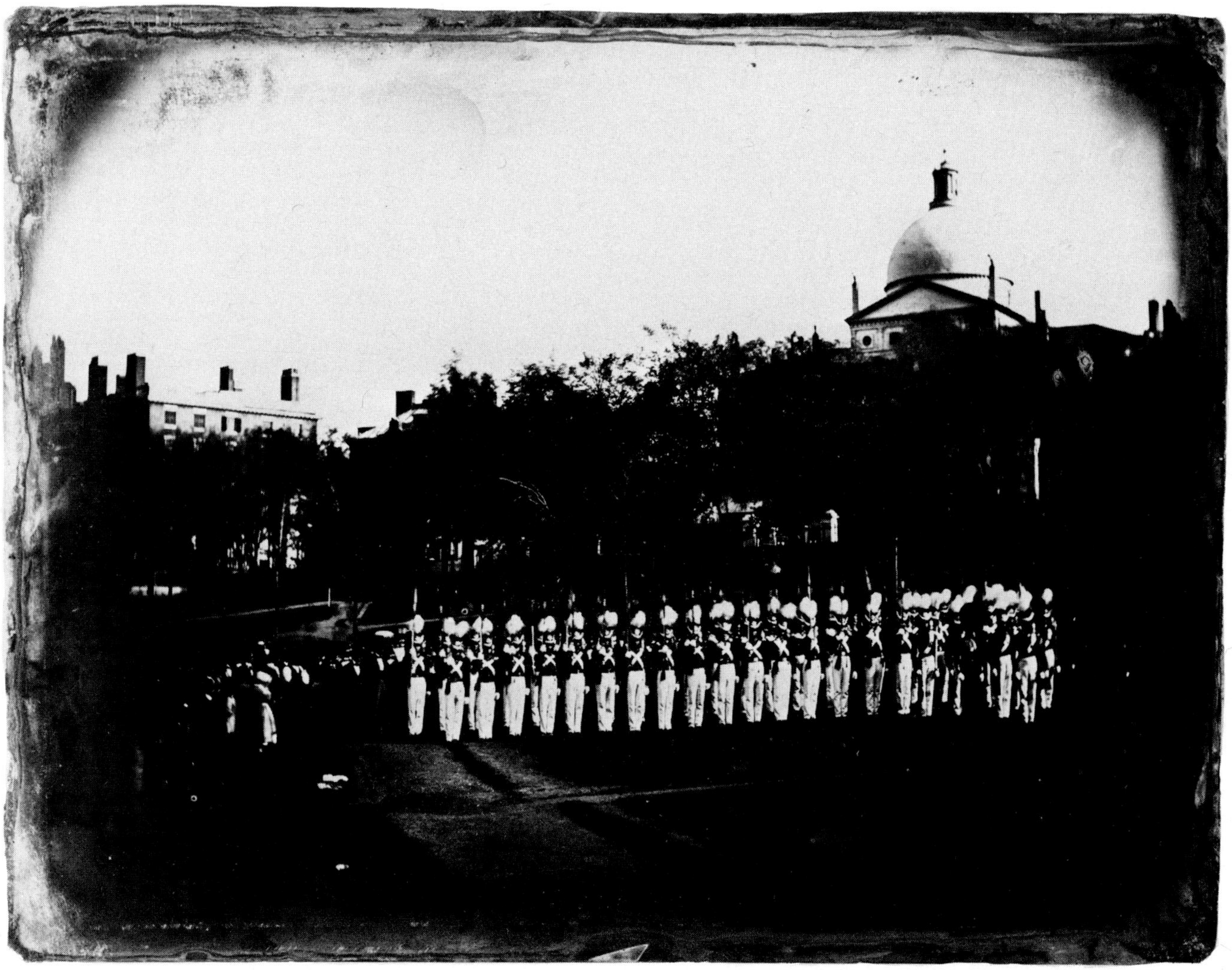

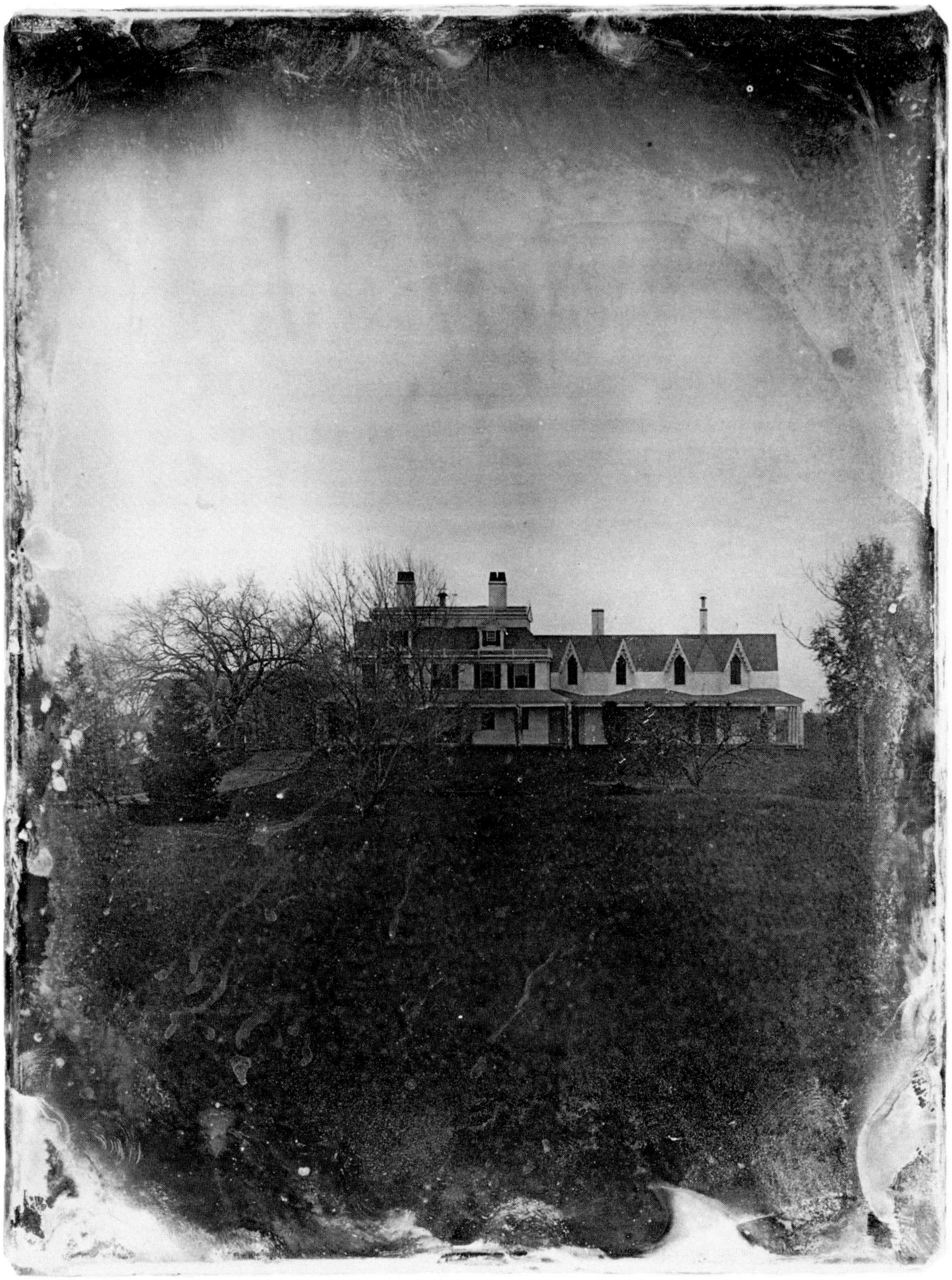

83. GREEN HARBOR, ESTATE OF DANIEL WEBSTER

Whole plate. Hallmark: u.l.: Double J. P. Richard Parker Collection, Marblehead, Massachusetts.

This view of Green Harbor, Webster's estate in Marshfield, Massachusetts, appears less inspired than the evocative portraits of the orator. Compared to the early Hawes landscape (Plate 84), the composition is dull, although somewhat similar. The house is presented more as an element within the landscape than as a structure of historical importance. It is set far back in the distance with a large open area in the foreground, perhaps to include Webster's favorite elm tree to the left of the house.

It was first assumed that this view had been made at Webster's request or quite unofficially during a trip that took the two partners past the great estate. The plate, however, is listed as one in a series of stereo daguerreotypes which were exhibited in the studio's Grand Parlor Stereoscope and this, along with the compositional elements, would indicate the partners exposed this view for their own use in the Stereoscope.

[Harvey, Peter. *Reminiscences and Anecdotes of Daniel Webster.* Boston: Little, Brown & Co., 1877, pp. 263–315. Lanman, Charles. *The Private Life of Daniel Webster.* New York: Harper & Brothers, 1852, pp. 69–82. Southworth & Hawes Account Book of 1851–1852, S&H, IMP/GEH.]

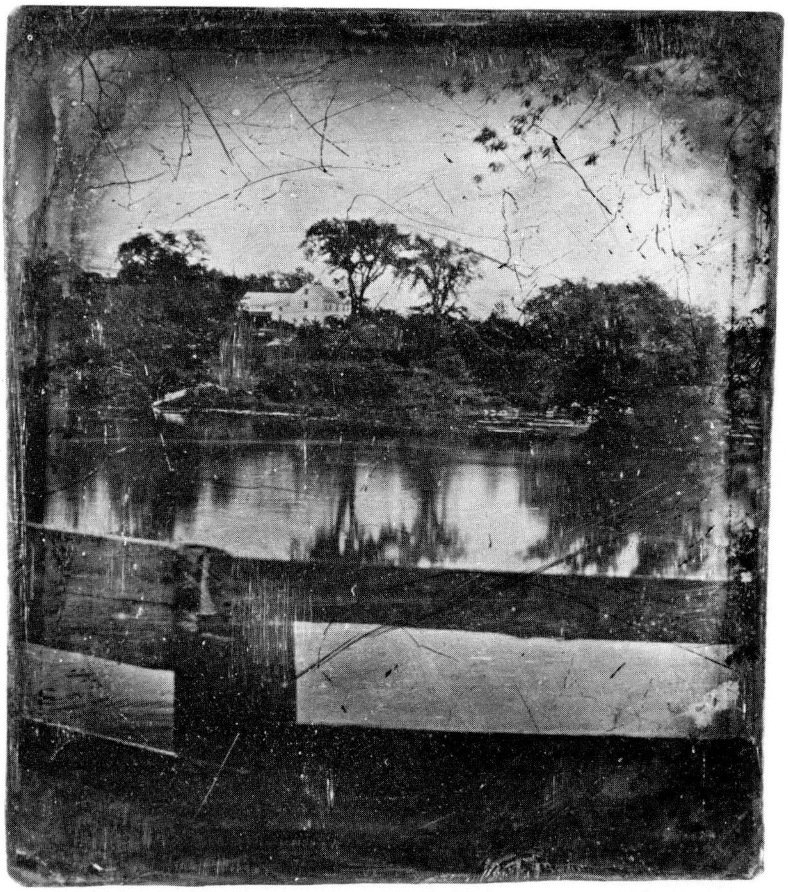

84. Unidentified Landscape

Sixth plate. Hallmark: none. Museum of Fine Arts, Boston. Gift of Edward Southworth Hawes in memory of his father, Josiah Johnson Hawes. 43.1432a.

The provenance of this sixth-plate landscape daguerreotype traces a direct line from the Hawes family to its present location. The image resembles the common daguerreotype views of rural estates and farm architecture that were popular in America during the 1850s. Yet there are features which associate this plate with Southworth & Hawes's other large landscapes: its verticality, its slightly off-centered point of interest in the far distance, the broad foreground and the graphic contrasts between the near and the far. If one could establish that this plate was made by Hawes while he was an itinerant daguerreotypist prior to joining Southworth in 1843, then other large views could be attributed to Hawes on stylistic grounds.

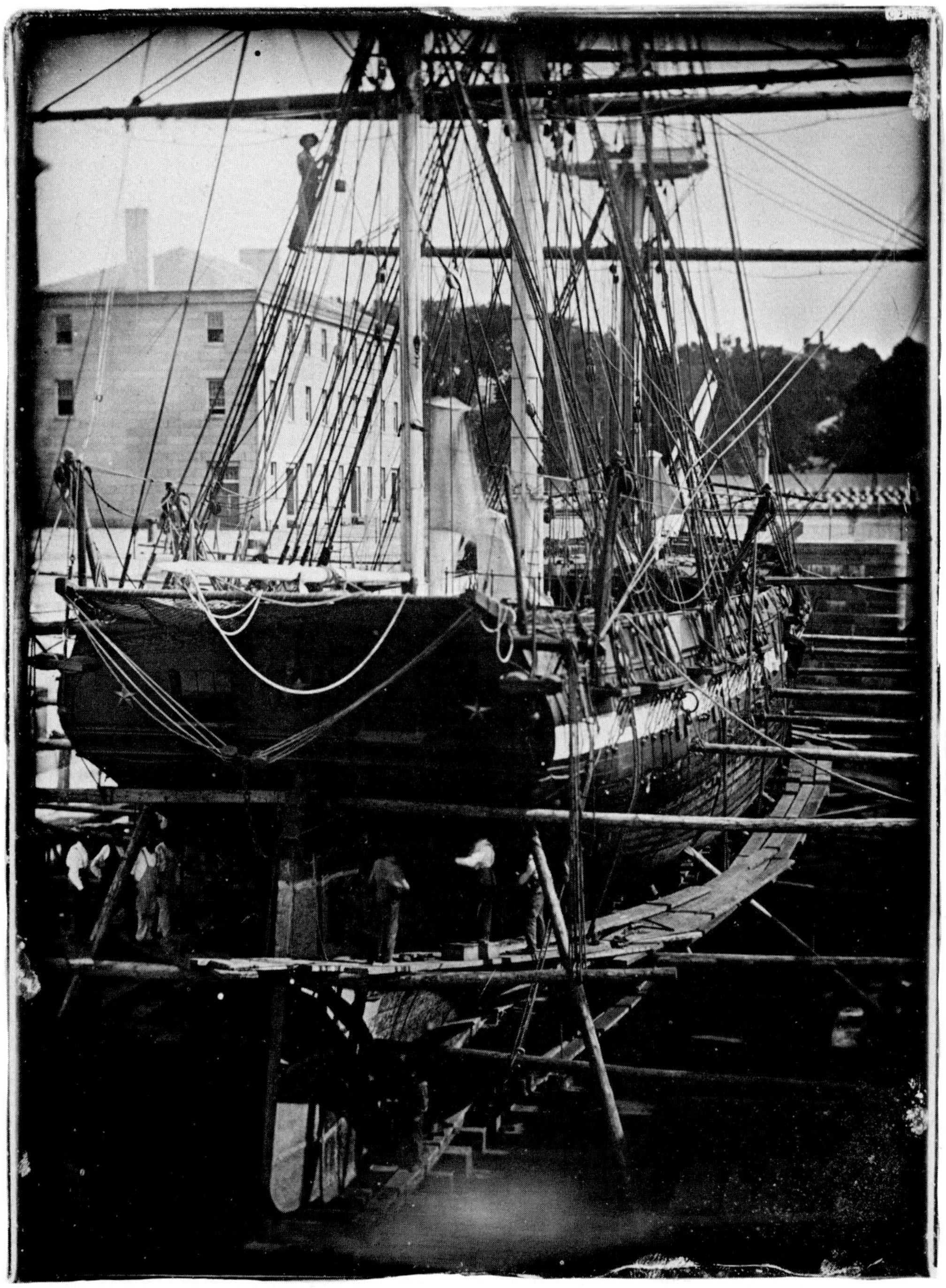

85. BOSTON NAVY YARD

Date: c. 1852. Whole plate. Hallmark: u.r.: Doublé J. P. International Museum of Photography at George Eastman House. Southworth & Hawes Collection. 74:193:1128.

The awkward framing of the sloop of war reveals a stronger interest in the dry dock than in the vessel. Designed and constructed by the great Massachusetts engineer Loammi Baldwin, the Dry Dock One was five years in construction before the S.S. *Constitution* gained first entrance in 1833. Built of Quincy granite, it was a notable engineering accomplishment in its day and is still in use. Although the image shows the sloop in dry dock for repairs rather than actual construction, the picture recalls the lines from "The Building of the Ship" by Longfellow (1849).

Day by day the vessel grew,
With timbers fashioned strong and true,
Stemson and keelson and sternson-knee,
Till, framed with perfect symmetry,
A skeleton ship rose up to view!
And around the bows and along the side
The heavy hammers and mallets plied,
Till after many a week, at length,
Wonderful for form and strength,
Sublime in its enormous bulk,
Loomed aloft the shadowy hulk!

[Bunting, W.H. *Portrait of a Port: Boston, 1852–1914.* Cambridge, Massachusetts: Harvard University Press, Belknap Press, 1971. (Same ref. for Plates 86–88.)]

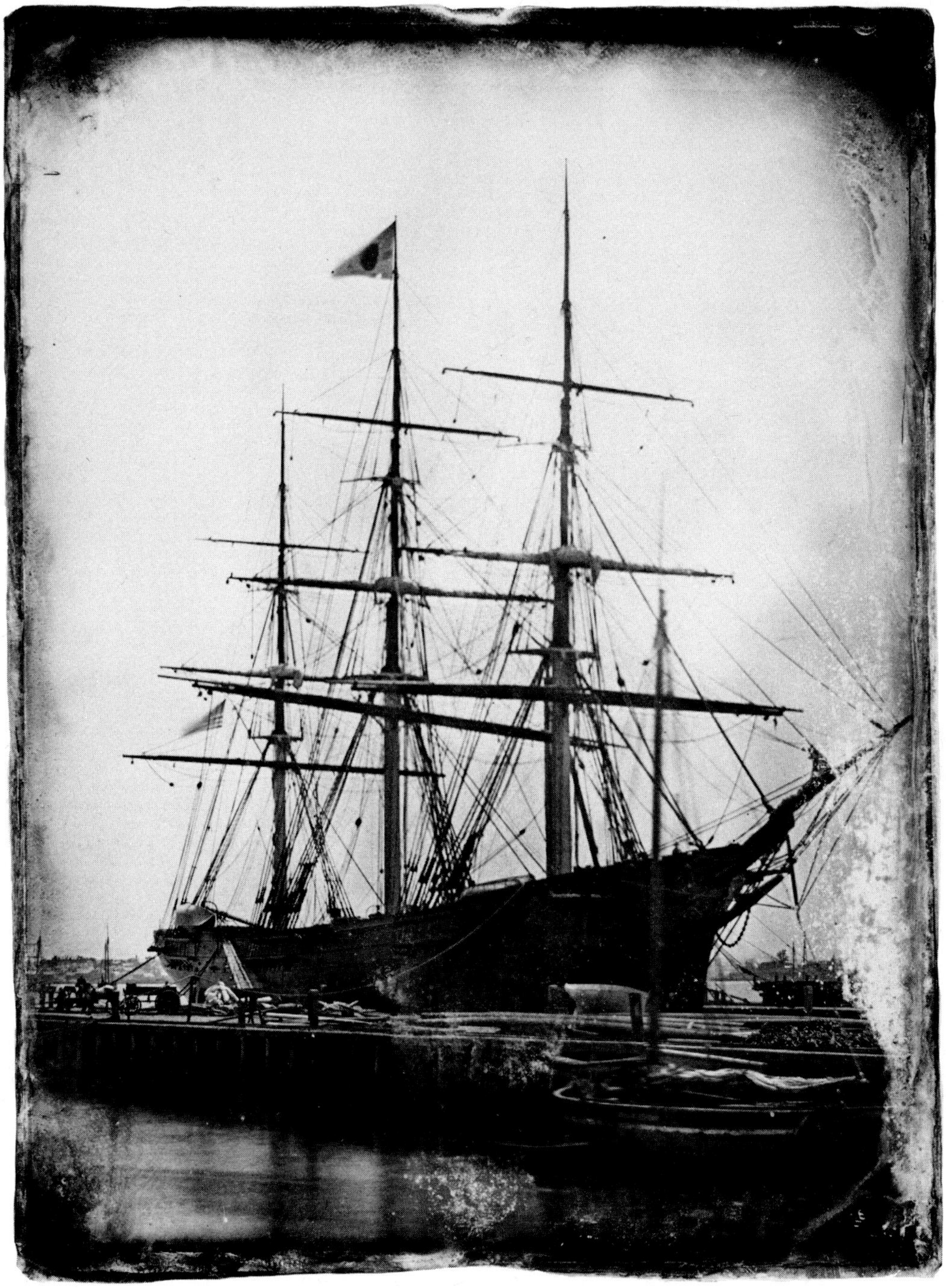

86. *CHAMPION OF THE SEAS,* EAST BOSTON

Date: 1854. Whole plate. Hallmark: u.r.: Christofle. Richard Parker Collection, Marblehead, Massachusetts.

When the *Champion of the Seas* was launched from her East Boston pier in May of 1854, she ranked as the world's largest sailing vessel, registering 2,447 tons. Built by Donald McKay (Plate 8), she was the second in a quartet of clippers constructed for James Baine and Company of Liverpool and Australia. According to *The Boston Daily Atlas* (May 20, 1854), the *Champion of the Seas* was a marked improvement over the *Lightning,* the first of the four clippers:

Her ends are as long, though not as sharp or concave, and are even more beautiful in their form. She is 238 feet long on the keel, and 259 feet on the deck between perpendiculars. . . . The run is long and clean, and blends in perfect harmony with the general outline of the model. Broadside on she has all the imposing majesty of a ship of war, combined with the airy grace of a clipper.

This daguerreotype is thought to be the only existing photographic image taken shortly before the *Champion of the Seas* was towed from the Grand Junction Wharf where she was loaded for her maiden voyage to Liverpool.

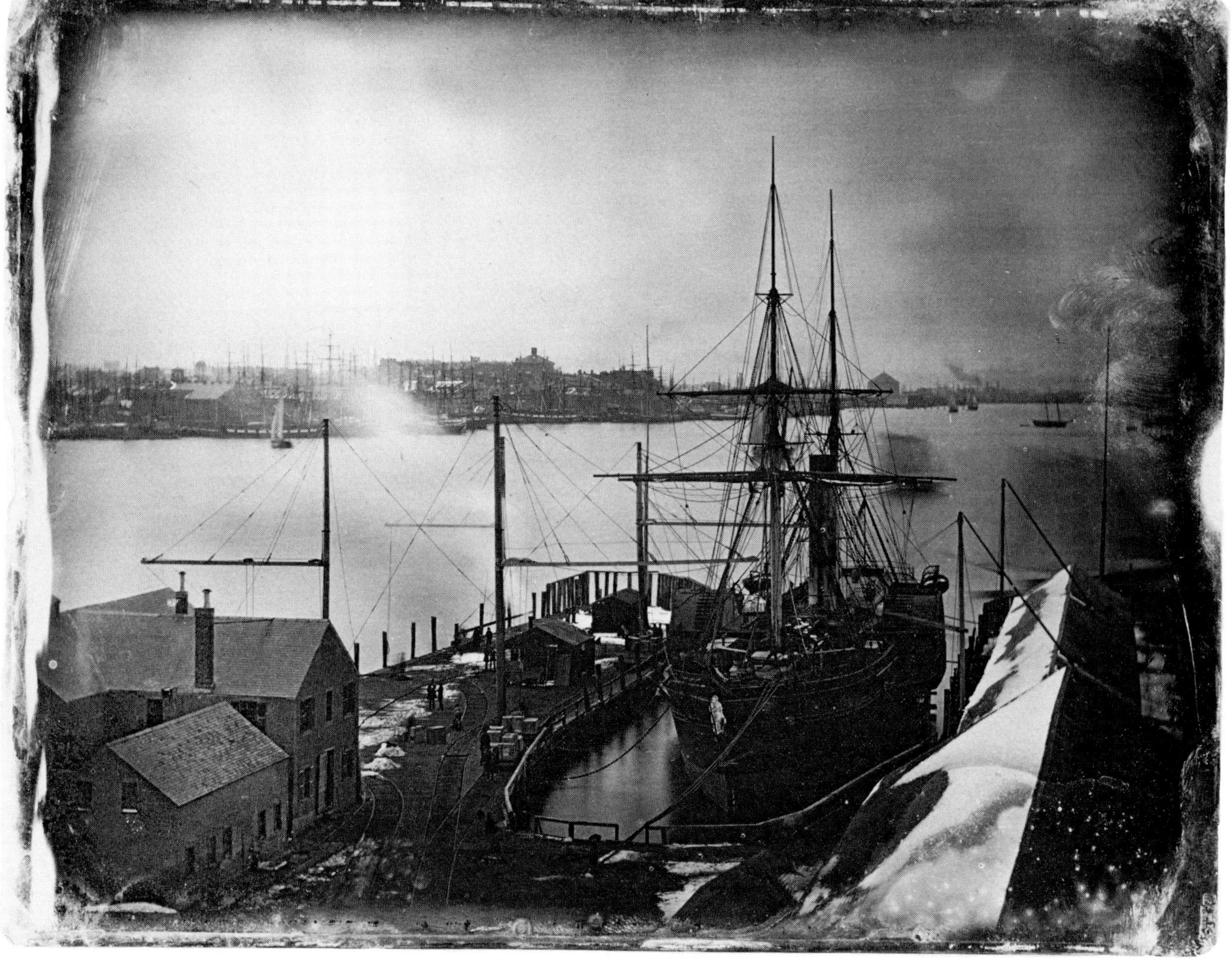

87. The *Niagara* in the Atlantic Dock, East Boston

Date: c. 1855. Whole plate. Hallmark: l.r.: A. Gaudin. Richard Parker Collection, Marblehead, Massachusetts.

This image is the only known winter view of the Boston harbor which Southworth & Hawes had photographed in at least six other whole-plate views (cf. Plates 85, 86, 88). One of the four standardized steamers built for Cunard in 1848, *Niagara* is shown here anchored in special derricks required for her protruding paddle wheel boxes. Beyond the docks and across the channel lie South Cove, the heights of Fort Hill and the outlines of Faneuil Hall in Haymarket Square and the house of Harrison Gray Otis. The harbor itself is jammed with shipping—most likely Boston cotton ships—which was of central importance to the development of New England textile industries and many local fortunes.

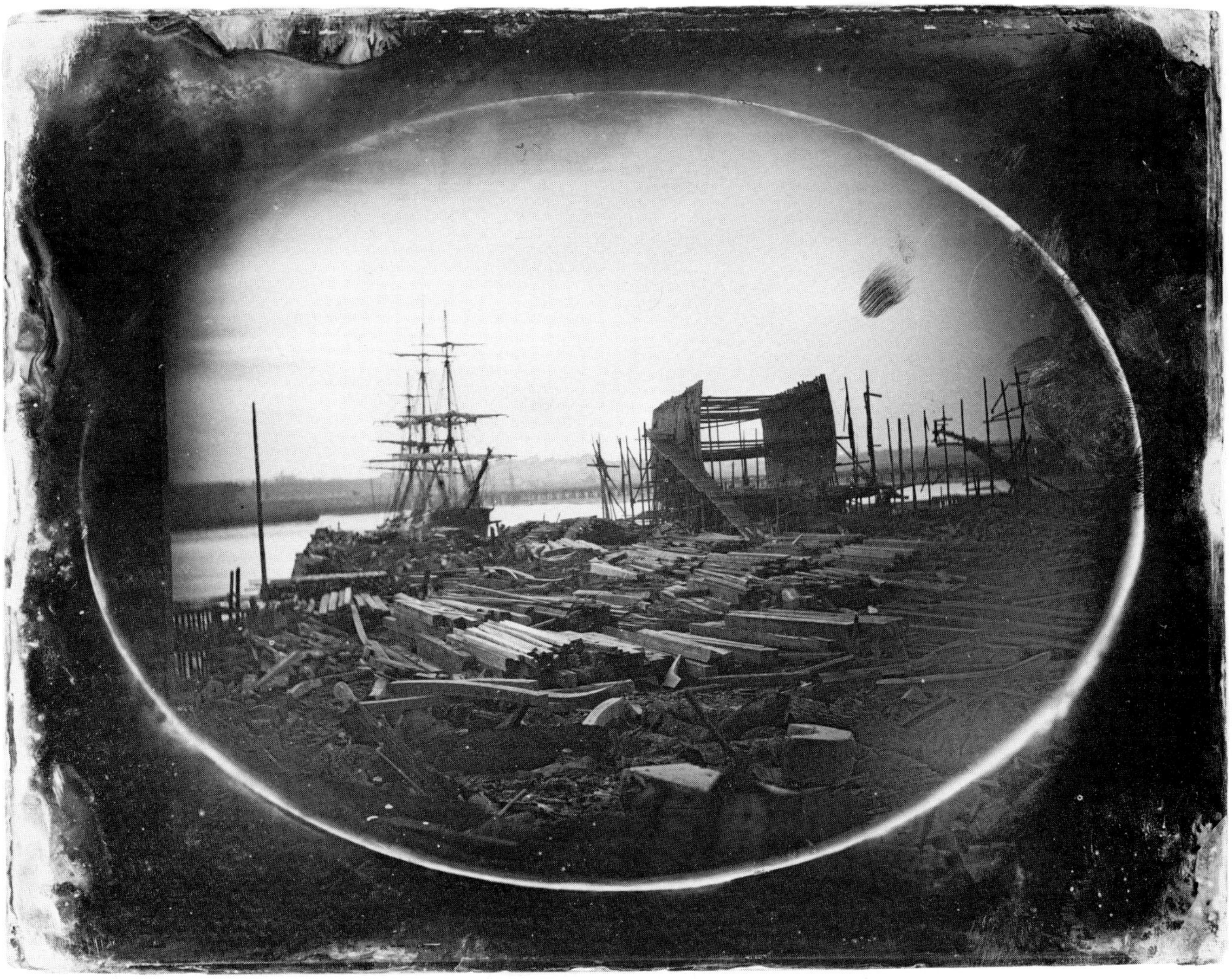

88. McKay's Shipyard, East Boston

Date: c. 1855. Whole plate. Hallmark: l.l.: A. Gaudin. Richard Parker Collection, Marblehead, Massachusetts.

In 1845 Donald McKay (Plate 8) established his shipyard in East Boston where he constructed clippers for the Diamond Line and later for the Californian and Australian trade. This view, thought to have been taken in 1855 when McKay produced only two vessels, is one of the most romantic Southworth & Hawes landscapes. The vessel under construction dominates the wooden shipyard against the Mystic River Bridge, stretched across the background. Carpeted with wood shavings and chips strewn amidst raw timber, the view becomes more remarkable by the intrusion of the edge of a building on the left, a repoussoir element orchestrating the spatial relationship between the viewer and the landscape.

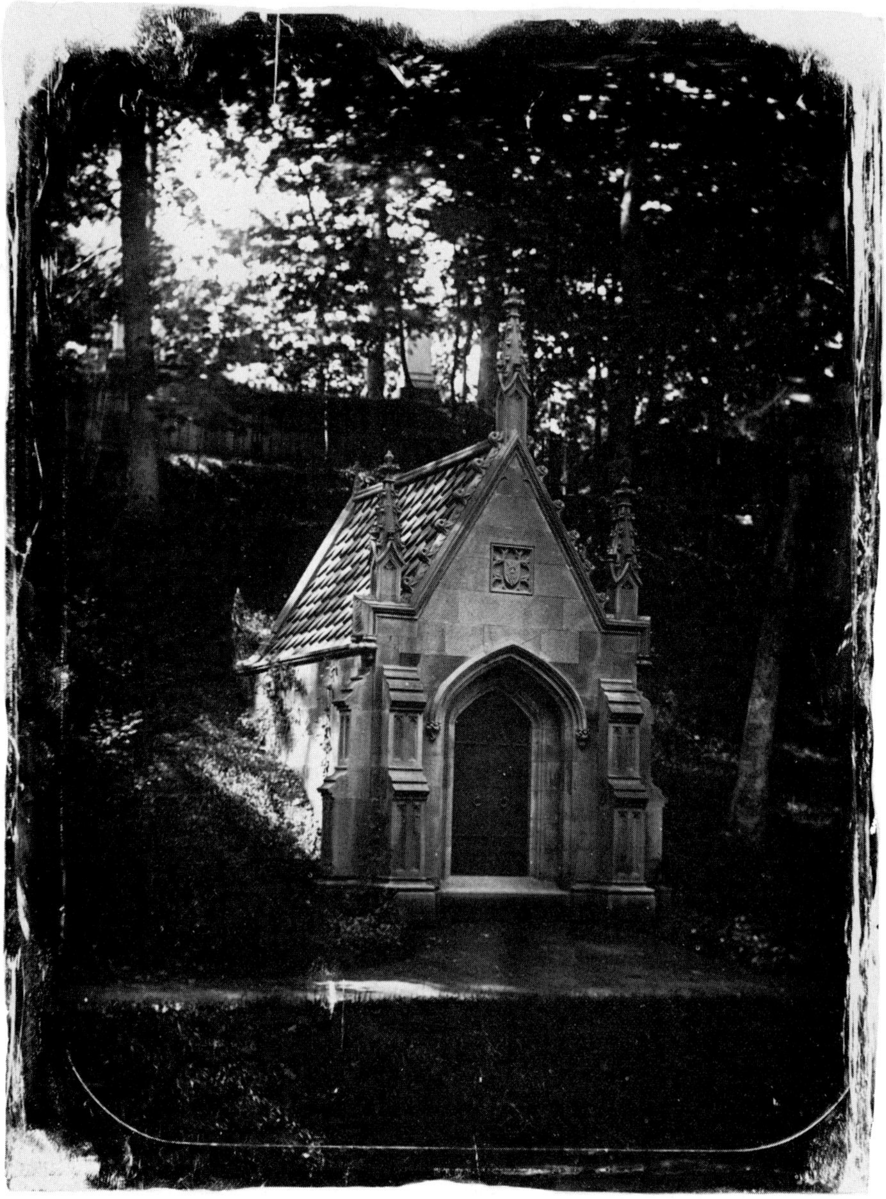

89. Winchester Family Tomb, Narcissus Path, Mount Auburn Cemetery

Whole plate. Hallmark: l.l.: Doublé J. P. International Museum of Photography at George Eastman House. Southworth & Hawes Collection. 74:193:12.

90. W. Read and S. O. Mead Tombs, Ailianthus Path, Mount Auburn Cemetery

Whole Plate. Hallmark: l.l.: Doublé J. P. International Museum of Photography at George Eastman House. Southworth & Hawes Collection. 74:193:82.

91. Unidentified Plots, Mount Auburn Cemetery

Whole plate. Hallmark: l.r.: Doublé J. P. International Museum of Photography at George Eastman House. Southworth & Hawes Collection. 74:193:96.

92. Unidentified Plots, Mount Auburn Cemetery

Whole plate. Hallmark: l.l.: Doublé J. P. International Museum of Photography at George Eastman House. Southworth & Hawes Collection. 74:193:107.

The founding of Mount Auburn Cemetery in 1831 indicated a departure from previous New England attitudes towards death. In practical terms, the increasing urbanization and rising populations made city cemeteries inadequate and an impractical use of land. Large cemeteries outside the city limits became an increasingly common solution and, although Mount Auburn was thought to be radical at its inception, it became the successful model for many subsequent rural cemeteries planned as permanent, park-like settings.

Philosophically, the tranquility of Mount Auburn reflected a desire on the part of New England leaders to replace the fearsome, Puritanical concept of death with a more uplifting Unitarian sentiment. In the words of Reverend Nehemiah Adams, an orthodox Congregational minister in Boston: "If it is possible by natural means to lose the dreadful associations of dissolution in the grave, a burial of someone in the lovely places in Mount Auburn seems sure to assist it. All that meets the eye there above and around the grave is beautiful." The beauty of the site and magnificence of the monuments soon gave the cemetery its nickname: "the garden of graves."

(*continued on page 86*)

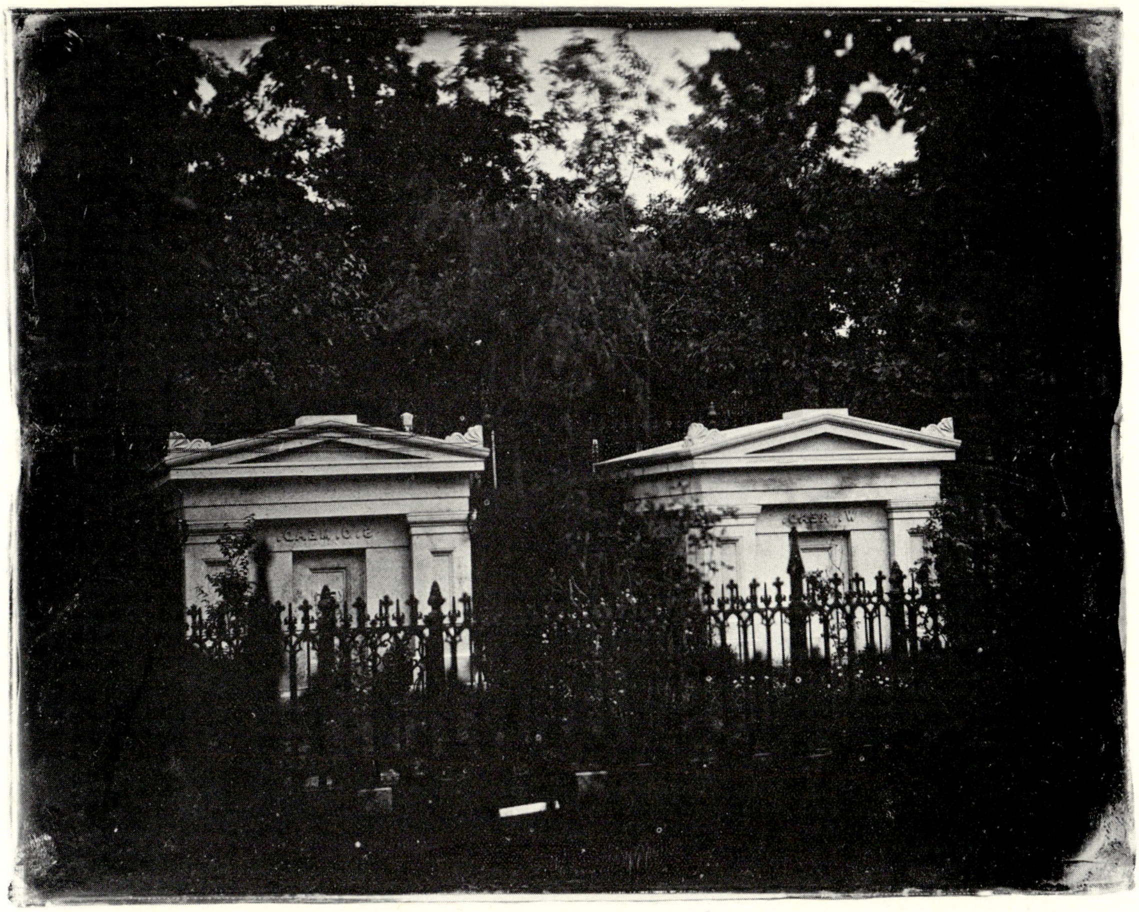

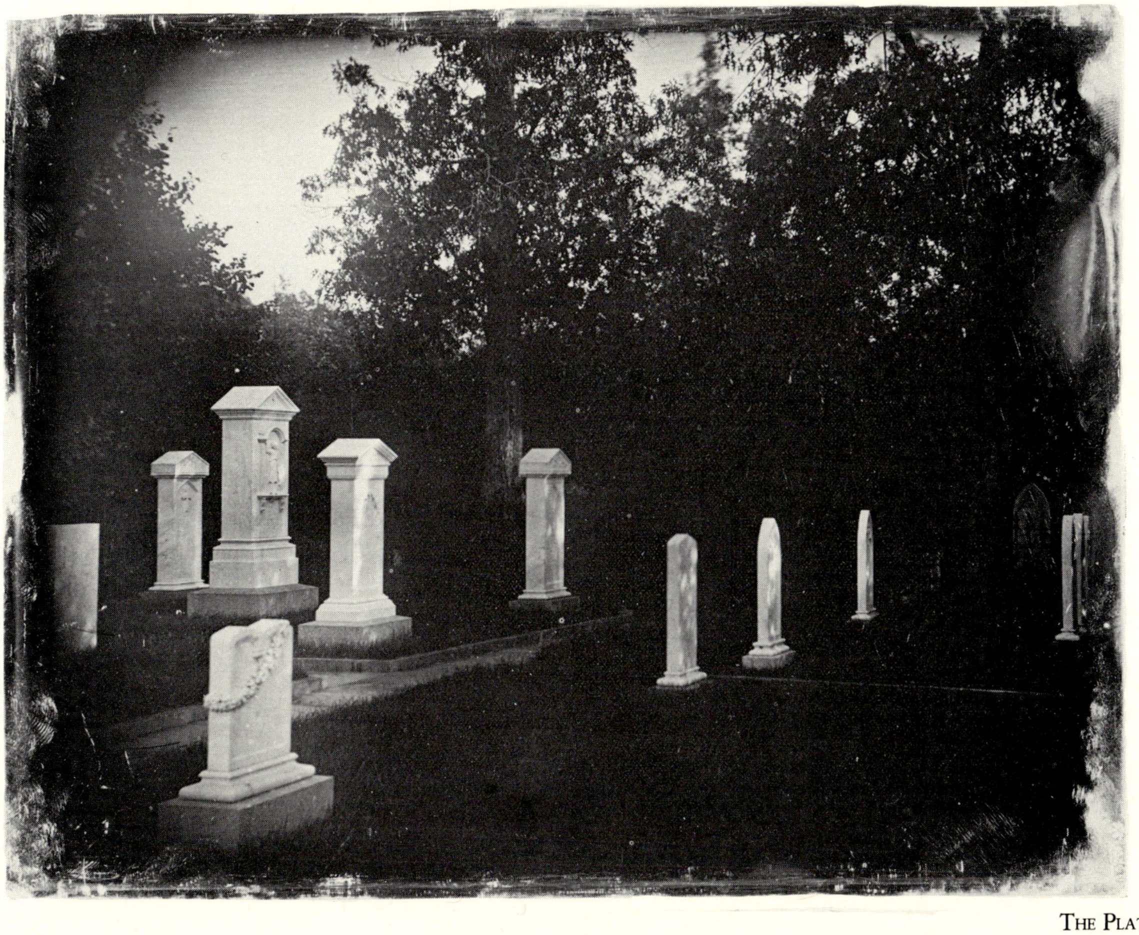

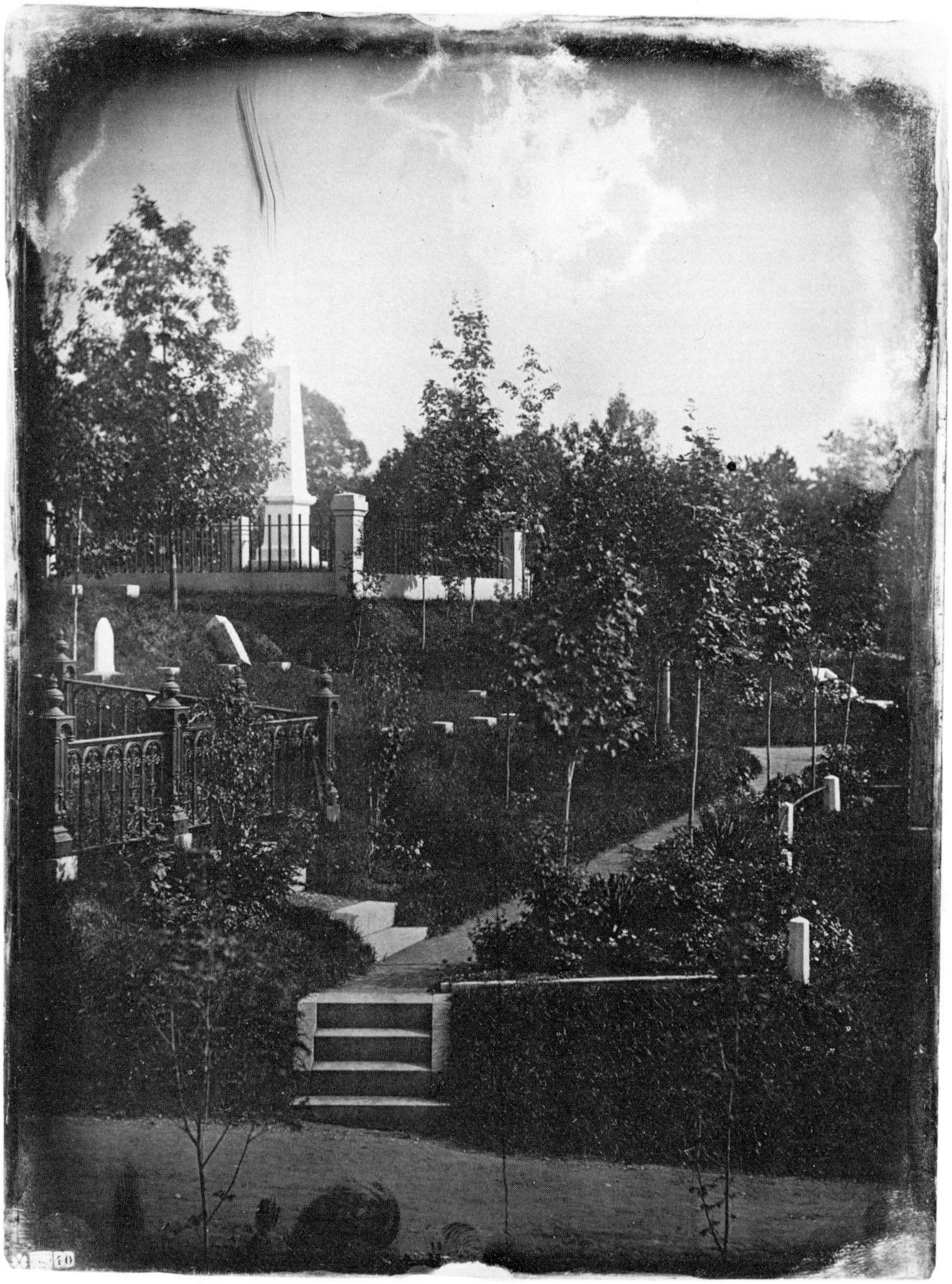

As a favorite rural retreat of Harvard students, "Sweet Auburn" played an integral part in Boston life long before the 107-acre plot was bought by a group of Boston Brahmins in 1825 for preservation. A family plot in Mount Auburn became essential to the proper Bostonian family. The Winchester family tomb, dating around 1850 (cf. Plate 89), shows the trouble some families went through to provide fitting resting places for their beloved ones.

These views of various plots and monuments in Mount Auburn exude gothic mystery, caused in part by the deep shadows and sylvan setting of the architecture. They resemble in feeling certain of Désiré Charnay's views of Mayan ruins done about a decade later and some of the moody, turn-of-the-century photographs by Frederick Evans.

[Adams, Nehemiah. "Mount Auburn," *American Quarterly Observer,* III (July 1834), note 156. Dearborn, Nathaniel. *Dearborn's Guide through Mount Auburn Cemetery,* 1851, passim. *Map of Mount Auburn Cemetery with a Guide to the Trees and Plants.* Brochure available at Mount Auburn Cemetery Offices. Rotundo, Barbara. "Mount Auburn Cemetery: A Proper Bostonian Institution," *Harvard Library Bulletin,* XXII, 3 (July 1974), pp. 268–272.]

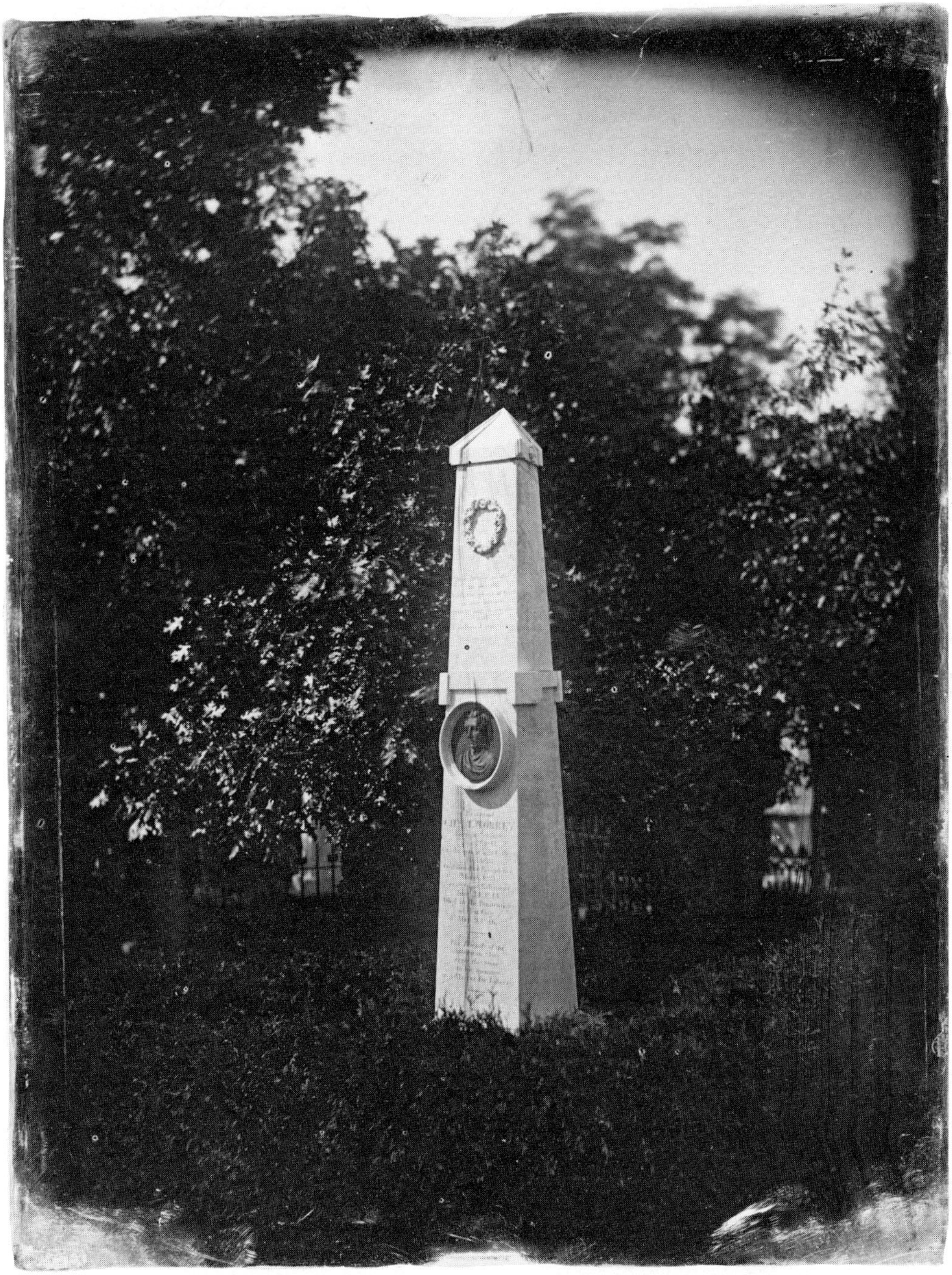

93. "SLAVE MONUMENT" TO CHARLES T. TORREY, MOUNT AUBURN CEMETERY

Whole plate. Hallmark: l.l.: Doublé J.P. International Museum of Photography at George Eastman House. Southworth & Hawes Collection. 74:193:97.

In addition to its role as a rural cemetery and experimental garden, Mount Auburn was designed to "afford the means of paying tribute of respect, by monumental erections, to the name and memory of great and good men, whenever or wherever they have died." The "Slave Monument" was erected by the Friends of the American Slave to honor Reverend Charles T. Torrey (1813–1846), "martyr of liberty." Originally from Scituate, Massachusetts, Torrey was arrested in Baltimore for supporting the anti-slavery movement and died five years later, while in prison. The epitaph on his tomb is taken from a letter he wrote on February 7, 1846:

It is better to die in prison with the peace of God in our breasts than to live in freedom with polluted conscience.

The choice of subjects—Captain Walker, Webster, Stowe, Clay, Emerson, Mann, Everett and the Free-Soilers, who were all actively involved in the anti-slavery movement—appears to indicate that Southworth & Hawes were sympathetic to the cause.

[Bigelow, Jacob. *History of the Cemetery of Mount Auburn.* Boston and Cambridge: James Munroe & Co., 1860, p. 142. Foxcroft, Frank. "Mount Auburn," *New England Magazine,* vol. XIV, 4 (June 1896), p. 426. Green, Martin. *The Problem of Boston: Some Readings in Cultural History.* New York: W. W. Norton & Co., 1966, pp. 41, 46, 74.]

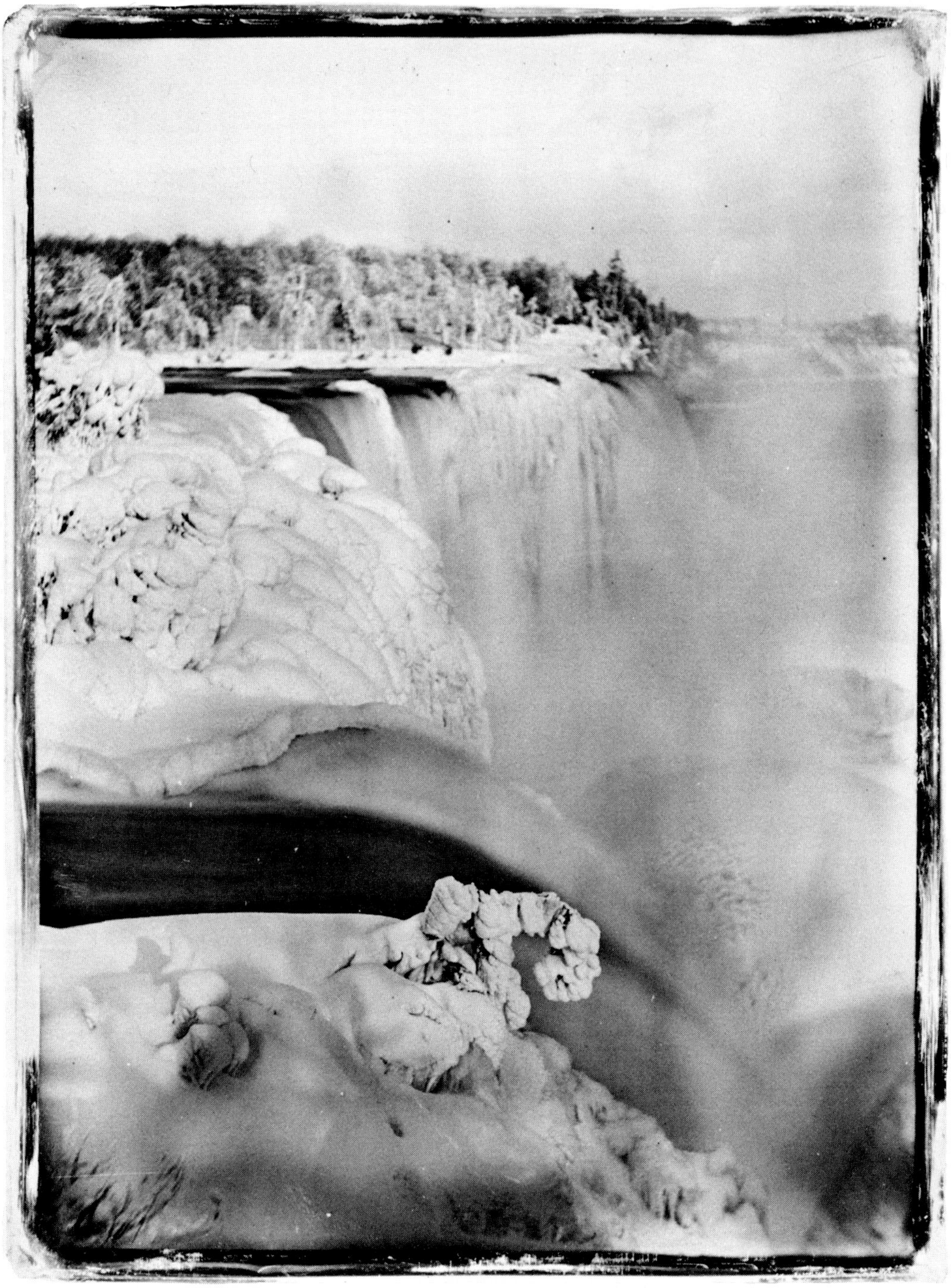

94. Niagara Falls

Whole plate. Hallmark: none. International Museum of Photography at George Eastman House. Southworth & Hawes Collection. 74:193:262a.

95. Niagara Falls

Whole plate. Hallmark: none. Metropolitan Museum of Art. Gift of I. N. Phelps Stokes and the Hawes family. 37.14.7.

Whether Southworth and/or Hawes ever went to Niagara is uncertain, but the provenance and stylistic evidence of these two winter scenes of the falls, including the two following views of the Roebling bridge, support Southworth & Hawes's authorship. The business affiliation between Platt D. Babbitt of Niagara and Southworth & Hawes with regard to the sale and distribution of the Grand Parlor Stereoscope possibly points to Babbitt as the author. However, no similar treatment of landscape photography exists in Babbitt's known work which is based on broader and panoramic backdrop landscape scenes with tourist figures. Southworth & Hawes have used these images of the brilliant winter forms around the falls to invest a natural scene with a monumental presence approaching the most sublime of romantic visions. Years later, the British photographer John Werge wrote: "No picture of language can possibly convey a just conception of the grandeur and vastness of these mighty cataracts. No poem has ever suggested a shadow of their majesty and sublimity." These images come close to depicting just these qualities.

[Werge, John. *The Evolution of Photography.* London: Piper & Carter, 1890, p. 150.]

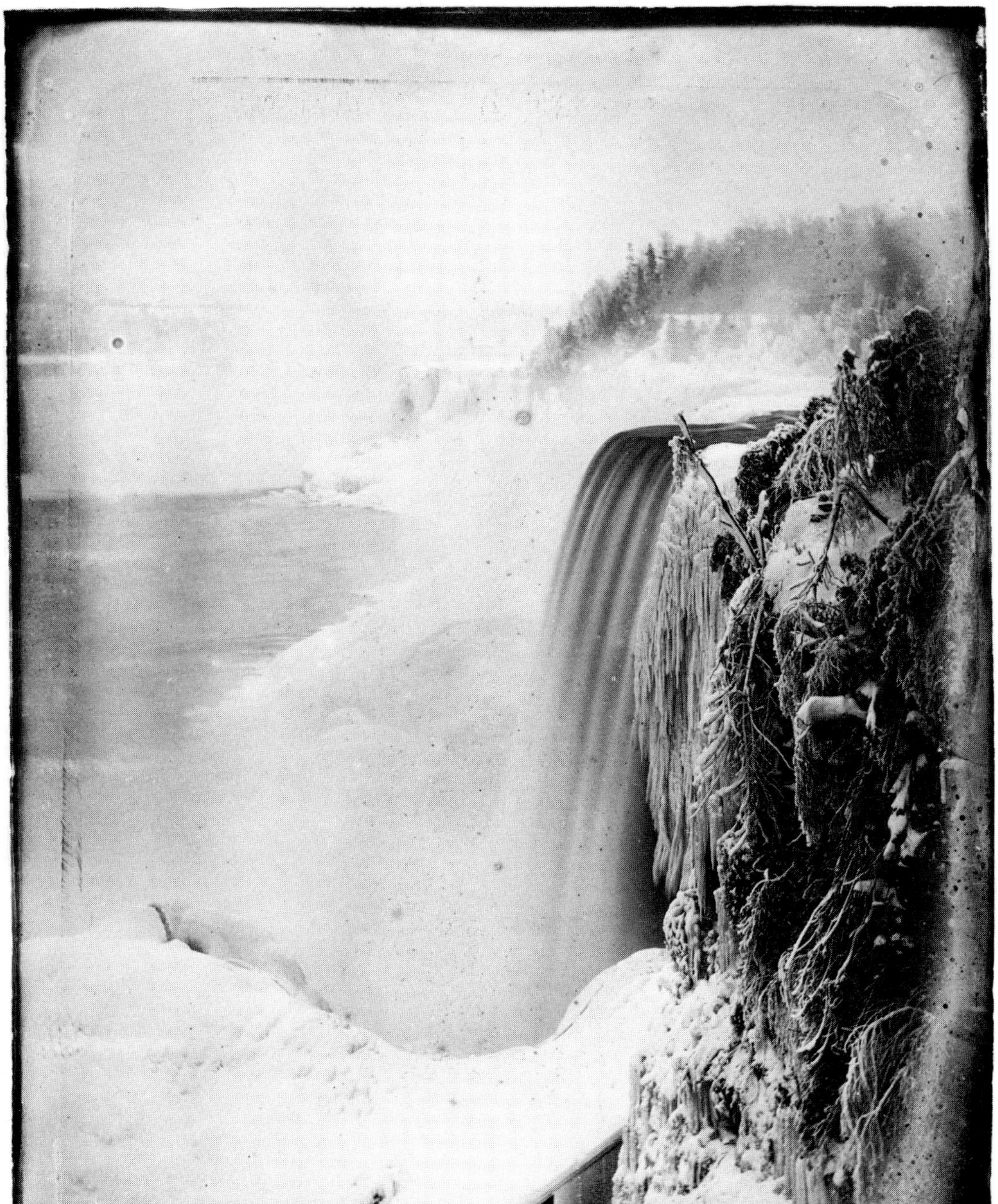

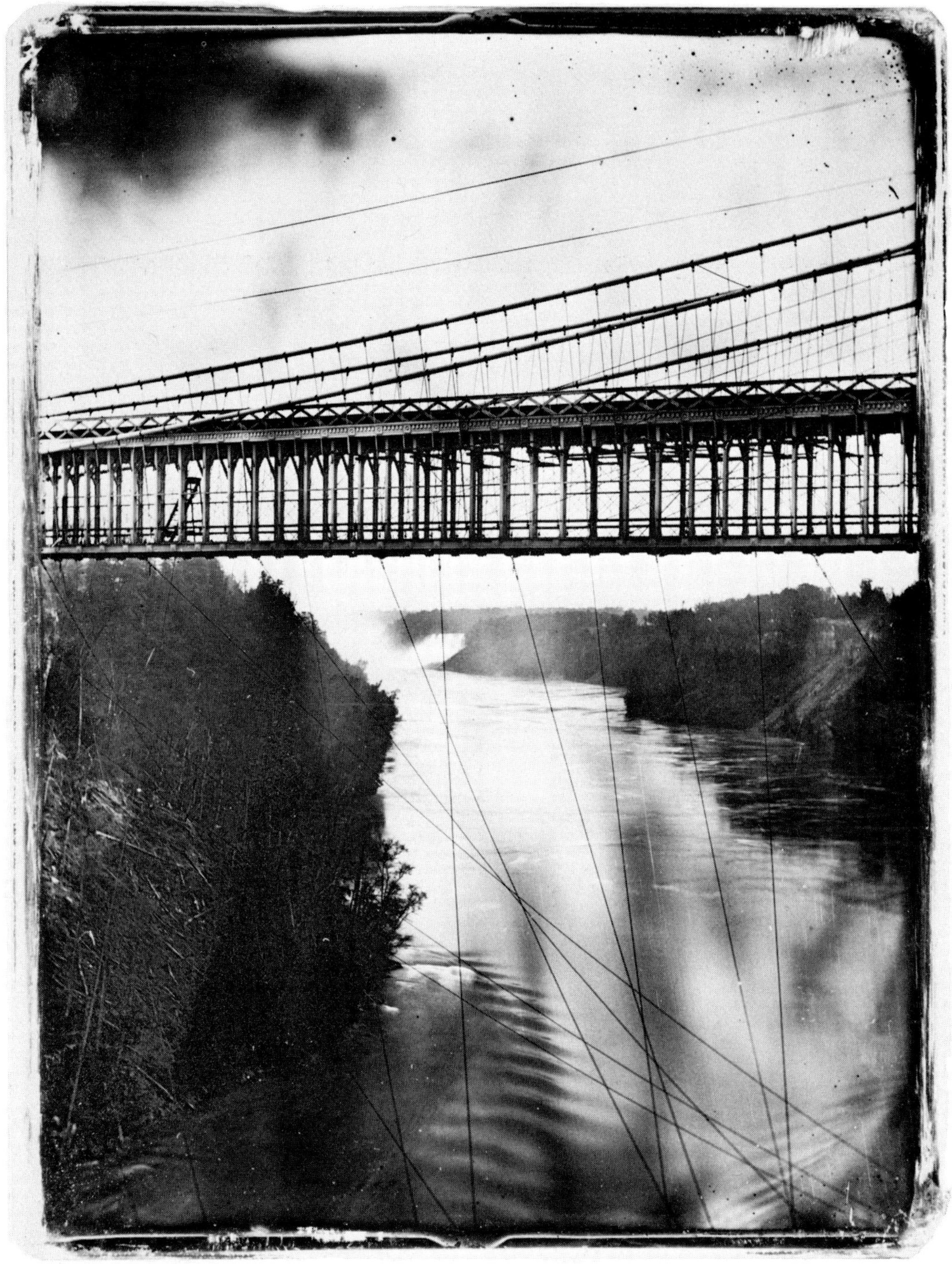

96. THE NIAGARA SUSPENSION BRIDGE

Date: c. 1856. Whole plate. Hallmark: u.r.: N° 40. International Museum of Photography at George Eastman House. Southworth & Hawes Collection. 74:193:257a.

Completed in March of 1855, the Niagara Suspension Bridge was described in an 1857 guide book as "the greatest artificial curiosity in America." The bridge was designed by John Augustus Roebling (1806–1869) who is better known for his Brooklyn Bridge. A vital commercial link between the expanding Canadian and American railways, Roebling's bridge established the cable suspension as the principal form of bridge construction until the end of the century.

The Niagara Bridge, with its delicate traceries of stays and guy wires, is dramatically silhouetted against the sky, above and in front of nature's wilderness extending into the far distance. Throughout the late 19th century, this engineering feat captivated both photographers and artists. Southworth & Hawes included this view in their Grand Parlor Stereoscope where the deep perspective of the view was sure to impress the spectator. John Werge in 1854, William England in 1859, and Charles Bierstadt in the early 1870s, all positively reacted to this scene, yet none produced an image as simple and yet visually complex as Southworth & Hawes's.

[Greenhill, Ralph and Thomas D. Mahoney. *Niagara.* Toronto: University of Toronto Press, 1969, pp. 61–64. Steinman, D. B. *The Builders of the Bridge: The Story of John Roebling and His Son.* New York: Harcourt & Brace, 1945, pp. 157–193. Werge, John. *The Evolution of Photography.* London: Piper & Carter, 1890, pp. 152–154.]

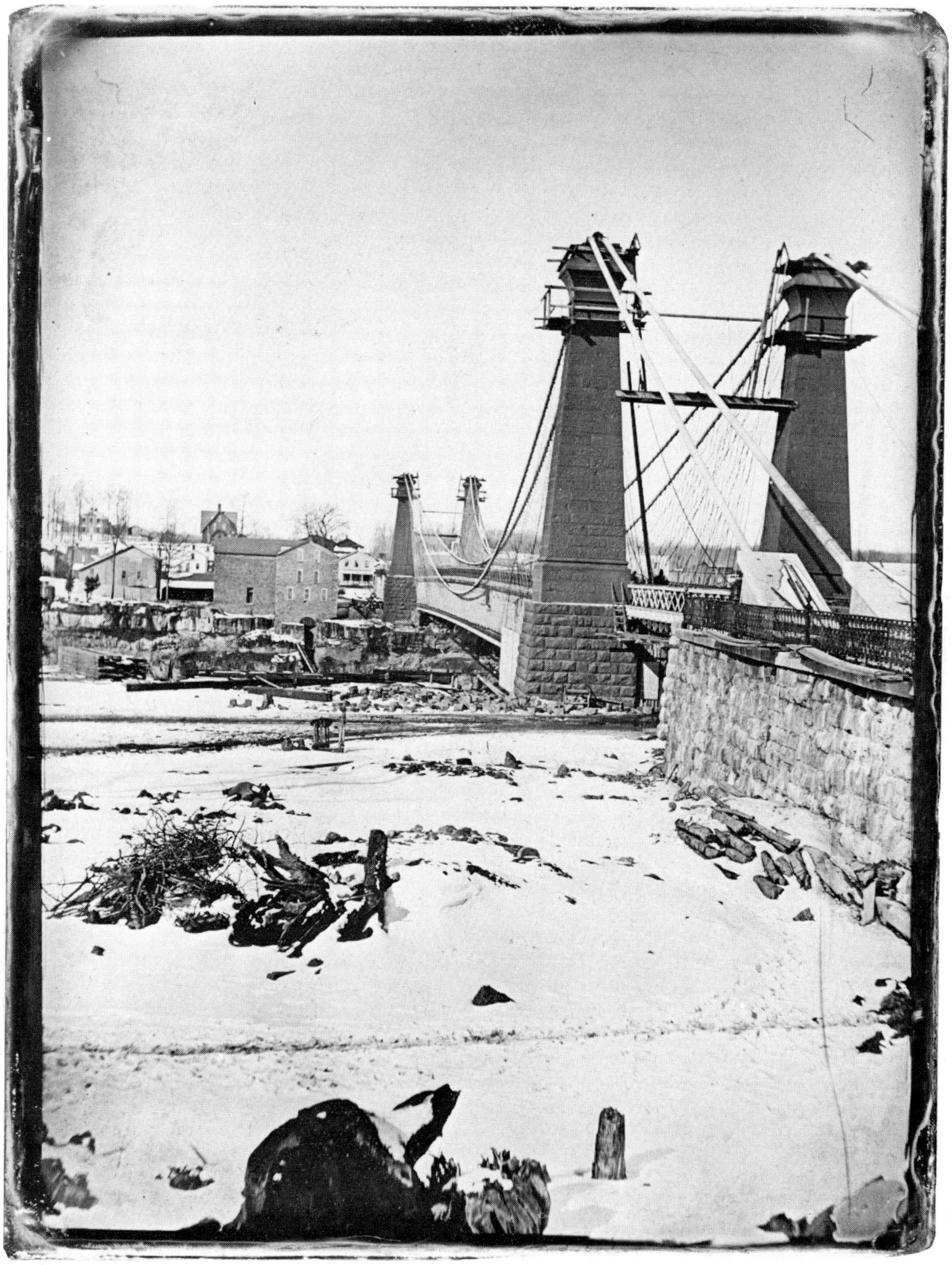

97. The Niagara Suspension Bridge

Whole plate. Hallmark: u.r.: N° 40. International Museum of Photography at George Eastman House. Southworth & Hawes Collection. 74:193:180.

Photographed shortly before the opening of the bridge on March 8, 1855, this view concentrates on the famous "Egyptian" towers at both ends of Roebling's structure. Still in place is the scaffolding set up to allow workmen access to the capitals in order to add the decorative scalloping so prominent in later views. The eccentric composition helps accentuate the virtual deep space necessary if the image is to be used in the stereoscope. A similar emphasis on foreground detritus is also seen in Southworth & Hawes's view of McKay's shipyard (cf. Plate 88).

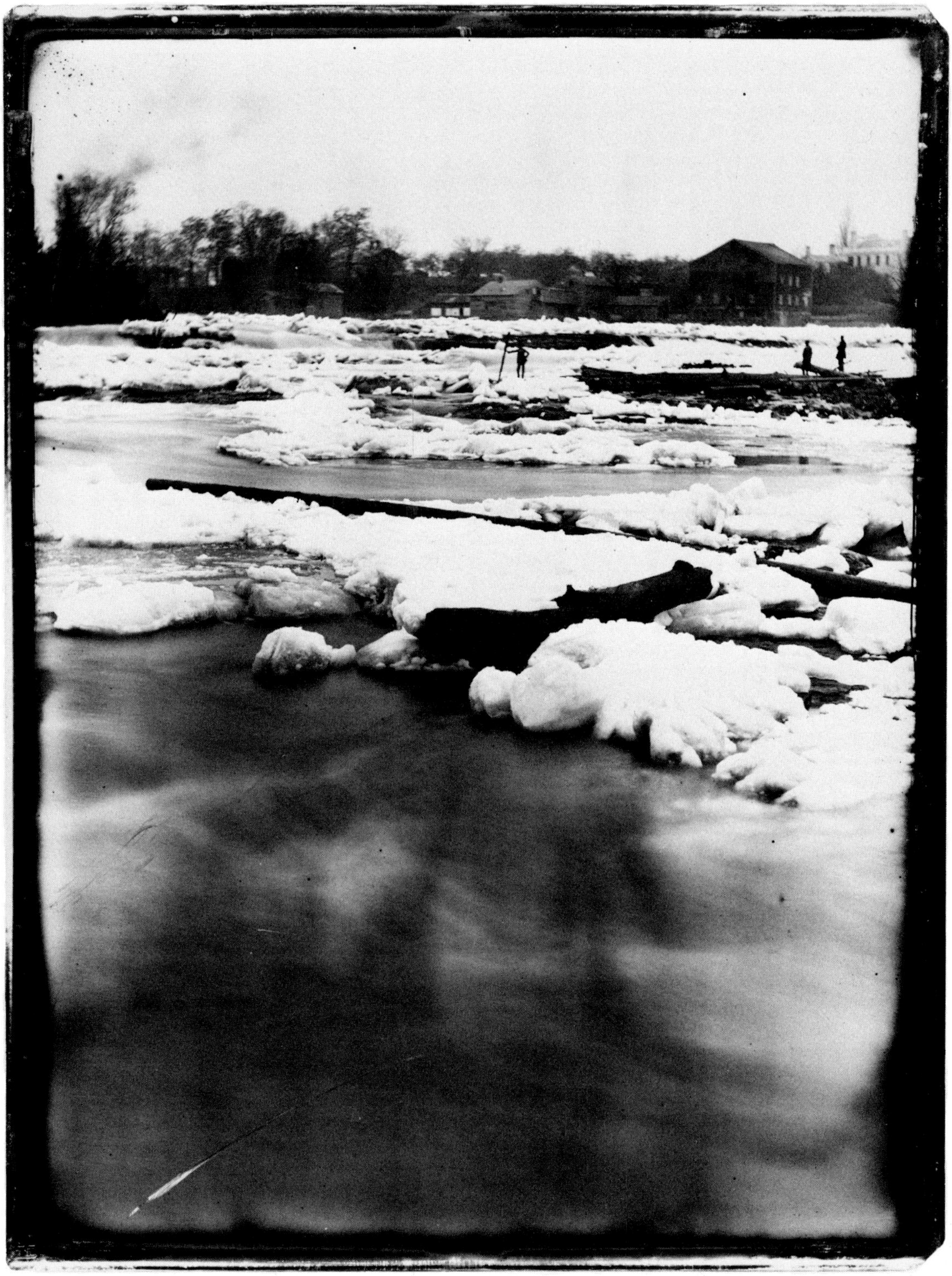

98. Unidentified River View

Whole plate. Hallmark: l.l.: N° 40. International Museum of Photography at George Eastman House. Southworth & Hawes Collection. 74:193:255a.

99. Unidentified Flood View

Whole plate. Hallmark: u.r.: N° 40. International Museum of Photography at George Eastman House. Southworth & Hawes Collection. 74:193:260b.

These two spectacular but unidentified landscapes display many of the same qualities as the previous four views. They share the vertical format, the long empty foreground with the high horizon line and the somewhat off-centered point of interest. Rarely found in other daguerreotype landscape views, many of these features may have been required for stereoscopic exaggeration in the Grand Parlor Stereoscope. The scene of the snow and ice-covered river is possibly that of Niagara Falls (cf. Plates 94, 95). What seems to be a flood scene has not as yet been identified.

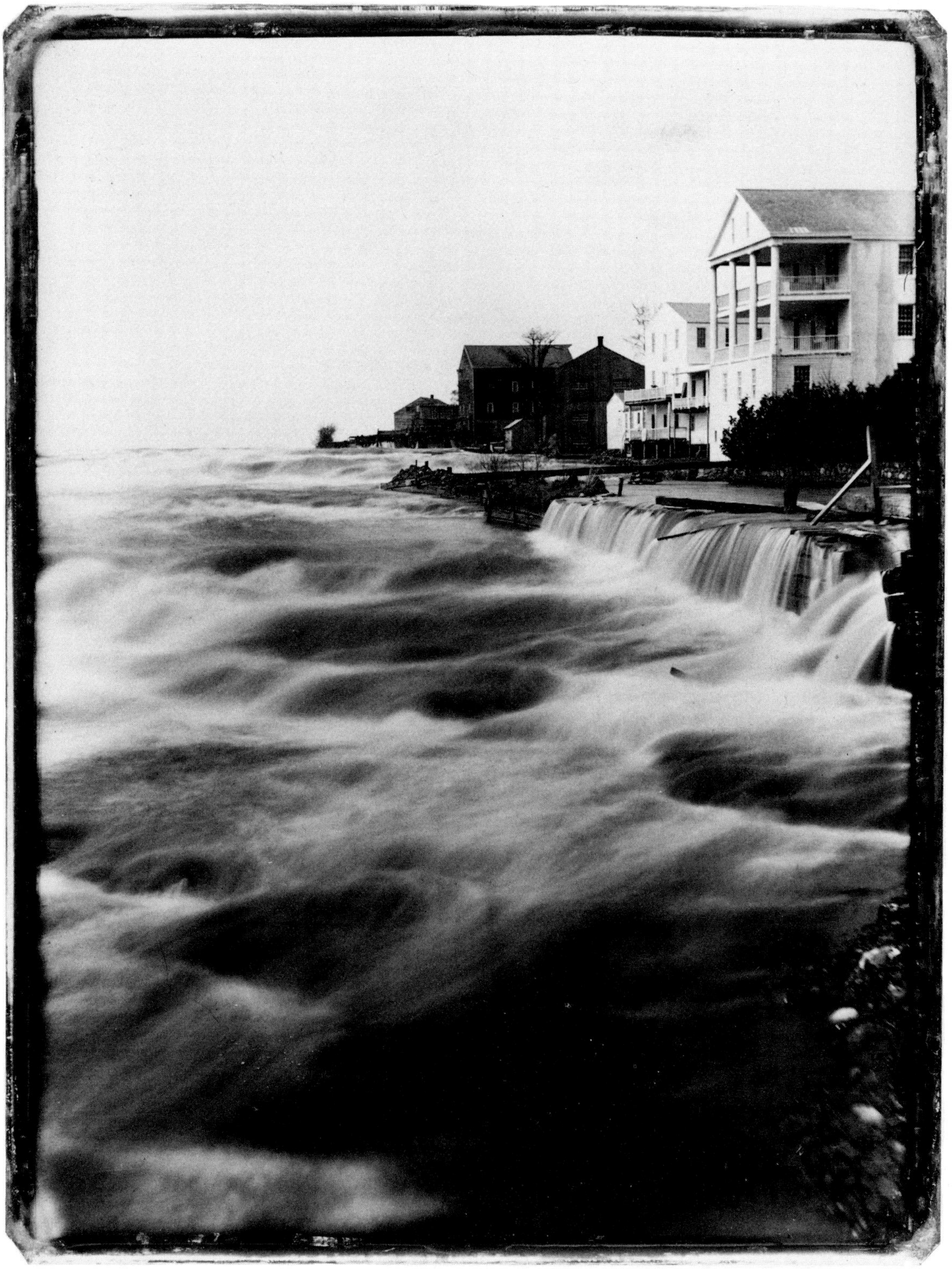

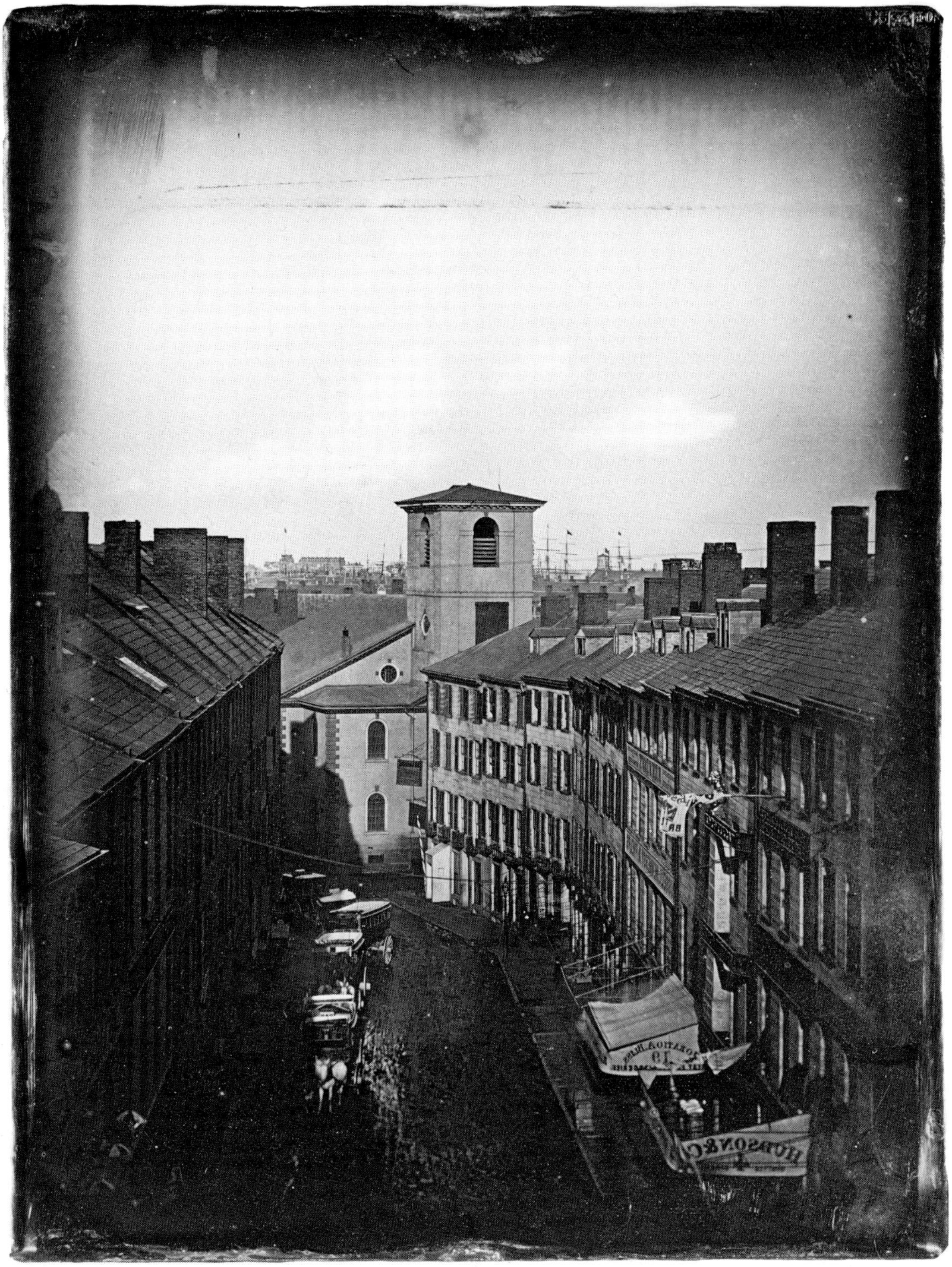

100. Brattle Street, Boston

Date: c. 1852. Whole plate. Hallmark: u.r.: Doublé J. P. Museum of Fine Arts, Boston. Gift of W. G. Russell Allen. 54.714.

The Tremont Row studio of Southworth & Hawes, overlooking the harbor of Boston, commanded a fine view of Brattle Street which was one of the city's main thoroughfares. When the funeral of Abbott Lawrence was held in the old Brattle Street Church in 1852, the slow moving funeral procession enabled the partners to capture the street scene below despite the relatively lengthy exposure. Earlier, many photographers had attempted views from the windows of their studios (Niépce in 1826 and Daguerre in 1838), but Southworth & Hawes are among the first to capture a time sequence by taking three exposures of the cortege as it progressed down Brattle Street. Only one of the other exposures is known to have survived and is now in the collection of the Metropolitan Museum of Art (37.14.3).

[Newhall, Beaumont. ''First American Masters of the Camera,'' *Art News Annual,* vol. XLVI, 9 (November 1947), p. 169.]

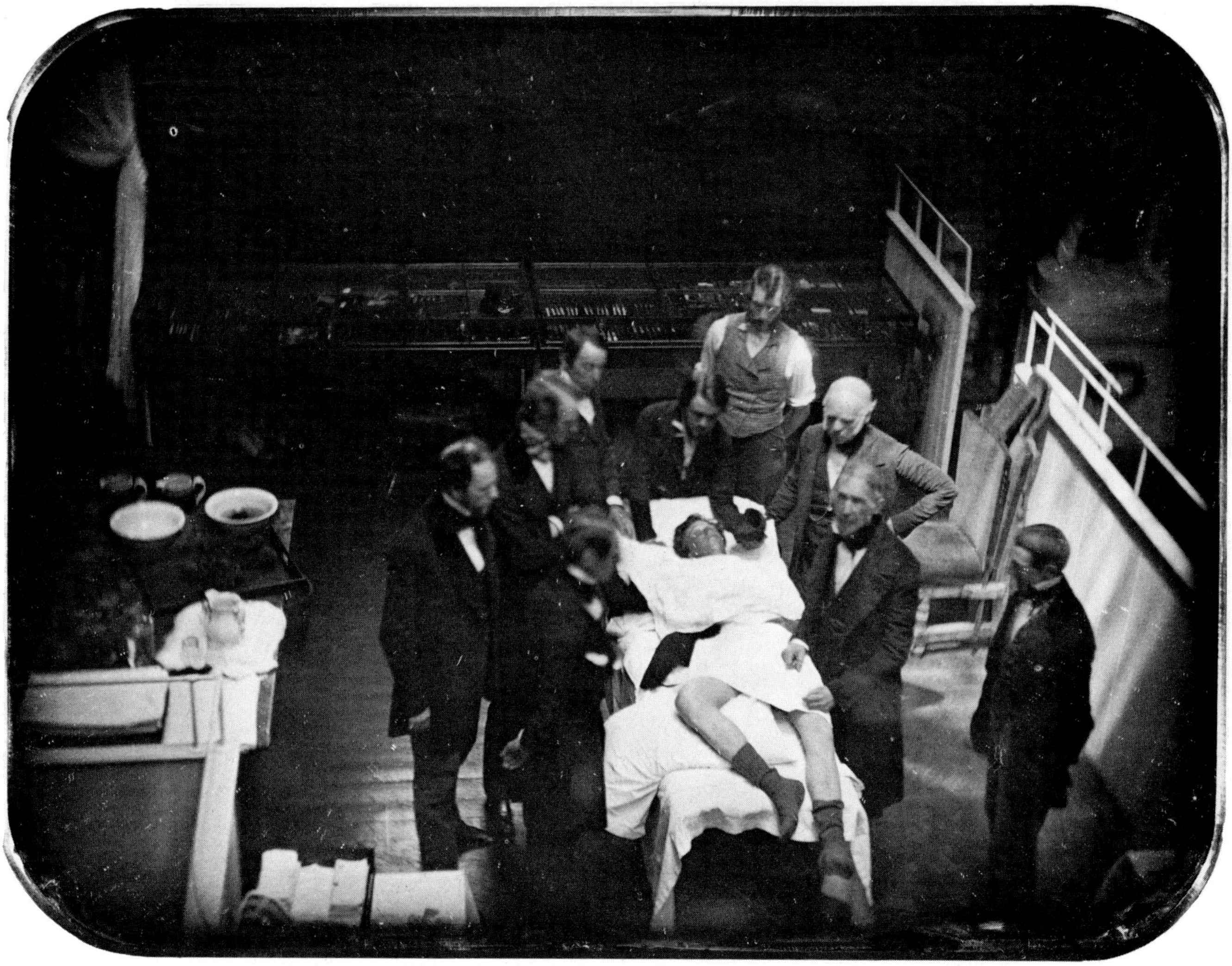

101. Operating Room of the Massachusetts General Hospital

Date: c. 1847–1848. Whole plate. Hallmark: inaccessible. Collection of Arnold H. Crane, Chicago, Illinois.

Remarkable for both its vantage point and subject matter, this interior view records an early operation with the aid of etherization, a technique labelled in its time as the "Death of Pain." The discovery of ether is credited to Dr. W. T. G. Morton (whose presence in this image is uncertain), who then received permission from Dr. John C. Warren (eighth from left) to use the anesthetic on Gilbert Abbott, a patient suffering from a tumor on his jaw. A daguerreotype image of a re-enactment of this first operation exists in the collection of the Massachusetts General Hospital Archives, and shows a male patient seated in a chair, a seemingly more appropriate position for an operation on the jaw. The physician behind him holds forward a vessel of ether. In the plate shown here, the doctor administering the ether uses an opened sponge, a technique not employed prior to February 1847. The authorship of the image showing the man seated in a chair is uncertain.

The Massachusetts General Hospital Archives also contain two further, full-plate depictions of ether-assisted operations. One is nearly identical to the plate shown here, with only slight variations of the doctors' poses, indicating clearly that it was made at the same session as the one illustrated here. A second daguerreotype shows a similar operation, but with a female patient and apparently the same doctors. Both of these daguerreotypes were most likely made by Southworth and Hawes.

The traditional interpretation that this image shows another re-enactment of the first, pioneering operation with ether of October 16, 1846, is not completely established. This image might depict an actual operation, which would account for the presence of displayed accessories at the left.

[Newhall, Beaumont. *The Daguerreotype in America,* pl. 64 caption. *Some Interesting Boston Events.* Printed for the State Street Trust Company, Boston, 1916, facing p. 61.]

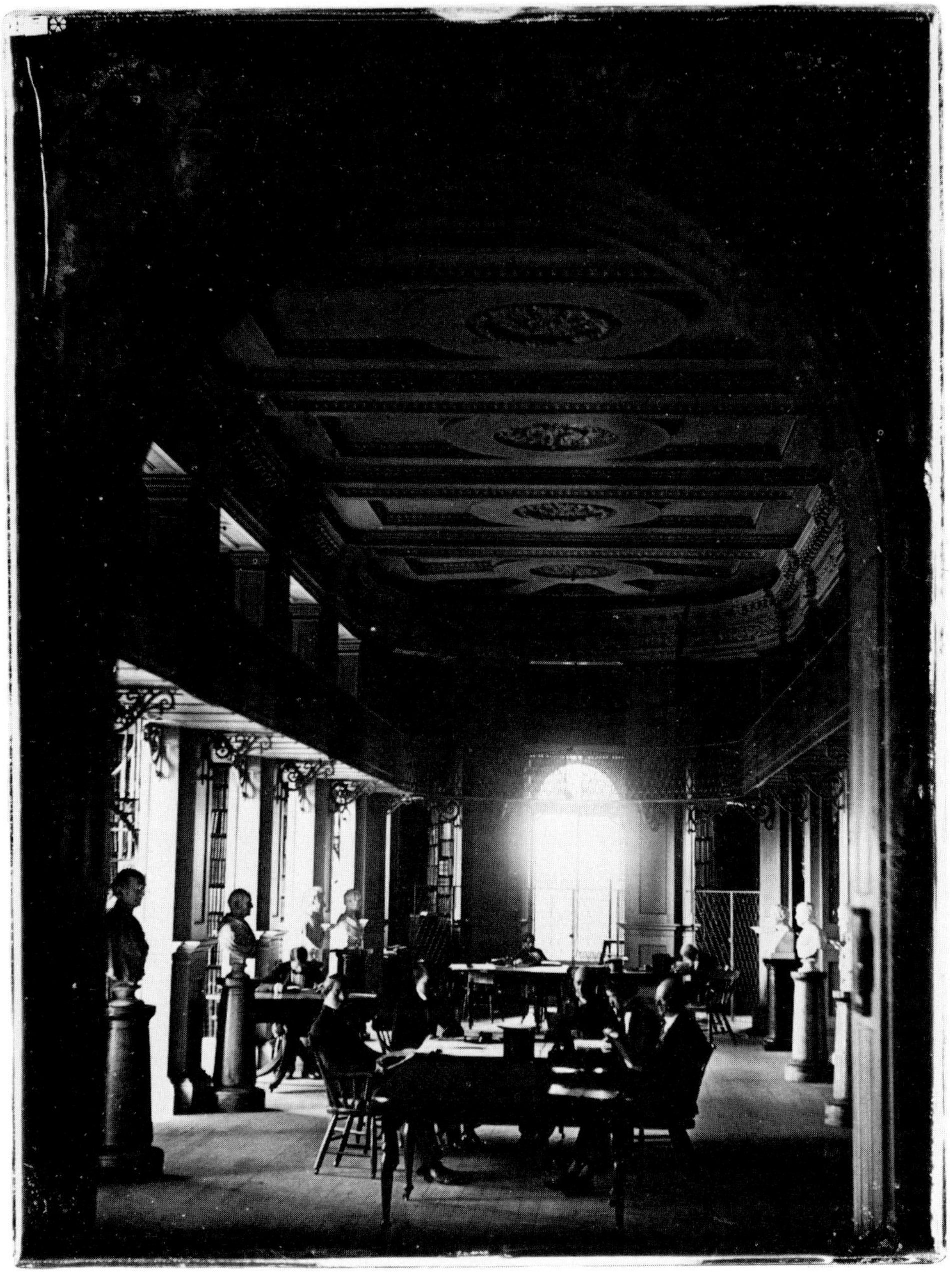

102a & 102b. Boston Athenaeum

Whole plate, stereo pair. Hallmark: a) u.l.: Doublé J. P., b) l.r.: Double J. P. International Museum of Photography at George Eastman House. Southworth & Hawes Collection. 74:193:1130a and 74:193:1130b.

Founded as a proprietary library in 1807, the Boston Athenaeum was designed in 1847 by Edward Clarke Cabot. The three stories contained a large reading room, a sculpture gallery and a series of picture galleries. Since its art collections which filled these galleries during Southworth & Hawes's times were transferred to the Museum of Fine Arts when it was founded in 1876, the Athenaeum has been solely a library. It has maintained its original address at 10½ Beacon Street, but two additional stories were built in 1913.

This stereographic pair of the second floor reading room of the Athenaeum is one of only a few extant whole plate interiors by Southworth & Hawes (cf. Plates 78, 101). In both plates each figure is in a nearly identical position except for the figure reading at the right rear table who had apparently moved during one exposure. An ultimate achievement in combining the mechanical and the artistic of their craft, the Grand Parlor Stereoscope won Southworth & Hawes a gold medal in 1853 and was highly praised in 1856 for its innovations when it was displayed.

> An entirely new method is adopted for taking the stereoscopic pictures, to which their beauty mainly is due. . . . In addition to this improvement in the pictures themselves, a new method of bringing them into the field of vision and withdrawing them therefrom has been devised. Heretofore this has been performed by hand, but, in the present case, it is done by the simple turning of a crank. The pictures are made to appear in pairs in the proper order, and after remaining a certain length of time in view, are withdrawn and replaced by others. The mechanism by which this is accomplished is as simple as it is effective.

The reference to the "entirely new method" for taking stereoscopic pictures is unclear, but it may be the sliding plate-holder Southworth patented two years later which took "stereoscopic pictures upon the same or different plates with

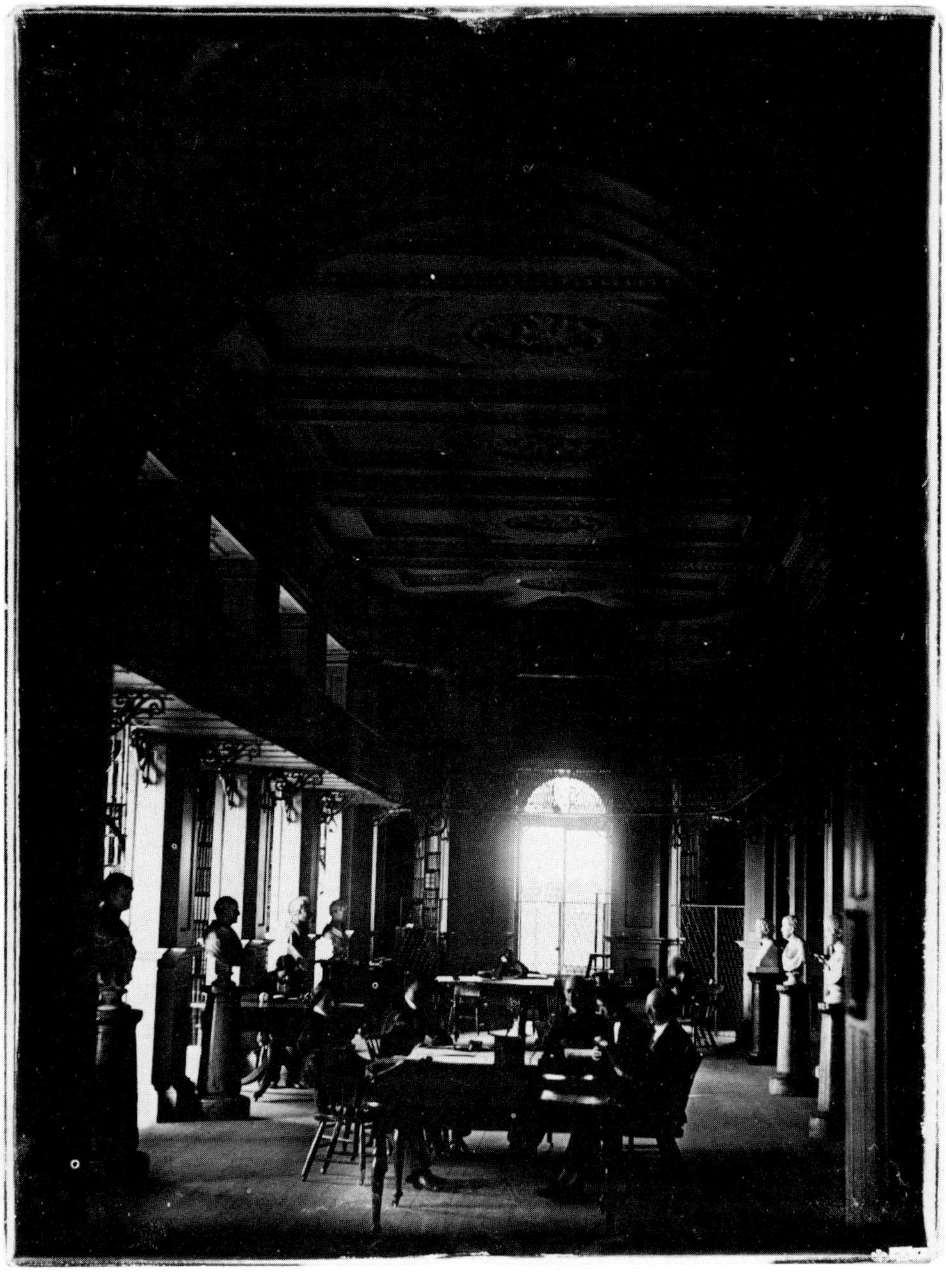

one camera . . . in rapid succession.''

Many of Southworth & Hawes's whole-plate daguerreotypes of portraits, statuary, landscapes and views were made expressly for the Grand Parlor Stereoscope which failed to become popular because of its large size and high costs (see Introduction, p. xiv).

[Judges Report. Machinery and New Inventions. Seventh Fair and Exhibition for Premiums of the Massachusetts Charitable Mechanics Association, Boston, 1853, typescript, S&H, IMP/GEH. Patent Specifications, for U.S. Patent No. 12,700, dated 10 April 1855, U.S. Patent Office, Washington, D.C. and entitled ''Daguerreotype Camera Attachment.'' Whitehill, Walter M. and Katherine Knowles. *Boston: Portrait of a City.* Barre, Mass.: Barre Publishing Co., 1966, p. 36.]

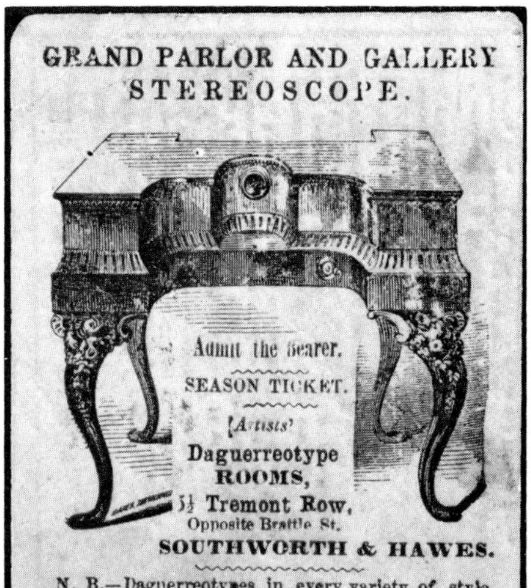

RIGHT: Season Ticket to Southworth & Hawes Studio for viewing of the Grand Parlor and Gallery Stereoscope, April 1854. Southworth & Hawes Collection, IMP/GEH.

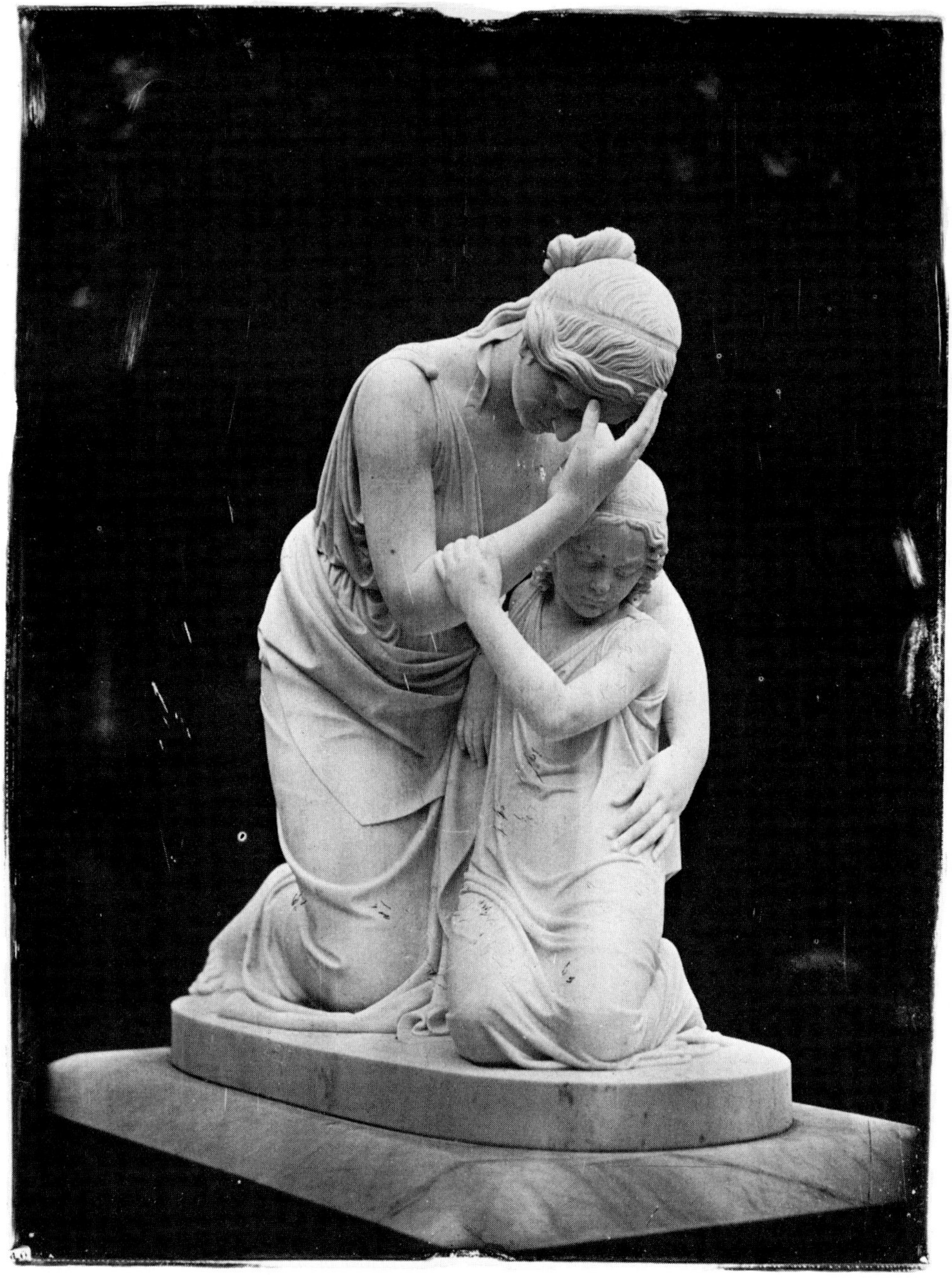

103. FUNERARY MONUMENT BY MARGARET FOLEY,
MAGOUN PLOT, FIR AVENUE,
MOUNT AUBURN CEMETERY

Whole plate. Hallmark: l.l.: 40; l.r.: star. International Museum of Photography at George Eastman House. Southworth & Hawes Collection. 74:193:253b.

Planned from the start to be enhanced by "works of taste," the bucolic setting of Mount Auburn Cemetery became a veritable sculpture garden which provided a rich source of commissions for local artists. Among them was Margaret E. Foley (?–1877), a native of Vermont best known for her cameo designs. Introduced to monumental sculpture during a visit to Rome in 1853, Foley settled in Boston and executed several large works, including this funerary monument inspired by the poem inscribed on the Magoun Tomb:

A household's tomb, to Faith how dear!
A part have gone; part linger here;
United all in love and hope,
One household still!

Together we shall sleep,
Together we may rise,
And sing our morning hymn,
One household still!

This public monument was photographed by Southworth & Hawes and installed as a stereographic pair in the Grand Parlor Stereoscope in their Tremont Street Studio.

[(Anonymous.) *Guide through Mount Auburn: A Handbook for Passengers over the Cambridge Railroad.* Boston: Russell & Richardson, 1873, p. 46. Fielding, Mantle. *Dictionary of American Painters, Sculptors and Engravers.* New York: Carr, 1965. Scharf, Frederic A. "The Garden Cemetery and American Sculpture: Mount Auburn," *Art Quarterly,* vol. XXIV (Spring 1961), p. 85.]

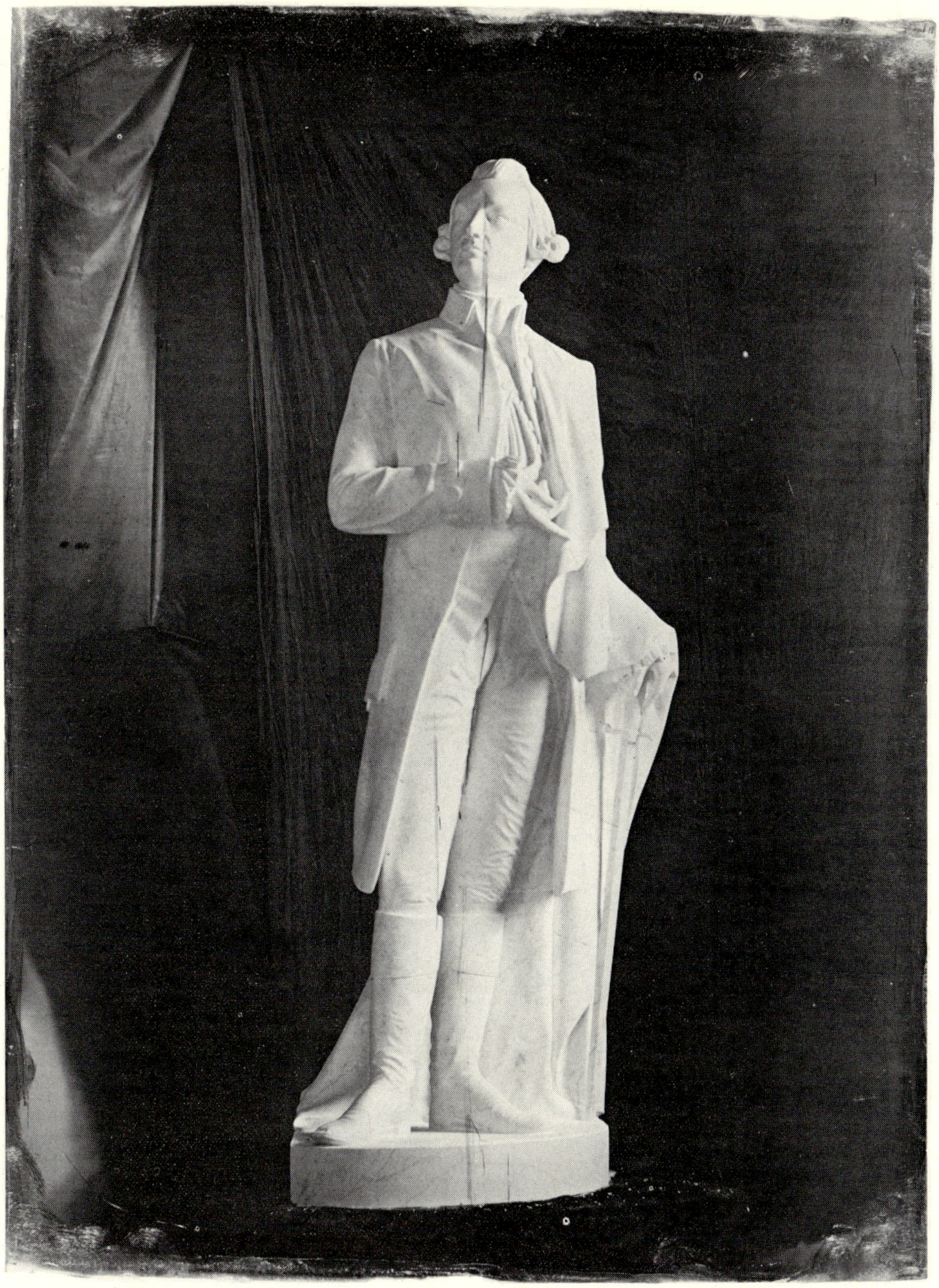

104. "GENERAL JOSEPH WARREN"
BY HENRY DEXTER,
STATUE IN BUNKER HILL MONUMENT

Date: 1851. Whole plate. Hallmark: l.l.: Doublé J. P. International Museum of Photography at George Eastman House. Southworth & Hawes Collection. 74:193:3.

The Bunker Hill Monument Association, on its 75th anniversary in 1850, voted to procure a statue of Dr. Joseph Warren (1741–1775) who had been killed while serving as a volunteer at Bunker Hill, although he had been elected a major general by the Provincial Congress. In the early 1850s, Henry Dexter was commissioned to execute a life-size marble statue of Warren. The finished work was unveiled on June 17, 1857.

Exposed before the statue was installed in the Bunker Hill Monument, this whole plate of General Warren is one of a pair of stereo daguerreotypes for the Grand Parlor Stereoscope. The numerous versions of the same statue in various collections indicate that the sculpture was one of the most popular pieces the partners daguerreotyped. A few of these versions show the statue and background laterally reversed.

[Whitehill, Walter Muir. *Boston Statues.* Barre, Massachusetts: Barre Publishers, 1970, p. 90.]

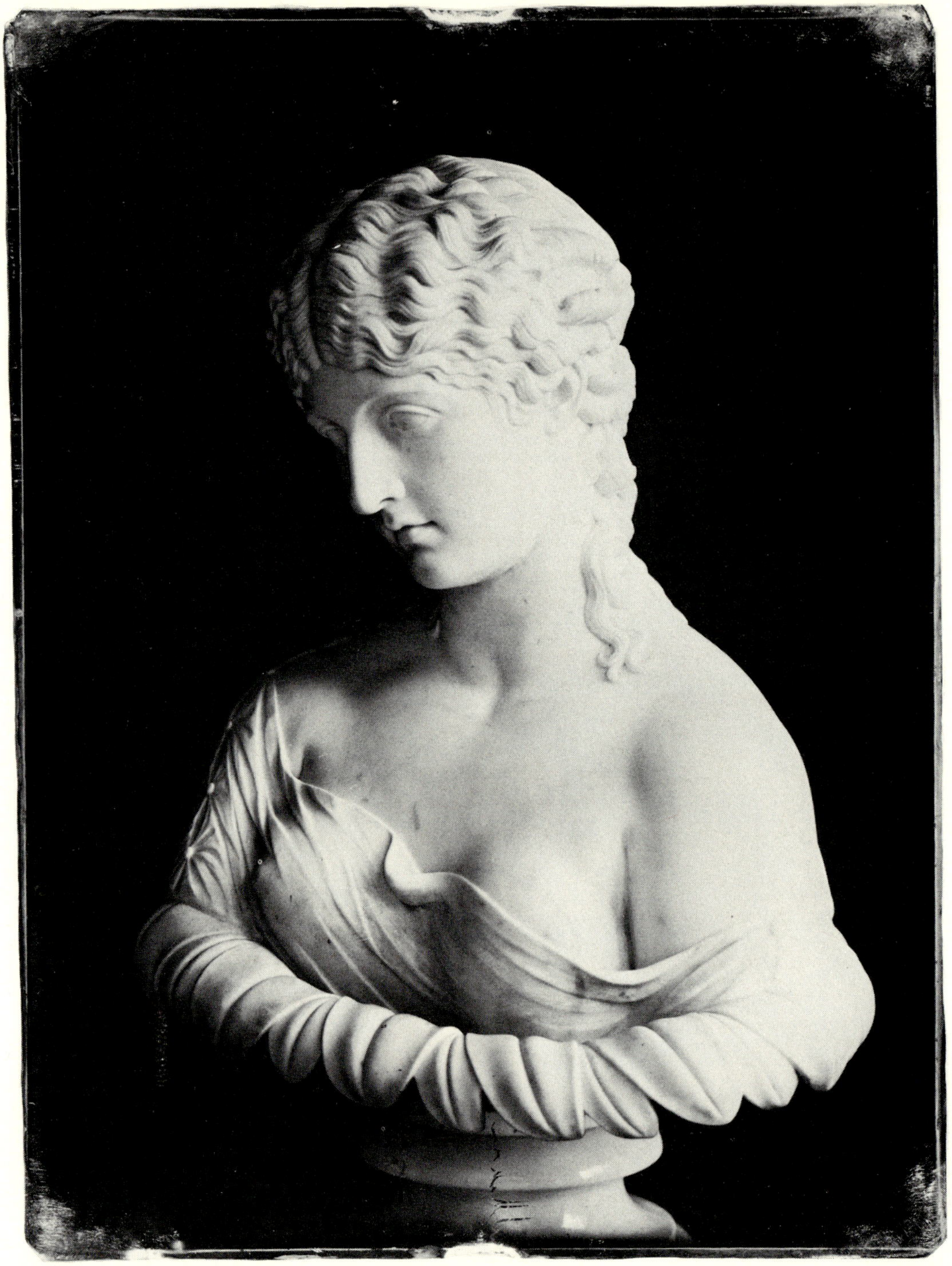

105. "CLYTIE," ANONYMOUS COPY OF ANTIQUE, SCULPTED BUST

Whole plate. Hallmark: u.l.: Garanti in rectangle. International Museum of Photography at George Eastman House. Southworth & Hawes Collection. 74:193:10.

Identified as "Clytie" on the reverse of the plate, this daguerreotype represents a popular form of mid-19th-century American neoclassical sculpture, the "ideal bust." Usually issued in limited editions, sometimes numbering over a hundred, the busts were available to the collector in either life-size or half life-size. Southworth & Hawes devoted the same care and attention to the lighting and viewing angle of this marble bust of Apollo's lover as to their living subjects.

[Gerdts, William H. *American Neo-Classic Sculpture: The Marble Resurrection.* New York: Viking Press, 1973, pp. 92–93.]

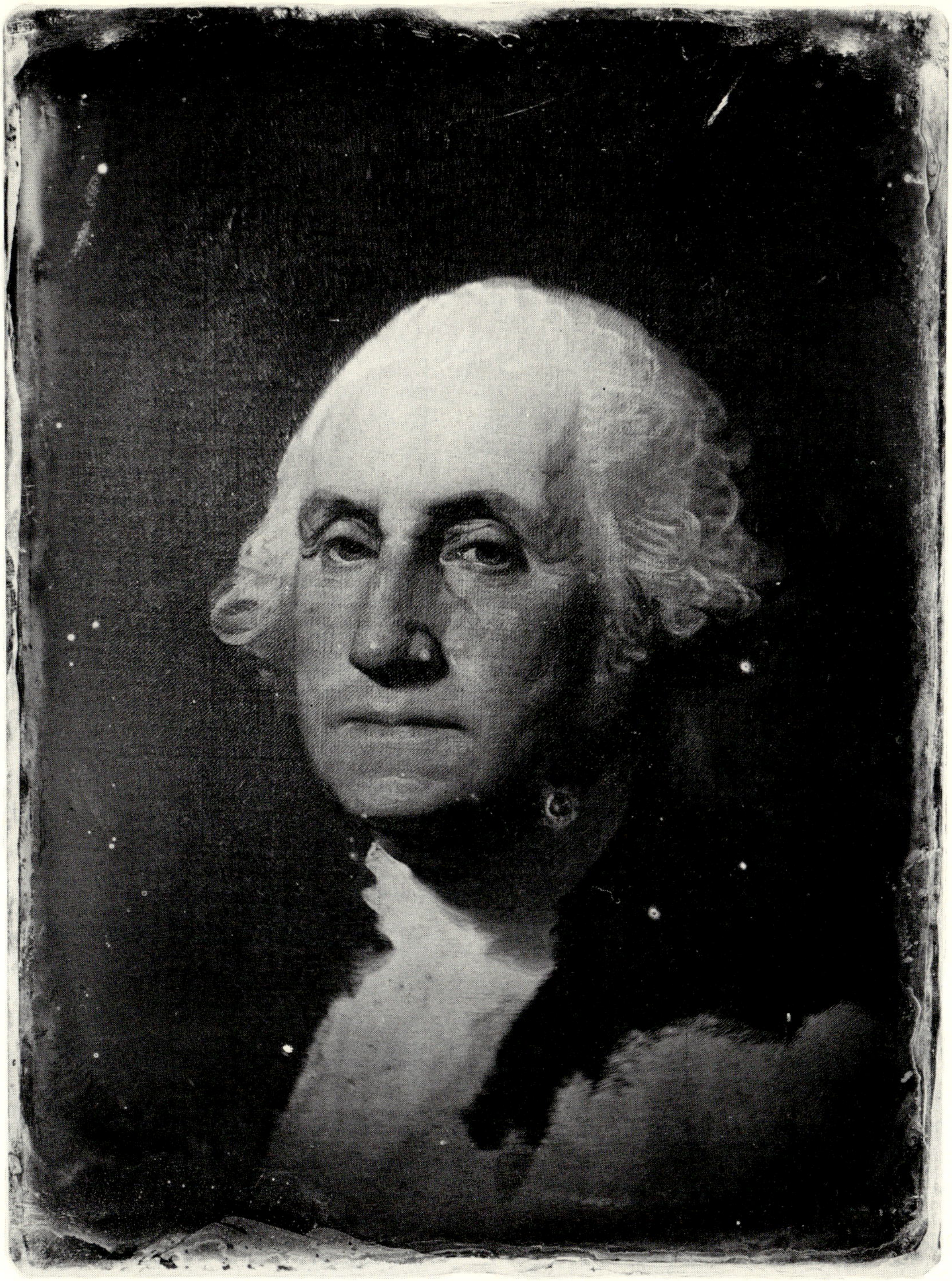

106. "George Washington"
by Gilbert Stuart, Painting

Date: 1853. Whole plate. Hallmark: u.l.: B.F. 40. Richard Parker Collection, Marblehead, Massachusetts.

In 1853, when this plate was made, the oil painting which hangs today in Boston's Museum of Fine Arts was part of the Boston Athenaeum collection (cf. Plate 102). Hawes had developed a triplet lens which minimized planar aberrations and was especially effective in copying two-dimensional works such as this painting by Gilbert Stuart or the Washington Allston drawing collection from which John Cheney engraved a portfolio in 1850 (cf. Plate 107).

Coinciding with a rising sense of nationalism, the introduction of the daguerreotype process in America during the mid-19th century led to a popular depiction of great Americans who had come to be regarded as symbols of an ideal national character. George Washington in particular epitomized "the honor, the modesty, the democracy and the loyal sense of duty that Americans saw as the cornerstones of their nation." This sense of veneration is apparent in another whole plate (cf. Plate 57) showing a young girl gazing at the Washington portrait copied here.

[(Hawes, Josiah.) "Stray Leaves from the Diary of the Oldest Professional Photographer in the World," *Photo Era,* XVI (February 1906), pp. 106–107. Rudisill, Richard. *Mirror Image,* pp. 5, 13.]

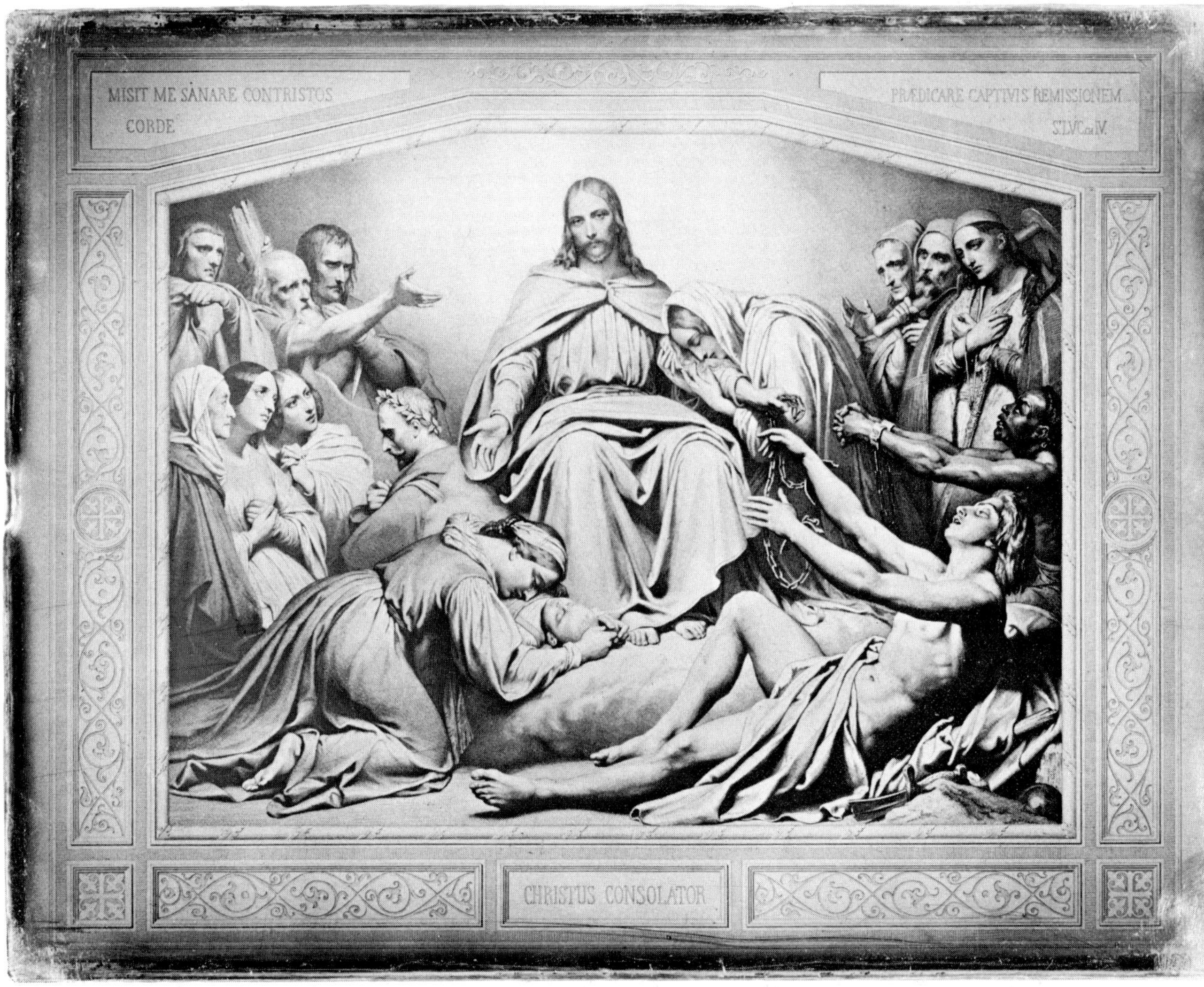

107. "CHRISTUS CONSOLATOR"
BY L. P. HENRIQUEL-DUPONT,
ENGRAVING FROM A PAINTING BY ARY SCHEFFER

Whole plate. Hallmark: l.l.: N. B.; u.r.: 30. International Museum of Photography at George Eastman House. Southworth & Hawes Collection. 74:193:27.

This copy of a 19th-century engraving, similar to the daguerreotype copy plates Josiah Hawes made for Cheney's 1850 portfolio of Washington Allston sketches, may have also been intended for reproduction. The preface to the portfolio reads: "Where it was necessary to reduce them [Allston's drawings] for engraving, the daguerreotype was used, by which the image was conveyed to the engraver's plates, prepared for that purpose, and there fixed by tracing the line through the silver."

[Cheney, J. and L. W. *Outlines and Sketches by Washington Allston.* Boston: Stephen H. Perkins, 1850, unpaginated.]

APPENDICES

FRANÇOIS GOURAUD'S
LECTURE AND MANUAL

SOUTHWORTH & HAWES
PLATES AND HALLMARKS

APPENDIX A

FRANÇOIS GOURAUD'S LECTURE AND MANUAL

Delivered in New York, Boston and Providence, Gouraud's lecture on the daguerreotype was the first concrete introduction of photography to America. Despite its sketchiness, the lecture not only provided a set of practical instructions on how to make daguerreotypes but also included a demonstration and an exhibit of finished daguerreotypes. Although a unique historical event in retrospect, the lecture was not an isolated instance but one of many public lectures given in Boston as part of a greater movement toward public education. The younger generation of 1840 witnessed an unprecedented plethora of lectures each season: "New England soon acquired the lecture-habit, the fruit of Edward Everett's enterprise [Plate 4]. . . . There were constant courses in every town and village . . . and almost every eminent man in New England joined in the general effort to propagate knowledge." The subjects covered in these lectures ranged from Greek antiquities to chemistry, from philosophy to botany. "As many as five hundred at a time learned that acids were not alkalis and that Homer did not write the *Iliad.* It was quite the rage. The boys invited the girls, and after the lecture they walked home together, ending the evening with an oyster-supper." In March of 1840, among the spellbound audience of Gouraud's lecture, two went home to begin new careers in photography—Albert Sands Southworth and Josiah Johnson Hawes.

[Brooks, Van Wyck. *The Flowering of New England.* New York: E. P. Dutton, 1936, pp. 179–181.]

DESCRIPTION

OF THE

DAGUERREOTYPE PROCESS,

OR

A SUMMARY

OF

M. GOURAUD'S PUBLIC LECTURES,

ACCORDING TO THE PRINCIPLES OF

M. DAGUERRE.

WITH A

DESCRIPTION OF A PROVISORY METHOD FOR TAKING

HUMAN PORTRAITS.

BOSTON:

DUTTON AND WENTWORTH'S PRINT.

1840.

PRELIMINARIES.

Contents.

THE APPARATUS.

A Daguerreotype Apparatus must be composed of the following objects:—the camera obscura, with its lens—the Iodine box, with its wooden dish—the substance box—mercury box, with its grooved board—a moveable camera sash, with its plate board—the plate box—the travelling box—two rinsing pans—a washing pan, with a cork at the corner—a phial containing olive oil—some very finely carded cotton—some impalpable pumice powder, tripoli, or other polishing substance, tied up in a bag of muslin, sufficiently thin to allow the powder to pass through when the bag is shaken—a phial of nitric acid, at 40 degrees, diluted with water, in the proportion of one liquor glass to sixteen of the same of distilled water—a small furnace—one spirit lamp—a phial of mercury—four metallic bands or cramps, the same substance as the plate—six wooden wedges—one glass funnel—a phial of Iodine—a bottle of hyposulphate of soda—a tea kettle—a vessel for distilled water—a little box of nails—a pair of iron pincers—a candlestick—chemical matches.

NOTICE:—*Each part of the apparatus afforded by M. F. Gouraud, bears an indication of its application; and as* PERFECTION AND CLEARNESS *in the* DESIGN *depend only on the* MATHEMATICAL EXACTNESS *of the apparatus, as in the extreme* PURITY *of the chemical substances employed in the process, each apparatus* PREVIOUSLY EXAMINED *and* TRIED *by M. Gouraud, bears his signature and seal as a guarantee of its perfection.*

PREAMBLE.

I.

The Daguerreotype, designs are executed upon thin plates of silver, plated on copper. The silver must be the purest that can be procured. As to the copper, its thickness ought to be the 24th number of the wire gage of brass manufacturers, and the proportion of silver, that must cover its surface, the 20th of it in weight. If the plates were not *faithfully* prepared by the manufacturers, according to the principle requisite for the Daguerreotype process, it is impossible to hope for any good success.

II.

The photogenic process is divided into five operations.

1. The first consists in polishing and cleaning the plate, in order to prepare it for receiving the sensitive coating, upon which the light traces the design.
2. The second is to apply this coating.
3. The third is the placing the prepared plate properly in the camera obscura, to the action of light, for the purpose of receiving the image of nature.
4. The fourth brings out this image, which at first is not visible on the plate being withdrawn from the camera obscura.
5. The fifth and last operation has for its object to remove the sensitive coating on which the design is first impressed, because this coating would continue to be affected by the rays of light, a property which would necessarily and quickly destroy the picture.

4

FIRST OPERATION.

Preparing the Plate.

The requisites for this operation are:
The phial containing olive oil.
Some of the finely carded cotton.
A small quantity of the polishing powder.
The phial of diluted nitric acid.
The furnace with charcoal.
A dozen at least of ordinary sheets of paper.

As already stated, these photographic delineations are executed upon silver plated on copper. The size of the plate will depend, of course, on the dimensions of the camera. We must begin by polishing it carefully. To accomplish this, the surface of the silver is powdered all over with the polishing substance, by shaking the bag without touching the plate.

Next, with some cotton dipped in a little olive oil, the operator rubs the plate gently, rounding his strokes, all over its surface. During this operation, the plate must be laid flat upon several folds of paper, care being taken to renew these from time to time, that the tablet be not twisted from any inequality in the support.

The polishing substance must be renewed and the cotton changed several times. It will be readily apprehended of what importance it is to attend to these directions, since upon the high polish of the silver depends in a great measure the beauty of the future design. When the plate is well polished, it must next be cleaned by powdering it all over once more with pumice, and rubbing with dry cotton, always rounding and crossing the strokes, for it is impossible to obtain a good surface by any other motion of the hand. A little pledget of cotton is now rolled up and moistened with the diluted acid already mentioned, by applying the cotton to the mouth of the phial and inverting it, pressing gently, so that the centre only of the cotton may be wetted and but slightly, care being taken not to allow any acid to touch the fingers. The surface of the plate is now rubbed *equally* all over with the acid applied by the pledget of cotton. Change the cotton and keep rubbing, rounding as before, that the acid may be equally spread, yet in so small a quantity as just to skim the surface, so to speak. If, as frequently happens, the acid run into small drops from the high polish, change the cotton repeatedly and break down the globules as quickly as possible,

5

but always by gently rubbing, for if allowed to rest or to run upon the plate, they will leave stains. It will be seen when the acid has been properly diffused, from the appearance of a thin veil spread regularly over the whole surface of the plate. Once more powder over pumice, and clean it with fresh cotton, rubbing as before, but very slightly.

The plate is now to be subjected to a strong heat. It is placed upon the furnace, the silver upwards, during at least five minutes, the operator holding it with a pair of long and strong pincers, and moving it at the same time, till all is equally heated. The plate is then to be cooled *suddenly*, by placing it on a cold substance, such as a mass of metal or stone, or best of all, a marble table. When perfectly cold, it is to be again polished, an operation speedily performed, since its gummy appearance merely has to be removed, which is done by the dry pumice and cotton repeated several times, changing the cotton frequently. The polishing being thus completed, the operation of the acid is to be repeated three different times, dry pumice being powdered over the plate each time, and polished off very gently with the cotton, which must be very clean, care being taken not to breathe upon the plate or to touch it with the fingers, or even with the cotton upon which the fingers have rested, for the slightest stain upon the surface will be a defect in the drawing.

When the plate is not intended for immediate use, the last operation of the acid is not performed. This allows any number of plates to be kept prepared up to the last slight operation, and they may be purchased in this state if required. It is, however, indispensable that a last operation by acid as described, be performed on every plate, immediately before it be placed in the camera. Lastly, every particle of dust is removed by gently cleaning the whole edges and back also with cotton, or by simply moving the plate in the air.

SECOND OPERATION.

Coating the Plate.

For this operation we require:
The iodine box.
The small board of the camera sash.
The small metallic bands.
The phial of iodine.

6

The plate is first to be fixed upon the board by means of the metallic bands with their small catches and tacks. The idione is now put into the little wooden dish of the iodine box. It is necessary to divide the iodine into pieces, in order to render the exhalation the more extensively and more equally diffused, otherwise it would form circles in the centre of the plate, which would destroy this essential requisite. The board is now fitted into its position, the plate face downwards, the whole being supported by small brackets projecting from the four corners of the box, which is then closed. In this position the apparatus remains till the vaporization of the idione which is condensed upon the plate, has covered its surface with a fine coating of a yellow gold colour. If this operation be protracted, the gold colour passes into violet, which must be avoided, because in this state the coating is not so sensitive to the impressions of light. On the contrary, if the coating be too pale, the image of nature in the camera will be too faint to produce a good picture. A decided *gold colour*—nothing more—nothing less—is the only assurance that the ground of the future picture is duly prepared. The time for this cannot be determined, because it depends upon several circumstances. Of these the two principal are the temperature of the apartment, and the state of the apparatus. The operation should be left entirely to spontaneous evaporation of the iodine—or at all events, no other heat should be used than what can be applied through the temperature of the room in which the operation takes place. It is also very important that the temperature of the inside of the box be equal to that of the air outside, for otherwise, a deposition of moisture takes place upon the plate, a circumstance most injurious to the final result. Secondly, as respects the state of the apparatus; the oftener it has been used, the less time is required, because in this case, the interior of the box being penetrated with the vapours of iodine, these arise from all sides, condensing thus more equally and more rapidly upon the surface of the plate, a very important advantage. Hence it is of consequence to leave always a small quantity of iodine in the cup, and to protect this latter from damp. Hence, likewise, it is obvious that an apparatus of this kind which has been some time in use, is preferable to a new box, for in the former the operation is always more expeditiously performed.

Since from these causes the time cannot be fixed, *a priori*, and may vary from five minutes to half an hour, rarely more, unless the weather be too cold, means must be adopted for examining the plate from

7

time to time. In these examinations it is important not to allow the light to fall directly upon the plate. Also, if it appear that the colour is deeper on one side of the plate than the other, to equalize the coating the board must be replaced, not exactly in its former position, but turned one quarter round at each inspection. In order to accomplish these repeated examinations without injuring the sensibility of the ground or coating, the process must be conducted in a darkened apartment into which the light is admitted side-ways, never from the roof—the door left a little ajar answers best. When the operator would inspect the plate, he raises the lid of the box, and lifting the board with both hands, turns up the plate quickly, and very little light suffices to shew him the true colour of the coating. If too pale, the plate must be instantly replaced, till it attains the proper gold tone; but if this tint be passed, the coating is useless, and the operations must be repeated from the commencement of the first.

From description this operation may perhaps seem difficult, but with a little practice one comes to know pretty nearly the precise interval necessary to produce the true tone of colour, and also to inspect the plate with great rapidity, so as not to allow time for the light to act.

When the coating has reached the proper tone of yellow, the plate with the board to which it is fixed, is slipped into the camera sash, and thus adjusted at once in the camera obscura. In this transference care must be taken to protect the plate from the light; a taper should be used, and even with this precaution, the operation ought to be performed as quickly as possible, for a taper will leave traces of its action if continued for any length of time.

We pass now to the third operation, that of the camera. If possible the one should *immediately* succeed the other, the longest interval between the second and third ought not to exceed an hour. Beyond this space the action of the iodine and silver no longer possesses the requisite photogenic properties.

Observanda.—Before making use of the box, the operator should clean it thoroughly, turning it bottom upwards, in order to empty it of all the particles of iodine which may have escaped from the cup, avoiding at the same time touching the iodine with the fingers. During the operation of coating, the cup ought to be covered with a piece of gauze stretched on a ring. The gauze regulates the evaporation of the iodine, and also prevents the compression of the air on the lid being shut from scattering the particles of iodine, some of which reaching the

8

plate, would leave large stains on the coating. For the same reason the top should always be let down with the greatest gentleness, not to raise the dust in the inside, the particles of which being charged with the vapour of the iodine, would certainly reach and damage the plate.

THIRD OPERATION.

The Camera.

The apparatus required in this operation, is limited to the camera obscura.

This third operation is that in which by means of light, acting through the camera, nature impresses *an image of herself* on the photographic plate, enlightened by the sun, for then the operation is more speedy. It is easy to conceive that this operation, being accomplished only through the agency of light, will be the more rapid in proportion as the objects, whose photographic images are to be delineated, stand exposed to a strong illumination, or in their own nature present bright lines and surfaces.

After having placed the camera in front of the landscape, or facing any other object of which it may be desirable to obtain a representation, the first essential is a perfect adjustment of the focus, that is to say, making your arrangements so as to obtain the outlines of the subject with great neatness. This is accomplished by advancing or withdrawing the frame of the obscured glass which receives the images of natural objects. The adjustment being made with satisfactory precision, the moveable part of the camera is fixed by the proper means, and the obscured glass being withdrawn, its place is supplied by the apparatus, with the plate attached as already described, and the whole secured by small brass screws. The light is of course all this time excluded by the inner doors; these are now opened by means of the two brass semicircles adapted to them, and the plate is disposed ready to receive its proper impressions. It remains only to open the aperture of the camera, and to consult a watch.

This latter is a task of some nicety, because as nothing is visible, and as it is quite impossible to determine the time necessary for producing a design, this depending entirely on the intensity of the light on the objects, the imagery of which is to be reproduced. At Boston, for example, this varies from three to thirty minutes.

9

It is likewise to be remarked, that the seasons, as well as the hour of the day, exert considerable influence on the celerity of the operation. The most favorable time is from seven to three o'clock; and a drawing which, in the months of June and July at Boston, may be taken in three or four minutes, will require five or six in May or August, seven or eight in April and September, and so on in proportion to the progress of the season. These are only general data for very bright or strongly illuminated objects, for it often happens that twenty minutes are necessary in the most favorable months, when the objects are entirely in shadow.

After what has just been said, it will readily occur to the reader that it is impossible to specify with precision the exact length of time necessary to obtain photographic designs; practice is the only sure guide, and with this advantage, one soon comes to appreciate the required time very correctly. The latitude is of course a fixed element in this calculation. In the south of America, for example, and generally in all those countries in which light has great intensity, as Spain, Italy, &c., we can easily understand that these designs must be obtained with greater promptitude than in more northern regions. It is, however, very important not to exceed the time necessary, in different circumstances, for producing a design, because, in that case, the lights in the drawing will not be clear, but will be blackened by a too-prolonged solorization. If, on the contrary, the time has been too short, the sketch will be very vague, and without the proper details.

Supposing that he has failed in a first trial, by withdrawing the tablet too soon, or by leaving it too long exposed, the operator in either case, should commence with another plate immediately; the second trial, being corrected by the first, almost insures success. It is even useful, in order to acquire experience, to make some essays of this kind.

In this stage of the process, it is the same as for the coating; we must hasten to the next operation. When the plate is withdrawn from the camera, it should immediately be subjected to the subsequent process; there ought, at most, not to be a longer interval than an hour between the third and fourth operations; but one is always surest of disengaging the images when no space has been allowed to intervene.

2

10

FOURTH OPERATION.

Mercurial or Disengaging Process.

Here are required :

The phial of mercury, containing at least 16 oz.

The lamp with spirit of wine.

And the mercury box with its grooved flat board.

With a great deal of care the mercury is poured into the cast iron cup at the bottom of the box : the quantity must be sufficient to cover the *bulb* of the thermometer ; afterwards, and throughout the remaining operations, no lights, save a taper, can be used.

The board, with the plate affixed, is now to be withdrawn from the mobile camera sash, and placed rapidly on the grooved board of the mercury box. Immediately, when this is done, the board is then placed within the ledges of the mercury box, at an angle of 45°, the tablet with sketch downwards, so that it can be seen through the semi-circular glass of the upper part; the top of the box is then gently put down, so as not to rise particles of the mercury, and the front glass previously carefully covered up with a piece of any kind of a dark cloth.

When all things are thus disposed, the spirit lamp is lighted, and placed under the cup containing mercury. The operation of the lamp is allowed to continue till the thermometer, the bulb of which is covered by the mercury, indicates a temperature of 65° centigrade (140° F.) The lamp is then immediately withdrawn ; if the thermometer has risen rapidly, it will continue to rise without the aid of the lamp, but this elevation ought not to exceed 75° centigrade (167° F.)

The impress of the image of Nature exists upon the plate, but it is invisible. It is not till after the lapse of several minutes that the faint tracery of objects begins to appear, of which the operator assures himself by looking through the glass, by the light of a taper, using it cautiously that its rays may not fall upon, and injure the nascent images of the sketch. The operation is continued till the thermometer sink to 45° centigrade (113° F.) ; the plate is then withdrawn, and this operation completed.

When the objects have been strongly illuminated, or when the action in the camera has been continued rather too long, it happens that this fourth operation is completed before the thermometer has fallen even to 65° centigrade (131° F.) One may always know this, however, by observing the sketch through the glass of the mercury box.

11

It is necessary after each operation to clean the inside of the apparatus carefully, to remove the slight coating of mercury adhering to it. When the apparatus has to be packed for the purpose of removal, the mercury is withdrawn by the small brass cock, inclining the vessel to that side.

One may now examine the sketch by a *feeble light*, in order to be certain that the processes hitherto have succeeded. The plate is now detached from the board, and the little bands of metal which held it there are carefully cleaned with pumice and water after each experiment, a precaution rendered necessary from the coating both of iodine and mercury which they have acquired. The plate is now deposited in the grooved plate box, until it undergoes the fifth and last operation. This may be deferred if not convenient ; for the sketch may now be kept for months in its present state without alteration, provided it be not too frequently inspected by the full daylight.

FIFTH OPERATION.

Fixing the Impression.

The object of this final process is to remove from the tablet the coating of iodine, which continuing to decompose by light would otherwise speedily destroy the design when too long exposed. For this operation the requisites are—

A saturated solution of common salt, or a weak solution of pure hyposulphite of soda—one measure whatever of *crystalized* hyposulphite, upon 14 of the same measure of distilled water.

The tin washing pans.

The vessel of distilled water.

In order to remove the coating of iodine, when the operator could not afford hyposulphite of soda, common salt is put into a bottle with a wide mouth, which is filled one fourth with salt and three-fourths with pure water. To dissolve the salt, shake the bottle, and when the whole forms a saturated solution, filter through paper. This solution is prepared in large quantities before-hand, and kept in corked bottles.

Into one of the square troughs pour the solution, filling it to the height of an inch ; into the other, pour in like manner your water. The solution of hyposulphite of soda, must be always preferred, than that of common salt, when possible, because it removes the iodine entirely,

12

which the saline solution does not always accomplish, especially when the sketches have been laid aside for some time between the fourth and fifth operations. It does not require to be warmed, and a less quantity is required.

First, the plate is placed in common water, poured into a trough, plunging and withdrawing it immediately—the surface merely requiring to be moistened—then plunge it into the saline solution, which latter would act upon the drawing, if not previously hardened by the washing in pure water. To assist the effect of the saline solutions, the plate is moved about in them by means of a little hoop of copper wire, or with the finger. When the yellow color has quite disappeared, the plate is lifted up with both hands, care being taken not to touch the drawing, and plunged again into the first trough of pure water.

Now, when the plate has been a moment into that water, the same washing pan is placed in an *inclined* position, sustained behind by any elevated thing, the *corked* corner being in the lower center point; the cock is then taken out, and then distilled water, hot, but not boiling, is made to flow in a stream over its whole surface, carrying away every remaining portion of the saline wash.*

Not less than a quart of distilled water is required when the design is of the now usual dimensions : $8\frac{1}{2}$ by $6\frac{1}{2}$ inches. The drops of water remaining on the plate must be removed by forcibly blowing upon it, for otherwise in drying they would leave stains on the drawing. Hence also will appear the necessity of using very pure water, for if in this last washing, the liquid contain any admixture of foreign substances, they will be deposited on the plate, leaving behind numerous and permanent stains. To be assured of the purity of the water, let a drop fall upon a piece of polished metal ; evaporate by heat, and if no stain be left the water is pure. Distilled water is always sufficiently pure without this trial.

After this washing the drawing is finished, it remains only to preserve it from the dust, and from the vapors that might tarnish the silver. The mercury, by the action of which the images are rendered visible, is partially decomposed ; it resists washing, by adhesion to the silver, but cannot endure the slightest rubbing.

To preserve these sketches then, place them in squares of strong pasteboard, with a glass over them, and frame the whole in wood. They are thenceforth unalterable even by the sun's light.

* If hyposulphite has been used, the distilled water need not be so hot as when common salt has been employed.

13

In travelling, the collector may preserve his sketches in a box similar to the one belonging to the apparatus, and for greater security may close the joints of the lid * with a collar of paper. It is necessary to state, that the same plate may be employed for several successive trials, provided the silver be not polished through to the copper. But it is very important after each trial to remove the mercury immediately by using the pumice powder with oil, and changing the cotton frequently during the operation. If this be neglected, the mercury finally adheres to the silver, and fine drawings cannot be obtained if this amalgam be present. They always in this case want firmness, neatness, and vigor of outline and general effect.

* Mr. Daguerre made attempts to preserve his sketches by means of different varnishes obtained from succinum, copal, Indian rubber, wax, and various resins ; but he has observed, that by the application of any varnish whatsoever, the lights in these sketches were considerably weakened, and at the same time the deeper tones were hidden. To this disadvantage, was added the still greater injury from the decomposition of the mercury by all the varnishes tried ; this effect, which did not become apparent till after the lapse of two or three months, terminated in a total destruction of the forms of the objects represented. Even had this not been the case, the author would have deemed it a sufficient reason for rejecting all varnishes, that they injured the vigor and clearness of the lights. The quality most to be desired in the new art is this intensity of tone in the contrast of the lights and shadows.

MANNER OF TAKING PORTRAITS

BY THE DAGUERREOTYPE,

Such as published in the Boston Daily Advertiser and Patriot, of March 26th, 1840.

Short Historical Introduction.

Within fifteen days after the publication of the process of M. Daguerre, in Paris, people in every quarter were making portraits. At first they were all made with *the eyes shut.* M. Susse, of the *place de la Bourse,* was one of the first amateurs who succeeded in making them in the most satisfactory manner. The achromatic lens, recommended by M. Daguerre was naturally first made use of. But these amateurs soon perceived, that in using a glass of this kind, a very long time was required to make the drawing. Every one began to look about for some means of shortening, as much as possible, the period of from fifteen to twenty-five minutes, which M. Susse, who had the whole disposal of his time, had employed in making his pretty portraits—with the eyes shut. Almost at the same time a young man, in the employment of the Minister of Public instruction, Mr. Abel Rendu, directed by the most simple optical principles, adopted an idea which seemed new to him, and produced to the admiration of some of the Paris circles, portraits of men and women, with the *eyes open,* executed in the most satisfactory manner. The mathematical perfection in the representation of the eyes, which M. Daguerre had been seeking for so long a time, was, to be sure, not to be found in these portraits; but this difference was so minute, that it was scarcely perceptible at first sight even by the most practised eye. On expressing the astonishment with which I was struck, and giving the warmest compliments of encouragement to M. Abel Rendu, that gentleman, without seeking to make the slightest mystery of the means he had employed, told me immediately that he had obtained these first results by means of a *Meniscus!* I immediately made a trial of this method. I used at first the Meniscus recommended by Wollaston, then the common one with one side plain, then one with a parabolic concavity, and obtained also the most satisfactory results, thanks to the information communicated in a manner so obliging by M. Abel Rendu. As these experiments were made just on the eve of my departure, it was impossible for me to repeat them, and not being able to resist the request of the person, in whose portrait I had succeeded in making the very best of my attempts, I left this most successful specimen behind with him, intending to supply myself with specimens at New York or elsewhere, when the fine summer sun should return, to offer us his brilliant light, so essential to the rapid execution of this operation. The portraits I had made in Paris, as well as those obtained by Mr. Abel Rendu, were formed in from ONE *minute to* TWO *minutes twenty-seven seconds,* at the

farthest. Considering the foggy atmosphere of Paris, this was already an immense step, but as M. Rendu did not attach any great importance to a discovery which did not offer the positively mathematical perfection which M. Daguerre required, and which M. Daguerre had undoubtedly himself, already disdained, he did not wish to make the thing an affair of *reputation,* but authorized me to make any use of it in America which I pleased. Before I quitted Paris, I made use of his Meniscus to take the pretty view of the *Pout Louis Phillippe,* and the magnificent *facade des Tuilleries,* which are found in my collection. From the slightly nebulous sides of these two pictures, in contrast with the clearness of the centre, may be seen at a glance the adaptation of the *Meniscus,* in preference to the other kinds of glasses, as regards the art of making portraits with the Daguerreotype. It will be perceived, that the centre of the design, offers in sharpness, in the lines, and in general clearness, a vigor in inverse proportion to the nebulosity of the sides. The reason why the Meniscus should give more clear lines, and act in a shorter space of time on the iodine plate in the camera obscura, will be obvious to all persons acquainted with the most simple principles of optics.

What is important, then, to the amateur in Daguerreotype drawing to know, is the manner of making use of it. The following is the process, (with the exception of some minute details, which it would be impossible to give in the columns of a newspaper,) as I communicated it on my arrival at New York to all who wished to hear it, and in fact as I have described it, (even to its details) in my crowded public lectures. I render it thus public, by means of the press, in order that those who may not have the opportunity of hearing my verbal information on the subject, may make experiments for themselves, and in fine, that by the means already made use of, they may know that I am able to make the *portrait of any person who wishes it.*

The shortness of the description will be equal to the simplicity of the method, and I am desirous that this new proof of my efforts to please the enlightened community in the midst of which I am placed, and by which I every day continue to be so kindly patronized—I desire, I say, in offering something of actual utility, as well as a source of intellectual amusement, that this new proof of my efforts, small as it may be in value of itself, may nevertheless be acceptable to all. Reserving for my public lectures a description of the general process, in obtaining drawings by the beautiful method of M. Daguerre, I will describe, in a few words, for the benefit of those who have already a notion of that process, how it is possible at the present time, to obtain a miniature portrait by the Daguerreotype.

SUMMARY DESCRIPTION OF THE PROCESS.

In the first place you will begin by preparing a room exposed to the sun, the south-east if possible. You will give to this room the form of a truncated pyramid, lying down, of which the base will be the whole breadth of the window—which window you will make as large as possible, and ex-

tending from the floor to the ceiling. The floor, the ceiling, and the two sides of the room, should be plastered with the whitest kind of lime plaster Those who cannot dispose a room in this manner, can fix the sides of the room with sheets or other cloth of perfect whiteness. The focus of the room must be covered with a tapestry of white cotton, with knotted or raised figures, which is designed to form the drapery. These are always agreeable to the eye, and should always be shewn in interior views. The chair on which the person sits must be of yellow wood. The person, if a man, must be dressed in a clear grey coat, pantaloons of a little deeper hue, a vest of a fancy ground, yellow, orange, if possible, with figures of a color to make a contrast, the whiteness of the shirt contrasting with a cravat of a grey ground, either a little less dark or more deep than the coat. The toilet of a lady should be of the same shades, and in all cases black must be constantly avoided, as well as green and red. This arrangement, however, is pointed out as the best means of obtaining the best effect; for, as in a portrait, the face is what is most cared for, the costume can be studied more or less at will, but the portrait, with other arrangements, will not be so agreeable to the eye. By means of mirrors properly disposed at the window or in the room, you will concentrate the strongest possible light on the person, and will considerably augment that of the chamber, which has already been made as clear as possible. If the sun should be too brilliant, and the *patient* is not able comfortably to bear the reflection of it. use may be made of the blue glass, recommended by M. Daguerre.

Having covered your plate well with the coating of iodine, you will fix the sitter. His head should be placed on a semi-circle of iron, fitted to the back of the chair. His arms may be arranged at pleasure. He should fix his eyes on some well defined object in any direction which he may prefer—the focus of the camera obscura must be regulated and provided with a good Meniscus. Now, if every thing has been arranged as it should be, your portrait will often be made, even in less than *twenty seconds,* and in the most satisfactory manner.

This is, *at present,* the most approved method of making a miniature by the Daguerreotype. Others may perhaps pretend to improve or invent, after my explanations have been made, because while employing the same means, they will change their places, or call them by other names. But until other methods shall have better success, it is certainly right that those who attach any importance to a futile celebrity should render to Cæsar the things which are Cæsar's, and it is right that the method of M. Abel Rendu, *rendered* public by me in this country, should be attributed entirely to him.

I will now say, at the close, that by adopting a confidential communication which I have received from M. D. G., the French Professor at Cambridge, since I arrived in Boston, I think it is very probable that we shall succeed in obtaining a Daguerreotype portrait in much less time than by the process above described. F. G.

APPENDIX B

SOUTHWORTH & HAWES PLATES AND HALLMARKS

Nearly 1,500 daguerreotype plates have been catalogued during the course of research on Southworth & Hawes. The importance of the physical plates themselves cannot be overemphasized. In addition to their role in the chemical process, their surface quality as determined by the luster and evenness of the silver coating is a decisive factor in the calibre of the resulting image. Moreover, the identification of the manufacturer's hallmark on the edge of the plate, when established, provides one of the few available aids in dating a daguerreotype. Caution must be exercised, however, in using this method of dating because a hallmark only indicates the manufacturing date of the plate.

Except for minor variations in trimming, the majority of Southworth & Hawes's daguerreotype plates conform to standard sizes determined by the cameras and plateholders of the day:

Whole plate	6½ x 8½″
Half plate	4½ x 5½″
Quarter plate	3¼ x 4¼″
Sixth or medium plate	2¾ x 3¼″
Ninth plate	2 x 2½″[1]

Contrary to the prevalent use of the sixth plate which was by far the most popular size for portraits in America,[2] the standard sizes used in the Southworth & Hawes studio were mostly quarter and whole plates. The inordinate use of whole plates remains a particular trademark of the Southworth and Hawes studio and accounts for most of their portraits of notables and their landscapes.

Only two oversize plates by Southworth & Hawes are known to exist. Oversize plates were available in all large daguerreotype studios after 1853 but were seldom used since they sold for as much as $50.00 and were obviously only for the wealthy and the extravagant.[3] The two extant oversize plates from the Southworth & Hawes studio are both male portraits, now located in the Metropolitan Museum of Art and listed as "mammoth plates." Plates larger than 6½ x 8½″ were made to order for special equipment and did not follow the standards for smaller plates. As a result, both measurements and names for oversize plates may vary according to source:

Double whole plate	8½ x 13″
	16 x 12″
Mammoth plate	11 x 13″
	13 x 17″
	13½ x 17½″
	15 x 17″
Without designation	12 x 15″
	13½ x 16½″
	12⅞ x 16⅝″
	12¾ x 16⅝″
Without measurement	Imperial plate
	8/4 plate[4]

The Southworth & Hawes mammoth plates come closest to the 13 x 17″ reference; the Boston innkeeper John L. Tucker (Plate 17) measures 12⅞ x 16⅝″ while that of poet Charles Sprague (Met 37.14.50) measures 12¾ x 16⅝″.

Receipts and letters in the firm's business correspondence, now in the International Museum of Photography collection at George Eastman House, Rochester, show the Scovill Manufacturing Company of Waterbury, Connecticut, to be the first documented source of plates for the Southworth & Hawes studio. Scovill had been manufacturing silver-plated metal since about 1833 and had already supplied Samuel F. B. Morse with thirty-eight whole plates in October of 1839.[5] In July of 1841 Southworth opened his account with Scovill, who continued to provide the plates for the work of the later Southworth and Hawes partnership. Until 1846 other sources for plates are indicated only by quantity on receipts from distributors such as Widdifield & Co. and Haddock & Andrews, both of Boston. Southworth & Hawes's dependence on local plate suppliers indicates that the first plates used by American daguerreotypists were manufactured in this country and that only later the imported French plate began to dominate the American market. Even Gouraud, who had brought along a small supply of plates for lecture demonstrations, apparently failed to secure a continuing source from France. By March of 1840 he was forced to appeal to Scovill for additional plates.[6] American photographers had so greatly modified Daguerre's method by 1847 that it was referred to as "The American Process." French plates, however, were generally preferred to those manufactured in the United States (the first order for French plates by Southworth & Hawes dates from 1847). The surface of the French plate was reputedly smoother than the American and the quality was considerably more reliable. The superiority of the imported plate was due to the use of softer copper which allowed for easier bending of the edges and the insistence by the French in using only pure silver to coat the copper plate. Its consistency was guaranteed by the French government which required that all silverware, including silver-plated goods such as daguerreotype plates, be stamped with official government hallmarks denoting silver content. Although the marks vary, most include a number within a square giving the proportion of silver to other metal: i.e., 30 denoting a 1:30 proportion. American manufacturers, on the other hand, used a cheaper silver amalgam which resulted in an uneven or peeling silver coating and a less-pliable copper which could not be easily bent at the edges to fit the plate-holder. There were, of course, American manufacturers who resolved these problems and produced high-quality plates such as the Scovill Manufacturing Company, Pemberton & Co. of Connecticut, Holmes, Booth & Hayden, and E. White of New York, among others.

The following represents an inventory of hallmarks on the plates used by Southworth & Hawes. The wide variety of both foreign and domestic plates reflects not only the range of material available to the partners during their twenty-year partnership but also their continuous experiments with the process for the best possible results. Photographic reproductions of the actual hallmarks have been used wherever possible; hand-drawings have been substituted only when the bent edges or trimming of the plate have hampered legibility.

Little information exists on the manufacturers and sources of the daguerreotype plates. Most identifications have come from advertisements for daguerreotype supplies in contemporary journals. Much research is needed before useful keys to daguerreotype hallmarks are developed. The substantial pioneering efforts of Beaumont Newhall have supplemented our research and are gratefully acknowledged.

SELECTED BIBLIOGRAPHY TO APPENDIX B

Hughes, Grayham. *Modern Silver, Throughout the World, 1880–1967.* New York: Crown Publishers, Inc., 1967.

Kovel, Ralph M. and Terry H. *A Directory of American Silver, Pewter and Silver Plate.* New York: Crown Publishers, Inc., 1961.

Newhall, Beaumont. *The Daguerreotype in America,* 3rd revised ed. New York: Dover, 1976.

Rinhart, Floyd and Marion. "Notes on the Daguerreotype Plate" and "The Plate Maker's Hallmarks," *The New Daguerreian Journal,* volume 3, no. 2, 1975, pp. 5–10; 11–16.

Unpublished Manuscript on "The History of the Scovill Manufacturing Company." Courtesy of E. H. Davis, Plant Historian, Scovill Manufacturing Co., Waterbury, Conn.

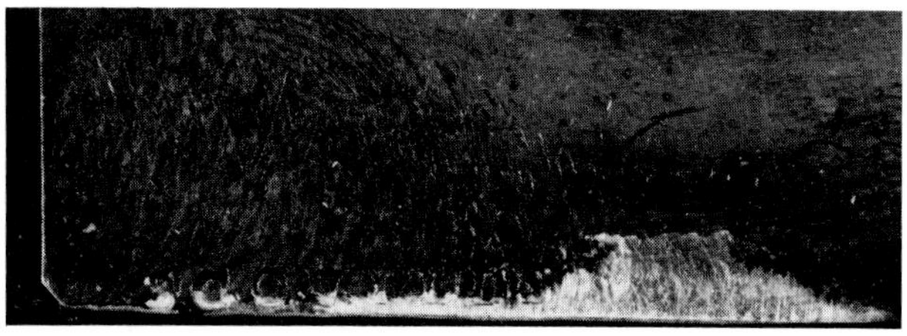

1. **SCOVILLS**
   c. 1839–1850
   J. M. L. and W. H. Scovill
   Waterbury, Connecticut
   This stamp was first used in the manufacturing of buttons where size was of essence. Scovill began manufacturing daguerreotype plates in 1839.

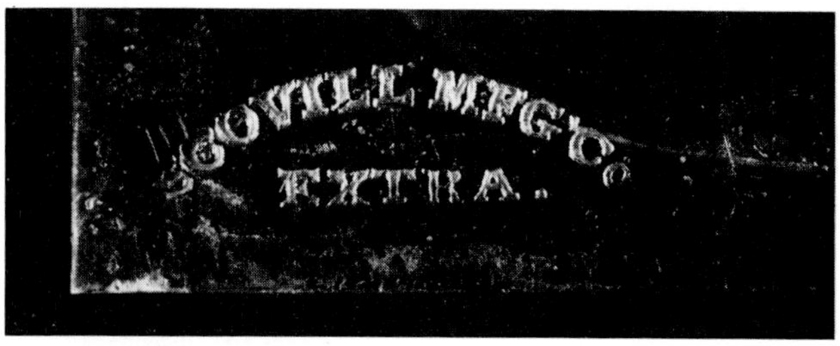

2. **SCOVILL MFG. CO. EXTRA**
   1850–1854
   Scovill Manufacturing Company
   Waterbury, Connecticut
   The firm changed its name in 1850 and retains the same address to this day. Scovill correspondence indicates plate production was halted in 1854 due to the rising popularity of the collodion process.

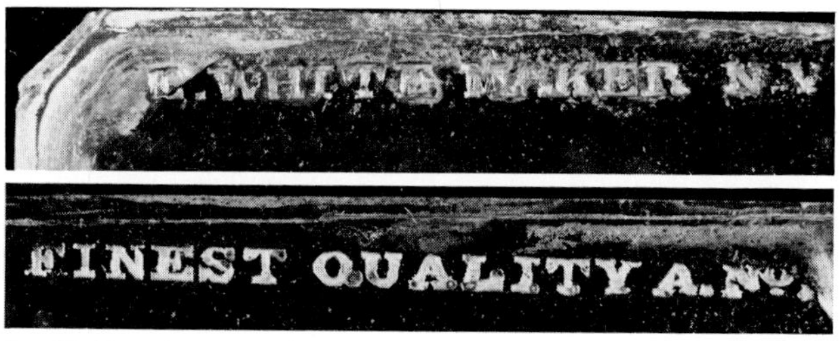

3. **E. WHITE MAKER**
   1844–c. 1850
   until 1847: 175 Broadway, New York
   until 1850: 247 Broadway, New York
   The first mention of White plates occurs in Southworth & Hawes correspondence of 1844.

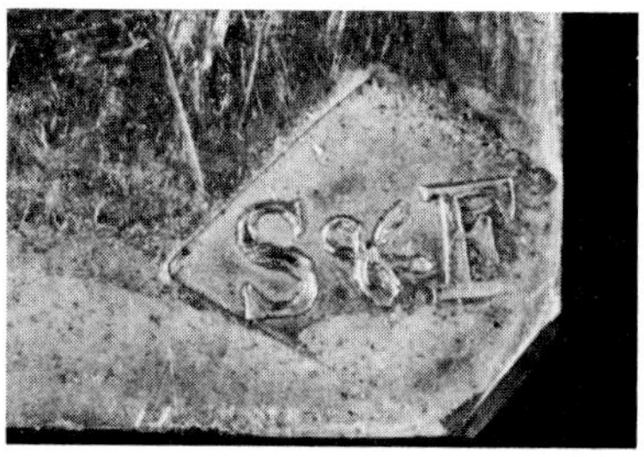

4. **S&F in lozenge**
   c. 1850
   possibly Sheldon & Feltman
   Albany, New York
   See: Kovel, *Directory of American Silver* for hallmark which duplicates the above except that a dash is used between the letters. Referred to in the *American Handbook of the Daguerreotype* by S. D. Humphrey, 5th ed. New York: 1858, p. 187.

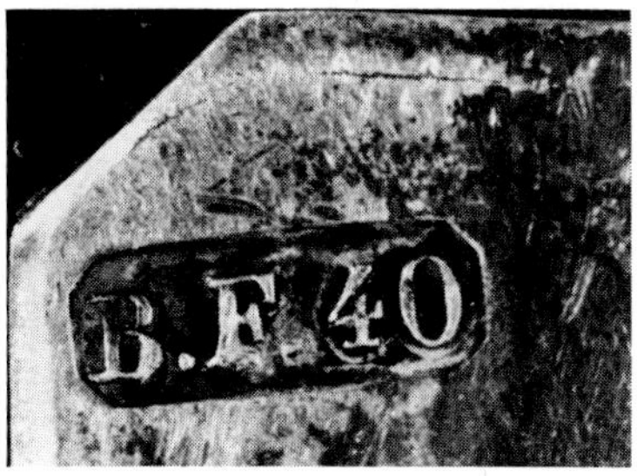

5. **B.F. 40**
1848–c.1854
Benjamin French
109 Washington Street, Boston
French began to deal in daguerreotype supplies in 1848 (*see* Beaumont Newhall, p. 119). French is the predominant supplier to the Southworth & Hawes studio according to receipts dating from 1851–1852.

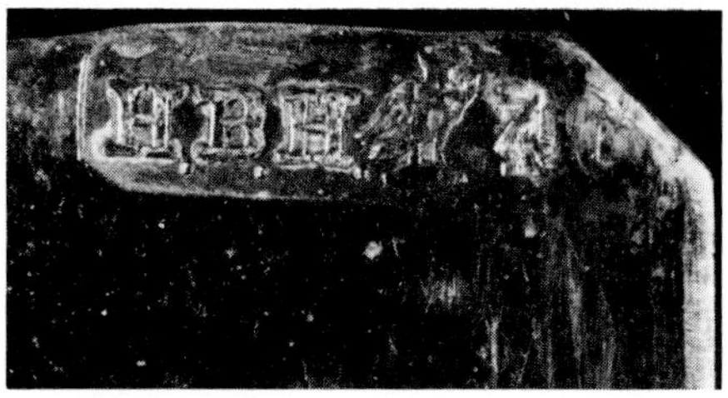

6. **H. B. H. / Eagle / 40**
? through 1858
Holmes, Booth & Hayden
81 Chambers and 63 Reade Street, New York
See: Humphrey, S.D., *American Handbook of the Daguerreotype*, 5th edition. New York: 1858, advertising pages at the end of the book.

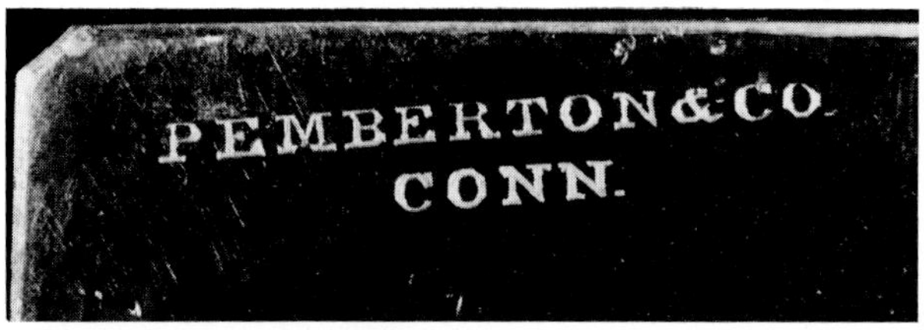

7. **PEMBERTON & CO.**
CONN.
Unidentified American plate.

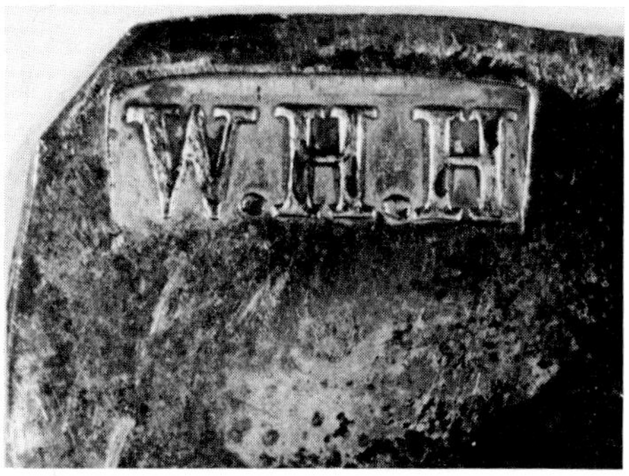

8. **W. H. H.**
Unidentified American plate. *See:* Rinhart, p. 13.

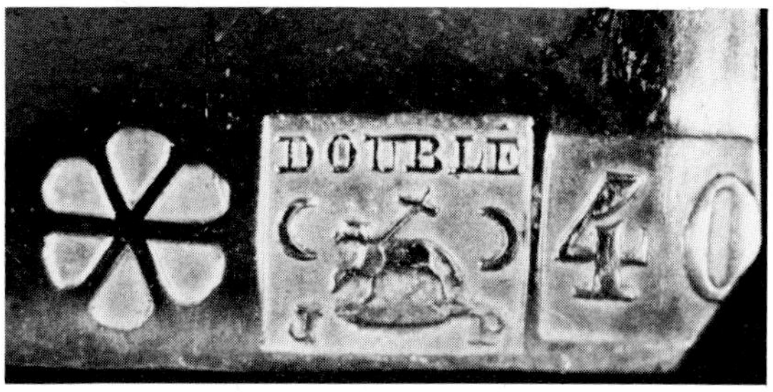

9. **DOUBLÉ / J. P.**
c. 1850
Unidentified French plate; among the most predominant of the Southworth & Hawes plates.

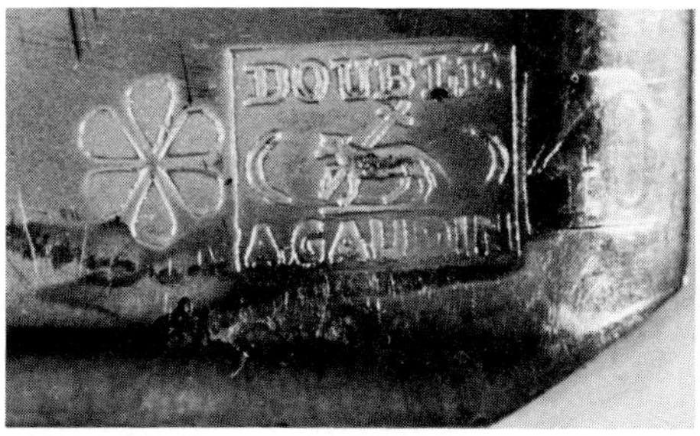

10. **DOUBLÉ / A. GAUDIN**
? until at least 1856
A. Gaudin & Bro.
9 rue de la Perle, Paris
One of the most popular of the imported plates, also distributed through American photographic dealers. The word "Doublé" means "plated."

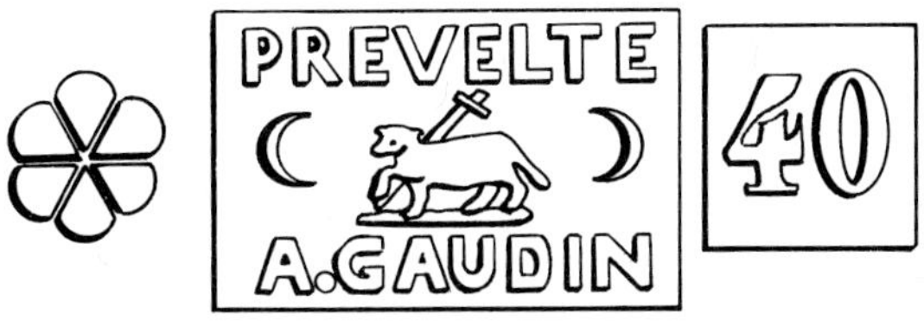

11. **GAUDIN / PREVELTÉ**
Unidentified French plate, probably a version of the A. Gaudin plate.

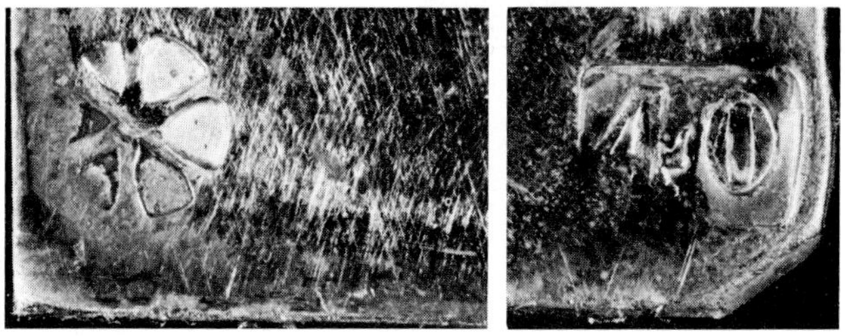

12. **STAR / 40**
from at least 1847 through 1856
Supposedly among the best-quality plate imported. Gaudin maintained to be the only French manufacturer of the "genuine Star plate." *See: Humphrey's Journal*, vol. VII, no. 19, February 1, 1856, p. 10.

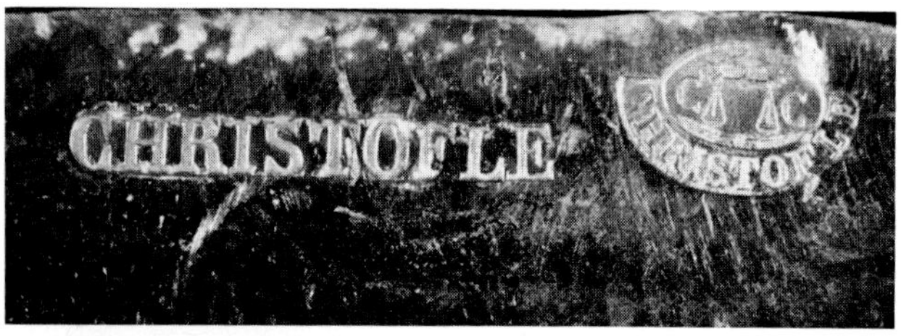

13. **CHRISTOFLE**
from 1851–?
Charles Christofle et Cie. 56 rue de Bundy, Paris
Like Scovill, the Christofle firm still exists today. The scale symbol was originated by the French government to indicate electroplating and was incorporated into the Christofle hallmark. As a result, the plates are often referred to as the ''Scale'' plate (Anthony, E., *A Comprehensive and Systematic Catalogue of Photographic Material Manufactured, Imported and Sold by E. Anthony.* New York: Snelling, 1854, p. 56).

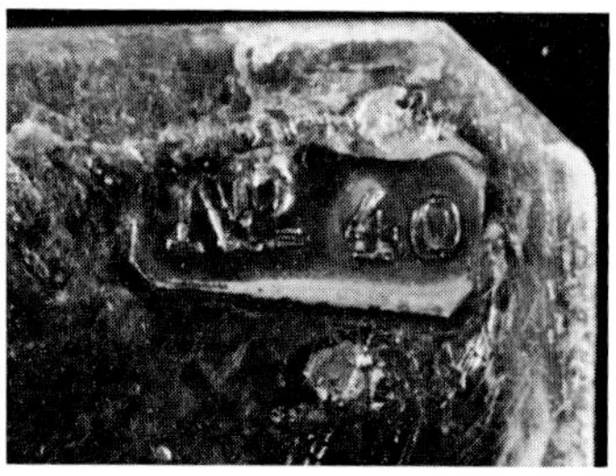

14. N° 40
Unidentified plate, probably French. The ''40'' would denote the proportion of silver to copper on the plate.

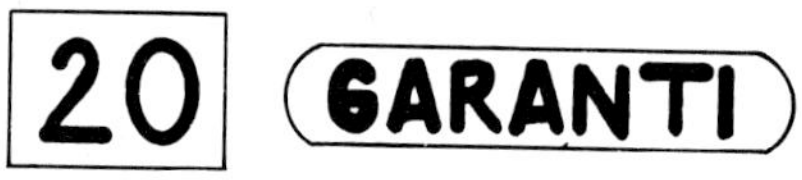

15. **20 GARANTI**
Unidentified French plate.

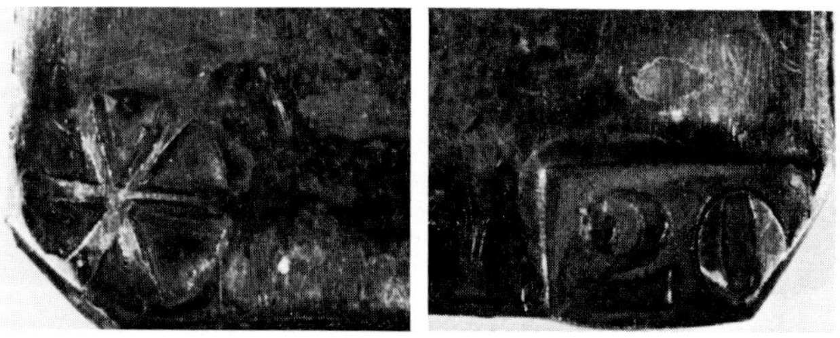

16. **STAR / 20**
Unidentified French plate. The ''20'' denotes a lesser amount of silver and therefore lower quality than the ''40'' plate.

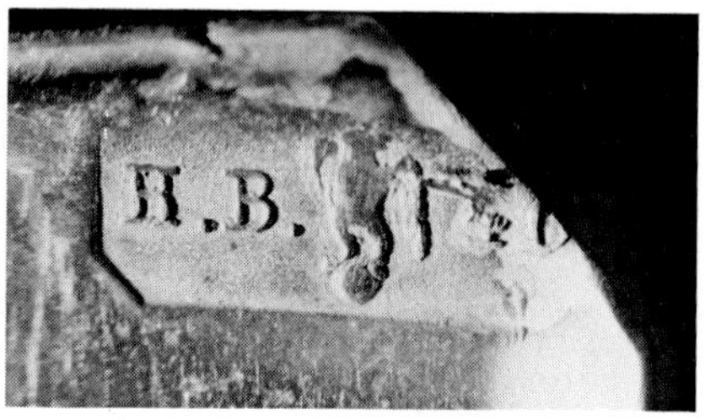

17. **H. B. / Bear / 40**
Unidentified plate. The Rinharts identify this as Holmes, Booth & Hayden (p.13); this identification does not coincide with the facts. Cf. above, no.6.

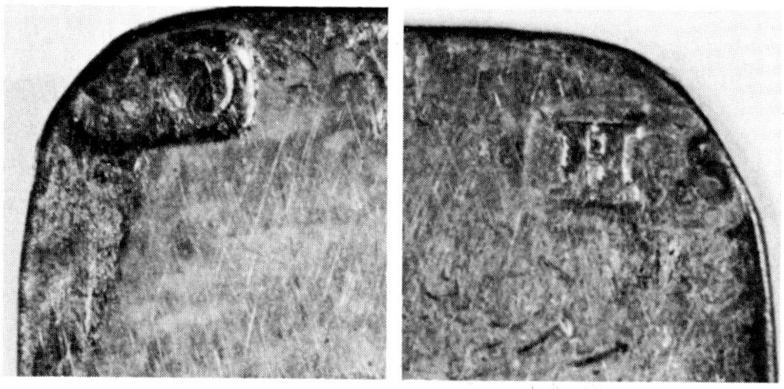

18. **40 / H. S.**
Unidentified plate. (*See:* Rinhart, p. 14).

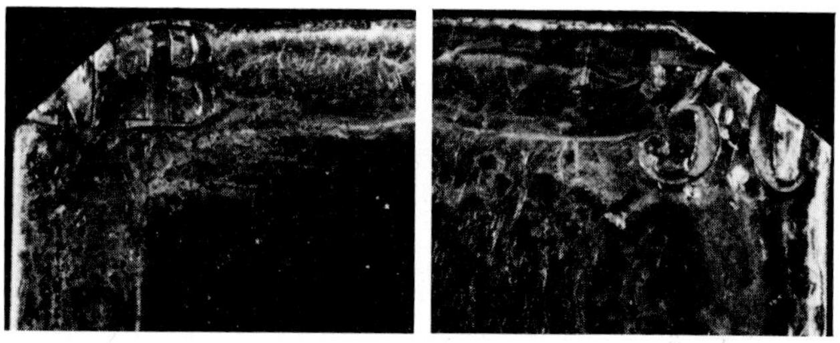

19. **NB / 30**
Unidentified plate.

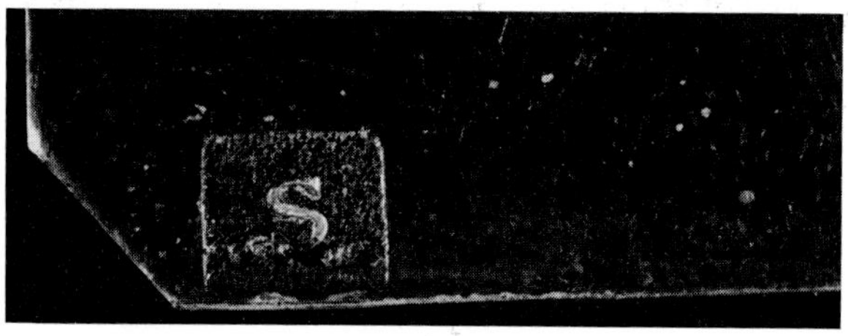

20. **S in square**
Unidentified plate.

Notes to Appendix B

1. Beaumont Newhall, *The Daguerreotype in America,* 3rd revised ed., New York: Dover, 1976, p. 118. See also: Robert Taft, *Photography and the American Scene,* New York: Dover, 1964, p. 78. Note that Taft lists the half plate as $4\frac{1}{2}$ x $6\frac{1}{2}$" but the material catalogued does not substantiate this.
2. Taft, *op. cit.,* p. 78.
3. *Ibid.,* p. 80.
4. *Ibid.,* pp. 78, 80. See also: Newhall, *op. cit.,* p. 118; Richard Rudisill, *Mirror Image. . . .* Albuquerque: The University of New Mexico Press, 1971, p. 145.
5. Unpublished manuscript on ''The History of the Scovill Manufacturing Company,'' p. 81. Courtesy of E. H. Davis, Plant Historian, Scovill Manufacturing Co., Waterbury, Conn. All information relating to Scovill and the firm of Southworth & Hawes was taken from this manuscript.
6. *Ibid.,* p. 88.

SELECTED BIBLIOGRAPHY

While little has been published on the work of Southworth & Hawes, a large body of clippings, letters, contracts, receipts and account books exists in the Southworth & Hawes collection at the International Museum of Photography at George Eastman House, Rochester, New York. Much of this material, especially the clippings from periodical literature of the period is often difficult, if not impossible, to trace to the original source. For a general bibliography on the early history of photography and daguerreotypy in America, refer to the extensive bibliographies in Richard Rudisill's *Mirror Image* and Taft's *Photography and the American Scene.* What follows is a brief listing of the sources that proved to be most valuable in studying the daguerreotype work of Southworth & Hawes. It is divided into two sections: general texts and manuals useful for background, and specific sources pertaining to Southworth & Hawes.

General Sources

The American Journal of Photography, n.s., vols. I and II (1858–1860).

Bisbee, A. *The History and Practice of Daguerreotyping.* Dayton, Ohio: L.F. Claflin, 1853.

Bogardus, Abraham. "The Lost Art of the Daguer reotype," *The Century Magazine,* vol. LXVIII, no. 1 (May 1904), pp. 83–91.

The Daguerreian Journal, 1850; later called *Humphrey's Journal,* 1851– 1858.

Davis, Mrs. D. T. "The Daguerreotype in America," *McClure's Magazine,* vol. VIII, no. 1 (November 1896), pp. 2 –16.

Draper, John William. "On the Process of Daguerreotype, and its Application to taking Portraits from the Life," *The London, Edinburgh, and Dublin Philosophical Magazine,* series 3, vol. XVII, no. 109 (September 1840), pp. 222–224.

Gernsheim, Helmut and Alison. *L. J. M. Daguerre: The History of the Diorama and the Daguerreotype,* 2nd ed., rev. New York: Dover, 1968, chapter 5.

Gouraud, François. *Description of the Daguerreotype Process, or a Summary of M. Gouraud's Public Lectures, According to the Principles of M. Daguerre. With a Description of a Provisory Method of Taking Human Portraits.* Boston: Dutton and Wentworth's Print, 1840. (See Appendix A.)

Haley, W.S. *The Daguerreotype Operator, A Practical Work. . . .* New York: for the author, 1854.

Hill, Levi L. *A Treatise on Daguerreotype . . .,* Parts I, II and III. Lexington, N.Y.: Holman & Gray, 1850.

Hill, Levi L. *Hill's Treatise on Daguerreotype; the Magic Buff . . .,* Part IV. Lexington, N.Y.: Holman & Gray, 1850.

Humphrey, S. D. *American Hand Book of the Daguerreotype . . .,* 5th ed. New York: S. D. Humphrey, 1858.

Humphrey, S. D. and M. Finley. *A System of Photography. . . .* Canandaigua, New York: for the authors, 1849.

Newhall, Beaumont. *The Daguerreotype in America,* 3rd. revised ed. New York: Dover, 1976.

Newhall, Beaumont. *The History of Photography from 1839 to the Present Day.* New York: Museum of Modern Art, 1964.

Peale, Rembrandt. "Portraiture," *The Crayon,* vol. IV (1857), pp. 44–45.

The Photographic Art-Journal, 1851–1856.

Rinhart, Floyd and Marion. *American Daguerreian Art.* New York: Clarkson N. Potter, 1967.

Rodgers, H. J. *Twenty-Three Years Under a Sky-Light, or Life and Experiences of a Photographer.* Hartford, Conn.: H. J. Rodgers, 1872.

Root, Marcus Aurelius. *The Camera and the Pencil; or The Heliographic Art. . . .* Philadelphia: M. A. Root, 1864.

Rudisill, Richard, *Mirror Image: The Influence of the Daguerreotype on American Society.* Albuquerque, N. M.: University of New Mexico, 1971.

Ryder, James F. *Voigtlander and I in Pursuit of Shadow Catching.* Cleveland: Cleveland Printing & Publishing, 1902.

Snelling, Henry Hunt. *The History and Practice of the Art of Photography.* New York: G. P. Putnam, 1849.

Taft, Robert. *Photography and the American Scene: A Social History, 1839–1889.* New York: Dover, 1964.

Werge, John. *The Evolution of Photography.* London: Piper & Carter, 1890.

On Southworth & Hawes

[Anon.] "Among Ye Ancients." *Boston Sunday Journal,* 15 March 1896.

[Anon.] "Good News for Backsliders." *Western Photographic News,* vol. II (April 1876), p. 233.

[Anon.] "Oldest American Photographer." *Boston Transcript,* 9 August 1901.

[Anon.] "Oldest in the World." *Boston Herald,* 10 August 1901.
[Anon.] "One of the Oldest." *Snap Shot,* vol. III (June 1896), p. 317.
[Anon.] "Portraits of Noted Men." *Worcester Spy,* 6 January 1886.
[Anon.] Untitled article. *Boston Transcript,* 27 November 1888.
Hawes, Edward L. "The Daguerreotype in America: 1839–1860." Un-published manuscript for honors seminar in history, University of Pennsylvania, May 1958, especially chapter 4.
Hawes, Janet Laurie. "J. J. Hawes, Pioneer Photographer." *American Annual of Photography,* 1953, pp. 46–51.
[Hawes, Josiah.] "Stray Leaves from the Diary of the Oldest Professional Photographer in the World." *Photo-Era,* vol. XVI, no. 2 (February 1906), pp. 104–107.
[Holman, Louis.] "Josiah Johnson Hawes: Daguerreotyper." *Within the Compass of a Print Shop,* vol. III, no. 1 (November 1934), pp. 3–9.
Homer, Rachel Johnston. *The Legacy of Josiah Johnson Hawes: 19th Century Photographs of Boston.* Barre, Mass.: Barre Publishers, 1972.
Moore, Charles LeRoy. *Two Partners in Boston: The Daguerreian Artistry of Albert Southworth and Josiah Hawes.* Unpublished doctoral dissertation, University of Michigan, 1976.
Newhall, Beaumont. "First American Masters of the Camera." *Art News Annual* (1948), vol. XLVI, no. 9 (November 1947), pp. 91–98, *et seq.*
Newhall, Beaumont and Nancy, eds. *Masters of Photography.* New York: George Braziller, 1958, pp. 22–31.
Southworth, Albert Sands. "An Address to the National Photographic Association of the United States." *The Philadelphia Photographer,* vol. VIII, no. 94 (October 1871), pp. 315–323.
Southworth, Albert Sands. "Early History of Photography in the United States," extracted from *The Philadelphia Photographer. British Journal of Photography,* vol. XVIII (10 November 1871), pp. 530–532; (8 December 1871), pp. 582–583.
Southworth, Albert Sands. "On the Use of the Camera." *The Photographic News* [London], vol. XVIII, no. 80 (6 March 1874), pp. 109–111.
Stokes, I. N. Phelps. *The Hawes Stokes Collection of American Daguerreotypes by Albert Sands Southworth and Josiah Johnson Hawes.* New York: The Metropolitan Museum of Art, 1939.